Qualitative Exploration of Grounded Theory in Organizational Research

Maryam Ebrahimi
Independent Researcher, Germany

A volume in the Advances in Business Strategy and Competitive Advantage (ABSCA) Book Series

IGI Global
DISSEMINATOR OF KNOWLEDGE

Published in the United States of America by
IGI Global
Business Science Reference (an imprint of IGI Global)
701 E. Chocolate Avenue
Hershey PA, USA 17033
Tel: 717-533-8845
Fax: 717-533-8661
E-mail: cust@igi-global.com
Web site: http://www.igi-global.com

Library of Congress Cataloging-in-Publication Data

Names: Ebrahimi, Maryam, 1980- author.
Title: Qualitative exploration of grounded theory in organizational research / Maryam Ebrahimi.
Description: Hershey : Business Science Reference, 2020. | Includes bibliographical references and index. | Summary: "This book focuses on the application of grounded theory in organizational case studies"-- Provided by publisher.
Identifiers: LCCN 2020001199 (print) | LCCN 2020001200 (ebook) | ISBN 9781799842521 (hardcover) | ISBN 9781799852810 (paperback) | ISBN 9781799842538 (ebook)
Subjects: LCSH: Organization--Research. | Qualitative research.
Classification: LCC HD30.4 .E3197 2020 (print) | LCC HD30.4 (ebook) | DDC 302.3/50721--dc23
LC record available at https://lccn.loc.gov/2020001199
LC ebook record available at https://lccn.loc.gov/2020001200

This book is published in the IGI Global book series Advances in Business Strategy and Competitive Advantage (ABSCA) (ISSN: 2327-3429; eISSN: 2327-3437)

British Cataloguing in Publication Data
A Cataloguing in Publication record for this book is available from the British Library.

Advances in Business Strategy and Competitive Advantage (ABSCA) Book Series

ISSN:2327-3429
EISSN:2327-3437

Editor-in-Chief: Patricia Ordóñez de Pablos, Universidad de Oviedo, Spain

MISSION

Business entities are constantly seeking new ways through which to gain advantage over their competitors and strengthen their position within the business environment. With competition at an all-time high due to technological advancements allowing for competition on a global scale, firms continue to seek new ways through which to improve and strengthen their business processes, procedures, and profitability.

The **Advances in Business Strategy and Competitive Advantage (ABSCA) Book Series** is a timely series responding to the high demand for state-of-the-art research on how business strategies are created, implemented and re-designed to meet the demands of globalized competitive markets. With a focus on local and global challenges, business opportunities and the needs of society, the **ABSCA** encourages scientific discourse on doing business and managing information technologies for the creation of sustainable competitive advantage.

COVERAGE

- Tacit Knowledge
- Competitive Strategy
- Innovation Strategy
- Customer-Orientation Strategy
- Outsourcing
- Entrepreneurship & Innovation
- Foreign Investment Decision Process
- Strategic alliances
- Small and Medium Enterprises
- Strategy Performance Management

IGI Global is currently accepting manuscripts for publication within this series. To submit a proposal for a volume in this series, please contact our Acquisition Editors at Acquisitions@igi-global.com or visit: http://www.igi-global.com/publish/.

The Advances in Business Strategy and Competitive Advantage (ABSCA) Book Series (ISSN 2327-3429) is published by IGI Global, 701 E. Chocolate Avenue, Hershey, PA 17033-1240, USA, www.igi-global.com. This series is composed of titles available for purchase individually; each title is edited to be contextually exclusive from any other title within the series. For pricing and ordering information please visit http://www.igi-global.com/book-series/advances-business-strategy-competitive-advantage/73672. Postmaster: Send all address changes to above address.

Titles in this Series

For a list of additional titles in this series, please visit:
http://www.igi-global.com/book-series/advances-business-strategy-competitive-advantage/73672

Developing Creative Economy Through Disruptive Leadership Emerging Research and Opportunities
Kristin Joyce Tardif (University of Arkansas – Fort Smith, USA)
Business Science Reference • © 2020 • 180pp • H/C (ISBN: 9781799834168) • US $185.00

Knowledge Management, Innovation, and Entrepreneurship in a Changing World
Murray Eugene Jennex (San Diego State University, USA)
Business Science Reference • © 2020 • 463pp • H/C (ISBN: 9781799823551) • US $215.00

Developing Entrepreneurial Competencies for Start-Ups and Small Business
Jarmila Šebestová (Silesian University in Opava, Czech Republic)
Business Science Reference • © 2020 • 316pp • H/C (ISBN: 9781799827146) • US $225.00

Leadership and Followership in an Organizational Change Context
Sajjad Nawaz Khan (University Malaysia Sarawak, Malaysia) and Abdul Halim Busari (University Malaysia Sarawak, Malaysia)
Business Science Reference • © 2020 • 300pp • H/C (ISBN: 9781799828075) • US $225.00

Digital Marketing Strategies and Models for Competitive Business
Filipe Mota Pinto (Polytechnic Institute of Leiria, Portugal) and Teresa Guarda (Universidad Peninsula de Santa Elena (UPSE), Ecuador)
Business Science Reference • © 2020 • 300pp • H/C (ISBN: 9781799829638) • US $225.00

Recent Advancements in Sustainable Entrepreneurship and Corporate Social Responsibility
Amulya Gurtu (Cofrin School of Business, University of Wisconsin-Green Bay, USA)
Business Science Reference • © 2020 • 219pp • H/C (ISBN: 9781799823476) • US $215.00

Challenges and Opportunities for SMEs in Industry 4.0
Noor Hazlina Ahmad (Universiti Sains Malaysia, Malaysia) Qaisar Iqbal (Universiti Sains Malaysia, Malaysia) and Hasliza Abdul Halim (Universiti Sains Malaysia, Malaysia)
Business Science Reference • © 2020 • 271pp • H/C (ISBN: 9781799825777) • US $215.00

For an entire list of titles in this series, please visit:
http://www.igi-global.com/book-series/advances-business-strategy-competitive-advantage/73672

IGI Global
DISSEMINATOR OF KNOWLEDGE

701 East Chocolate Avenue, Hershey, PA 17033, USA
Tel: 717-533-8845 x100 • Fax: 717-533-8661
E-Mail: cust@igi-global.com • www.igi-global.com

Table of Contents

Preface

OVERVIEW

The outcomes of expeditions that are high risk to cross unknown domains are new discoveries. Explorers like Darwin, Columbus, and Freud were carrying out qualitative investigations in different ways (O'Reilly et al., 2012). One kind of qualitative research is the grounded theory (GT) methodology, which enables the discovery of inductive theory about a particular social reality that is grounded in data, which are collected and analyzed systematically throughout the iterative process (O'Reilly et al., 2012; Wiesche et al., 2017). The GT has the ability to build theory by specified and flexible tools for analysis (O'Reilly et al., 2012; Bollingtoft, 2017). The literature relevant to the GT provides guidance, recommendations, and perspectives concerning its application to ensure the accuracy and thoroughness of the research contribution. When there are limited previous studies on issues related to a research and for which there is a need to develop theory, the GT is especially useful (Wiesche et al., 2017).

Organizations are recognized as messy entities which are worth studying. There are many challenges ahead of organizational researcher while studying people, the information flow, and power within organizations. Additionally, there is another challenge caused by the external economic forces and their influence on an organization. Organizations are complex, open, and dynamic systems which are hard to be studied (Swanson, 2005). Instead of taking no account of or making easier to understand the complexities of organizational context, research methods must incorporate them to generate precise or effective results. GT is a general methodology which means that although sociologists initiated many early studies using GT, the use of this methodology has never been limited to them. Therefore, GT has been applied to psychology, anthropology, information science, social work, education, marketing, entrepreneurship, management and organizational studies, and many communities of practice in health care and in particular nursing (Bollingtoft, 2017).

This book aims to provide the theoretical foundation and practical applications of the GT in the area of organizatioal research. The strength of GT is that the theorizing process explains what is really happening in practice. It is useful to develop perspectives and to learn the ways participants manage their lives within the context of current and future organizational challenges. It helps especially research in fields that have not already been studied, where there is an apparent and clear gap, and where a new perspective could indicate areas for management involvement and improvement (Kenealy, 2008).

APPLICATIONS

Although the history of applying the GT goes back to sociology, its applications have extended beyond this field and into other areas of science as well for instance: tourism and hospitality management, medical studies, psychology, and business and organization studies. GT has been applied in the area of management for example: management research, innovation, business mergers, and management action (Douglas, 2003).

Qualitative research methods such as GT give an opportunity for the researcher to have information and collect insights that might be ignored as a result of using traditional data analysis techniques. The use of GT is increasing in the field of information systems (IS). The issues that experts operate in the IS environment are of a socio-technical nature. GT can overcome these problems by presenting a lens that do not give rise to prejudice due to previous assumptions and it does not provide a selection of predetermined theories that the researcher must explain social and technical phenomena.

It can be said that the GT approach can be used to present new theories. In fact, the GT approach poses an intellectual challenge and relates to management researchers. The GT approach empowers the researcher to think in both ways of analytic and conceptual and can be used by management academics to interpret and evaluate current management theory as a basis for teaching new approaches. It also provides a consistent way of theory development while also allowing people using the GT approach to evaluate alternative research methods more accurately (Trim and Lee, 2004). The main point of the GT is to emphasize on building theory, not to verify the theory that already existed.

Since key issues in technology management (TM), such as complex decision making processes, interactions in relationships, and social networks require in-depth analysis of empirical data from a real environment, GT's features make it particularly relevant to this field. GT offers valuable research opportunities for TM research. Studies have shown that GT is more suitable for sociological applications, and knowledge management (KM) has a strong sociological nature. While KM is widely regarded as the planned, formal, or recognized activities, processes, or management involved in the use of knowledge in organizations, it shows a fundamental social process that in this regard using GT methodology is very appropriate and beneficial.

There have been studies dealing with the corporate social responsibility (CSR) using GT. The GT approach can be used in a new way to analyze annual reports. GT has the ability to offer a reasonable explanation for what forms this reporting, and define drivers and desired outcomes of CSR practices. GT provides us insights into what CSR means to employees. GT is very popular in social and behavioral research, for instance in order to study the social aspects of each household and their ideology in buying/ building, operating, improving housing for having efficient energy consumption, a qualitative approach such as GT is appropriate to have a more comprehensive image of the real context.

GT focuses on identifying and describing processes of interaction between or among individuals or groups within a given social context. GT approach is used in order to identify factors affecting employee empowerment. It can be applied to explain the exercise of power in an organizational setting in order to have a better understanding of what fosters or limits employees' empowerment and to develop empowerment theory. The GT can be selected to investigate the relationship between different factors and burnout because it allows the researcher to discover a phenomenon and construct theoretical models or theories for work areas.

GT has been at the forefront of feminist research since the mid-1990s. Researchers in various disciplines claim methodological consistency and incorporate feminist principles into their GT studies. GT can be applied to gain a better understanding of the effect of sexual assault on a victim's life and establish a theory to explain it. Constructivist GT which fits with feminist inquiry helps theorists attempt to understand and describe both the meanings of the silence and actions of the participants.

TARGET AUDIENCE

This book is a collective resource with comprehensive knowledge in the field of grounded theory (GT) in organizational research in theory and practice. GT can assist researchers and practitioners to discover or construct theory from data in the social sciences and related fields. GT focus is useful for those who need to understand the experiences and interactions of people embedded in a particular social context, to reveal strategies developed before experienced situations. Target audiences are academics (researchers, lecturers, and advanced students), practitioners (managers and experts of organizations), and professional institutions (professional bodies of GT).

ORGANIZATION OF THE BOOK

The book is organized into 10 chapters. A brief description of each of the chapters follows:

Chapter 1, 'The Grounded Theory Methodology in Organization Studies Within Qualitative Research', explains GT and its applications in organizational research. It discusses the Glaserian classic GT, Straussian GT, Charmazian constructivist GT, and Clarkeian situational GT as the four GT schools. Additionally, the theory-research-development-practice cycle, the factors affecting the choice of organization research methodology and the types of qualitative research methods are studied by comparing four qualitative methods of case study, GT, phenomenological study and content analysis.

Chapter 2, 'The Use of Grounded Theory Methodology in Theory Building', directly addresses the GT as a systematic methodology in the construction of theories especially in understanding the social systems. It introduces approaches of theory development including induction, deduction, and abduction. In addition, functions, levels, components, and evaluation of theories are introduced. Then, research methods for theory development, in particular GT and its theoretical coding in addition to presenting trustworthiness in GT methodology are discussed.

Chapter 3, 'Exploratory Analysis in Information Systems Area: Using Grounded Theory Methodology', focuses on GT approaches in IS research including research contributions of GT in IS research, qualitative perspective to conduct research in IS, types of GT approaches used in IS research, and guidelines for GT studies in IS. Applications of GT in IS research especially in software engineering are presented.

Chapter 4, 'Grounded Theory in Practices of Technology Management', discusses how GT is used for theory building in the field of TM research by providing a review to the use of GT in the special concepts of TM such as research and technology commercialization, technology adoption, and technology readiness and transfer.

Chapter 5, 'Grounded Theory in Sustainable Energy Initiatives', analyzes studies performed in the area of energy transition by applying GT. Focusing on GT, it reviews studies about green building policy and capital investment decision-making, perceptions and behaviors of energy saving, the diffusion of renewable energy technologies to provide a diffusion pattern, and developing policy interventions to mitigate climate change with renewable-energy technologies.

Chapter 6, 'Grounded Theory Approach in Knowledge Management', provides an understanding of the use of GT methodology in KM. It focuses on understanding process of transforming knowledge into wisdom, presenting KM model, determining factors of knowledge sharing, and therefore developing a framework of knowledge sharing, and defining critical success factors of KM and their relationships in a shape of a model.

Chapter 7, 'Explaining Empowering Employees by Grounded Theory Methodology: In Particular for Health Services', starts with an examination of the concept of empowerment; moved on to a review of empowerment approaches, strategies and process; provides an overview of GT application in employee empowerment and particularly empowerment in nursing and the health services.

Chapter 8, 'A Grounded Theory Approach for the Study of Organizational Burnout: Particularly for Caregivers in the Workplace', focuses on the application of GT approach in the field of occupational burnout by examining current studies of job burnout that have applied GT. Particularly, it refers to caregivers' burnout in the workplace.

Chapter 9, 'Using Grounded Theory Methodology to Explore Women's Sense of Insecurity', examines the studies on sexual harassment and sexual violence, focusing on definitions, statistics, forms, consequences, and prevention strategies. In addition, it focuses on GT and compares it with constructivist GT. Additionally the application of GT in various studies such as understanding of the effect of sexual assault on the couple relationship; paradigm modeling of sexual harassment; understanding intimate partner violence; women's descriptions of women's journey of recovery from sexual assault; understanding marital violence; perceptions of adult female sexual assault victims/survivors about their wellbeing are discussed.

Chapter 10 is 'Analysis of Corporate Social Responsibility With Grounded Theory Approach: Focusing on CSR and Sustainable Behavior'. The objective of this chapter is to review the present studies of the applications of GT in CSR. It focuses on paradigm modeling in the areas of CSR and sustainable behavior and provides an explanation of the phases of GT in CSR research.

This book presents different case studies about applications of GT in organizational research. It attempts to help people from the novice to the GT professionals to have a better understanding of GT and its potential to be used in social sciences and related areas. It discusses how GT is used for theory building in organizational research by examining relevant studies. It shows that GT not only allows individuals' subjective experiences interpretation but also, due to its special aspects such as theoretical sampling and constant comparison, it can be as a means of abstraction of the subjective experience into theoretical statements.

Through GT process, a researcher can develop a theory that is shaped by the views of participants to explain a process, action, or interaction. The approach utilizes an ongoing and more complex set of data collection, coding, categorizing, memo-ing, sorting, validating, and writing, from which theory emerges. GT is commonly known as an induction method that attempts to bridge the gap between research and theory. It is also a systematic theory development of data that has both inductive and deductive thinking. Researchers who want to use GT do so with the aim of providing a usable theoretical explanation for a complex problem. Instead of relying on past analysis or assumptions to highlight the right answers to the wrong questions, GT leads researchers to be enthusiastic and to seek the right answers to the right questions (Sepastian, 2019).

In the field of management, models and theories have gained widespread acceptance and have been widely used in organizational research. However, some researchers claim that some research problems cannot be addressed using existing theories or models. This is especially the case when examining new phenomena or topics that do not exist in existing literature. Thus, exploration based GT is required to produce and create new meaning that helps perceive the phenomenon. The GT has improved over the years to meet the scientific demands of the IS field. It has been used in IS studies in real-life contexts, especially when the boundaries between the phenomenon and its contexts were not fully clear, and it was not thought to be obviously defined between information and communication technology practices and the organization.

Certain mechanisms should be designed for facilitating successful practices of TM. For this purpose, GT can be used to analyze the drivers and obstacles and therefore develop a conceptual model relevant to each function. The use of GT has led to the production of models relating to KM focusing on for example key knowledge processes and a set of success factors.

Since 1970, the GT approach has been applied in nursing research and the studies have focused on nursing practice and education. Instead of being a static factor, empowerment is clearly a process; therefore, a GT approach can be the preferred methodology. GT can be conducted to better understand occupational burnout and resilience in response to workplace issues. GT asked the researchers to work without a predetermined hypothesis, as well as with the iterative processes of data collection and data analysis to explain victim's life of sexual violence. With regard to GT's growing popularity as a research method in management and the examples that have been mentioned, its applications in the field of CSR and sustainable energy transition can also be referred.

REFERENCES

Bollingtoft, A. (2017). Grounded theory analysis in entrepreneurship research. In H. Neergaard & C. M. Leitch (Eds.), *Handbook of Qualitative Research Techniques and Analysis in Entrepreneurship*. Edward Elgar Publishing.

Douglas, D. (2003). Inductive theory generation: A grounded approach to business inquiry. *Electronic Journal of Business Research Methods*, *2*(1), 47–54.

Kenealy, G. J. J. (2008). Management research and grounded theory: A review of grounded theory building approach in organizational and management research. *The Grounded Theory Review*, *7*(2). http://groundedtheoryreview.com/2008/06/28/1004/

O'Reilly, K., Paper, D., & Marx, S. (2012). Demystifying grounded theory for business research. *Organizational Research Methods*, *15*(2), 247–262. doi:10.1177/1094428111434559

Sebastian, K. (2019). Distinguishing between the types of grounded theory: Classical, interpretive and constructivist. *Journal for Social Thought*, *3*(1), 1–9.

Swamson, R. A. (2005). The challenge of research in organizations. In R. A. Swanson & E. Holton (Eds.), *Research in Organizations: Foundations and Methods in Inquiry*. Berrett-Koehler Publishers.

Trim, P. R. J., & Lee, Y. L. (2004). A reflection on theory building and the development of management knowledge. *Management Decision*, *42*(3/4), 473–480. doi:10.1108/00251740410518930

Wiesche, M., Jurisch, M. C., Yetton, P. W., & Krcmar, H. (2017). Grounded theory methodology in information systems research. *Management Information Systems Quarterly*, *41*(3), 685–701. doi:10.25300/MISQ/2017/41.3.02

Chapter 1
The Grounded Theory Methodology in Organization Studies Within Qualitative Research

ABSTRACT

It is believed that the grounded theory (GT) approach works best for researchers who are concerned about the gap between academic and practical research because of the importance they place on applied research. The chapter aimed to explain the GT methodology and identify its application in organizational research context. In this regard, the theory-research-development-practice cycle, the factors affecting the choice of organization research methodology, and the types of qualitative research methods have been studied by comparing four qualitative methods of case study, GT, phenomenological study, and content analysis. Also, in this regard, the four main GT schools including Glaserian classic GT, Straussian GT, Charmazian constructivist GT, and Clarkeian situational GT, as well as the GT process involving the phases of data collection, coding, memo-ing, sorting, and validation are discussed in detail.

DOI: 10.4018/978-1-7998-4252-1.ch001

INTRODUCTION

Grounded Theory (GT) is recognized as an influential methodology for research inquiry of much academic debate aiming at providing practical explanations. Because the GT approach is interdisciplinary, it is not expected that it will be possible to develop mature theoretical frameworks within specific academic areas. Rather, it emphasizes the importance of accessing the tacit knowledge of different organizational actors. According to Burden and Roodt (2007), the GT approach was used until the 1970s in the studies related to management and organizational behavior which were published in major journals, and GT is one of, if not the most important, approaches cited in qualitative studies used in these fields.

The GT approach since its introduction in 1967, and then its application in the fields of management and organization in the 1970s, has gradually become a research method of interest in the toolkit of analysts. The best application of the GT is to understand the social processes and subsequent psychological consequences inherently associated with organizational change in a seemingly turbulent environment. Rather than describing what is happening, the process of theorizing in GT ensures that it explains what is actually happening in practice as a strength of this method. In addition to expanding the perspective, this approach can help participants learn how to manage their lives in the current environment and with future organizational challenges. Therefore, this method is very suitable for organizational research. According to Kenealy (2008), GT is applicable to areas that have not been explored before and there is a research gap and new perspectives are needed to identify areas of management involvement and improvement. Until recent times, most organizational and management research training focused heavily on quantitative techniques specially in UK universities, that has caused ignoring qualitative methods, particularly GT. There is still a lack of experienced grounded theorists and GT training although despite the growing trend of applying qualitative research and teaching them.

Organizations are very complex and diverse environments involving complex entities that operate in different ways within them. Therefore, the use of multilateral approaches that can provide a broad, dynamic analytical picture of organizational hierarchy should be valuable to researchers and organizational consultants. In this regard, research methods should be more aware of the complexities of organizational environments and, as far as possible, rather than simplify them, consider them in order to achieve more accurate results. As the theorist should approach an inquiry with a fairly open mind it is likely that a kind of general theoretical account will be emerged in the particular investigation during the grounded initially approaches. In the organizational context, the research related to the pilot stages of large scale survey inquiries, the case studies of organizational behavior in order to produce more than an impressionistic account from their inquiries, the research related to the world organizational features as corporate cultures, that are well-suited particularly to qualitative investigation, and the studies concerned about detailed, locally based fact collection and interpretation essential to perform excellent organizational research can be appropriate subjects in which the GT approach can be implemented (Martin and Turner, 1986).

The purpose of this chapter is to explain the methodology of GT and to identify its application in organizational research. In this way, the theory, research, development, and practice cycle, the factors affecting the choice of organization research methodology and the types of qualitative research methods have been studied by comparing four qualitative methods of case study, GT, phenomenological study, and content analysis. Also, in this regard, the four main GT schools including Glaserian classic GT, Straussian GT, Charmazian constructivist GT, and Clarkeian situational GT, as well as the GT process involving the phases of data collection, coding, memo-ing, sorting, and validation are discussed in detail.

ORGANIZATIONAL STUDIES AND GT

In order to study all types of organizations, it is possible to use the GT approach. Research conducted based on the applied methodology of the GT approach, leads to an increased understanding of the research situation and the underlying problems affecting the research topic. All aspects of human resource management, from employment planning through the recruitment and selection of employees, appraisal and rewards, to motivation and career planning can be involved with such issues. The researcher during the research process, (through comparative analysis) on the specific issues of the field under study, can obtain data that can lead to more attention to these issues using systematic interviews or observations. Susabowska (2016) aimed aims to verify whether the use of this methodology can also be appropriate in the area of human resource management, because the GT methodology in management science significantly influences the organization of qualitative research and it is possible to apply its procedure to explore study most research areas.

By using and application of GT approach, and observing the focus of this approach on the way of change perception by the people who are affected by the process and recognizing that available change management models do not adequately capture the complexity of the change process from the perspective of change recipients, the GT-based research design is mainly focused on helping change management theory (Rosenbaum et al., 2016).

The GT approach is suitable for consumer research, for example in areas where discovery of relevance is applied to consumer behavior. These areas can include analysis of the consumption of technological products, women's clothing in the workplace, and the symbolic meaning found in advertisements. Of course, it is likely that many consumer research studies have employed GT methods without recognizing or acknowledging them and what was mentioned are merely studies that explicitly state the use of the GT method (Shivany and Velnampy, 2015).

Also, the special features of the GT method make it particularly suitable for addressing key problems in industrial marketing, such as complex decision-making processes and interactions in social networks and relationships, because in these areas, in-depth analysis of the data is needed. It is a real-life experiment. For this reason, GT has been suggested in previous research as a useful method for industrial marketing research because it has provided valuable research opportunities for this research. Of course, the GT use in industrial marketing in particular has not been as extensive as marketing or management fields, and even with the potential for using in such research, it has sometimes been misunderstood and ignored (Keränen and Oinonen, 2019).

GT-based studies in the fields of organizational tensions, conflicts, dialectics, and paradoxes in organizational science have increased. In this regard, Fairhurst and Putnam (2019) have developed an integrated approach that helps identifying different types of organizational opposition and responds to them, as well as promoting assessment of the potential impact of the power and dynamics of micro-organizing.

With the increasing popularity of qualitative research in the field of medical research, the GT method has also been emphasized by most researchers in this field (Sbaraini et al., 2011). For instance, transition to motherhood for women with post-natal depression, clients' experiences of disengaged moments in psychotherapy, perceptions of the schizophrenia recovery concept, and the experiences earned by nurses with working in acute psychiatric settings are among the subjects of newly published GT articles (Tweed and Charmaz, 2011).

Companies have found it challenging to attract and retain top talent Millennials due to the costly job-hopping. Rivers (2018) developed a theory that demonstrates the Millennials' process for deciding whether to job-hop or stay in a company. Mohammed and Norman (2016) investigated the practices of organizational information sharing of the millennial generation with the use of GT. Haider et al. (2019) considered the motivation for sustainable work of local government employees via a rigorous GT method of inquiry. They argued that with Millennials' default perception of the public sector as relatively conservative, bureaucratic and slower to change, the recruitment and retention of young people and Millennials in the public sector is becoming increasingly difficult.

Kwanjai (2011) applied GT on cultural intelligence in general and cross-cultural intelligence that was practiced at selected Dutch firms in Thailand in particular. Plessis and Marais (2015) focused on the challenges facing leaders engaged in multicultural education by conducting a GT research. Ziyatdinova (2017) aimed at identifying the role of the cultural intelligence from the viewpoint of a leader and examining the influence of culture on leadership with the use of GT. Rozkwitalska et al. (2016) applied the GT approach to analyze and propose a model of the social interactions in multicultural environments of multinational corporations. Draucker et al. (2014) proposed that GT research could be beneficial more to health disparities research.

As it utilizes the natural context in which the phenomena studied happened, GT is attractive to researchers in order to examine and understand social constructions. This method is considered as one of the most effective and widely used methods in qualitative research in specific fields such as sociology. Although often overlooked in the field of sport management, the GT method components (usually coding techniques) are often used for data analysis in sport-related studies. As such, researchers combine GT with other research methods. Of course, combining different methods as long as it is justified and appropriate to the research problem is a valid way of doing research. The main consequence of this mixture of GT with other research methods is that the analysis departs from the basic principles of GT, namely the emergence of theory (Sotiriadou and Shilbury, 2008).

THEORY-RSEARCH-DEVELOPMENT-PRACTICE

Organizations are (1) complex systems, (2) open systems, and (3) dynamic systems that are worth studying. However, many claim that academic research has failed to provide useful solutions to problems in practice in organizations because of the widening gap between science and practice in organizations. This criticism is increasing, since the findings of academic studies and consulting are not applicable for experts in the organizations. There is also growing debate between advocates of normal science and action science methods (Swanson and Holton, 2005). As a vital cycle, theory, research, development, and practice together compose allows refining ideas progressively through evolving from concepts to practices and from practices to concepts. This cycle of theory-research-development-practice shows a systematic application of research methods applied to advance the knowledge used by both organizational researchers and practitioners.

Some researchers warn us about building relationships between theory, research, development and practice. For example, Kahn (1970) forced philosophers and researchers to rethink the assumptions underpinning the scientific method and in this way, paved the way for alternative, post-positivistic approaches to research in the behavioral sciences when proposing the notion of a scientific paradigm. Swanson and Holton (2008) believe that using qualitative methods such as GT allows the theory to emerge from the data obtained from practice and experience; the theory does not necessarily exist prior to research and can be derived from it. Therefore, the model of theory, research, development, and practice in organizational research contains such a warning.

This model demonstrates the need for awareness to enrich all professional areas. Also, exchange between domains is multilateral; as such, each domain can be a good starting point for subsequent domains in the cycle. Whether one begins with theory, research, development, or practice, the improvements can occur in the profession. Hence, according to Swanson and Holton (2008), each of the domains of the cycle can either informs or is informed by the other domains.

As an important use of research that can be done through GT, and research can also proceed along it, is the theory building cycle. Although the current benefits of the rich theoretical foundations are more widely used in organization-focused practice areas, much of this research is rooted in relevant areas of study. In order to gain greater understanding of a wide range

Figure 1. Theory-Research-Development-Practice cycle (Swanson, 2007)

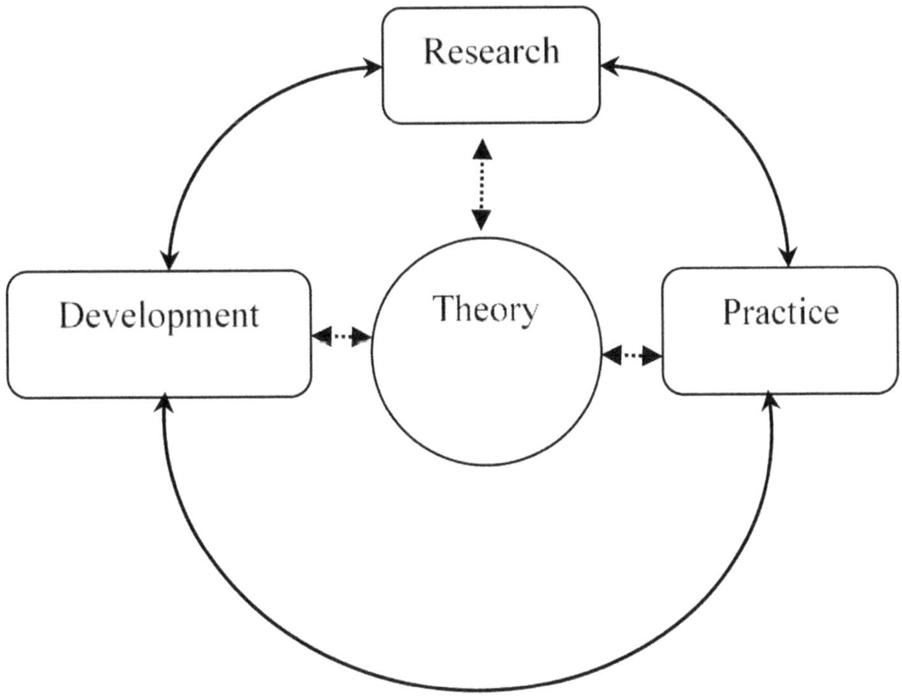

of human and organizational phenomena, additional theories are needed and in this regard, research can play a dual role in proceeding the organizational knowledge. Research leads to the creation of knowledge that can be directly applied to the practical improvement and development of basic theories. Organizational development efforts are one of the unique opportunities to enter this cycle. In this domain, the conditions are already in place due to the demand and the need for radical changes and conditions to create fundamentally new organizational models and methods. The problems and challenges facing functioning organizations is completely felt when starting with practice. These challenges are an inexplicable source of research problems. During a cycle period from practice to research or practice to development, it traces the path of familiarity with the problems that persist in organizations and stimulates their research and development efforts (Swanson and Holton, 2005).

QUALITATIVE RESEARCH METHODOLOGY

The three trends of widening boundaries, the multi-paradigmatic profile, and the methodological inventiveness are characterized the field of organizational research. Thus, as can be seen in figure 2, selecting the research methods, formed by aims, epistemological concerns, and norms of practice, is also affected by organizational, historical, political, ethical, audience, and personal factors, generally seen as a problem that must be overcome. Also, researchers in a field can have a variety of goals, for example some of them consider the creating solidarity, identifying causal links, building models,

Figure 2. Factors influencing the choice of organizational research methods adopted from (Buchanan and Bryman, 2009)

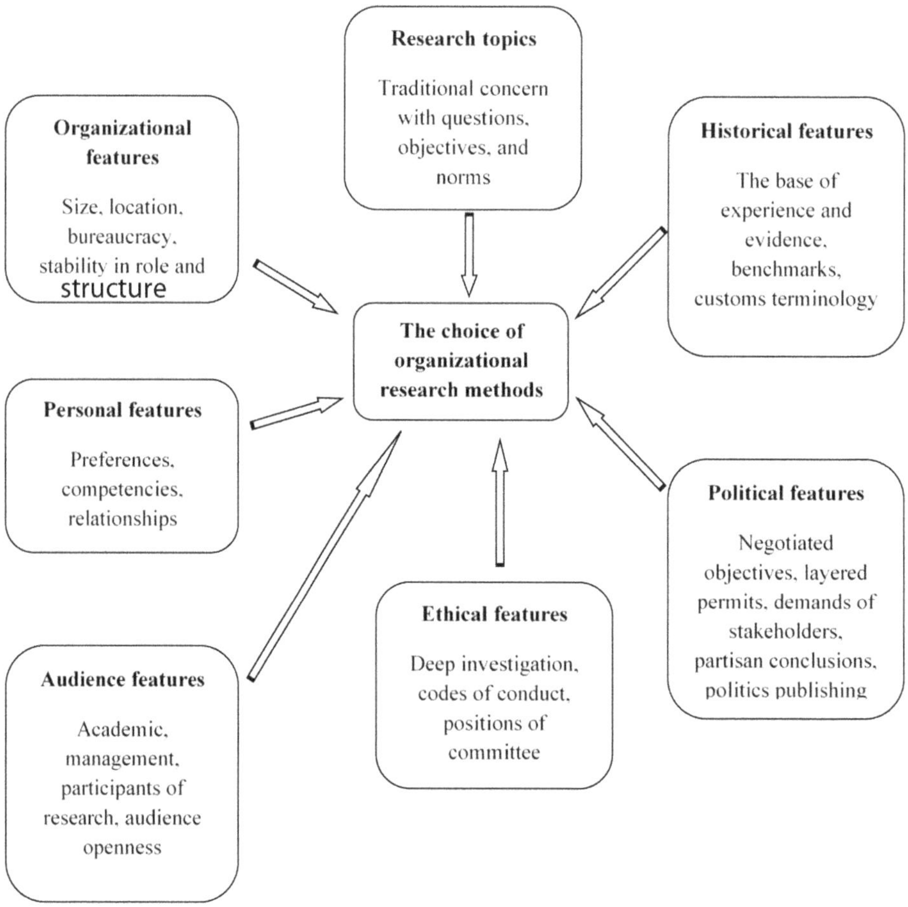

or testing hypotheses. Others are more concerned with rich descriptions and capturing complex texture of the corporate world as a valuable goal of its kind. The different positivist, critical, phenomenological, constructivist, interpretative, feminist, and postmodern perspectives can be displayed within the organizational research.

The features of the focal organization such as size, location (single or multiple sites), and whether it is a commercial organization or a professional bureaucracy have always been more or less significantly effective in the logistics of fieldwork. In this regard, the choice of method can be highly dependent on the stability of the research setting. In case that the organizational context is changing, the predetermined and inflexible methods are less or perhaps inappropriate.

Because of this, organizational research is less cumulative, and researchers often overlook the risk of historical records and evidence obtained from long-term research and past results in the field. Therefore, organizational researchers can be advised to consider past experiences, frameworks, conceptualizations, and findings that may influence current choices of research focus and appropriate research methodology. Due to the nature of organizations as political entities, it may be difficult for scholars to observe contractual norms of observer neutrality by avoiding entanglement in power and politics issues. Negotiating on research objectives, obtaining permissions to access respondents, aligning with stakeholder groups, and attempting to publish findings are four ways through which researchers are routinely engaged in political actions.

Of course, the open-ended nature of some qualitative research, which raises some ethical questions, has led to the focus on ethical scrutiny in the field of organizational research. For example, in some research approaches, such as GT, it is emphasized that research questions are not as clear as possible prior to data collection which leads to issues during the investigation. Before selecting methods so relevant audiences will perceive their approach as having been appropriate, the organizational researchers often need to concern about how and by whom their findings will be used. Therefore, the potentially conflicting interests and expectations of academic, management, and research practitioner audiences need to be considered by researchers.

Often when selecting a research topic, researchers look at topics that interest them, and use a method in which they are competent and skilled as it is easy to use. Although some researchers may opt for face-to-face encounters and challenges when identifying patterns and collecting qualitative data, others may prefer computer screening, and discovery of relationships in quantitative data. The choice of subject as well as how the research is influenced by the researcher's training and skills also apply. Generally, beginner researchers are not allowed to apply their personal preferences and biases to technical decisions related to research methods.

Because of providing a guidance to conduct of the research and its effect on the quality and the accuracy of research results, the selection of a research methodology is crucial. Qualitative methods have long been used in industrial and organizational psychology research. As one of the qualitative research

Table 1. Comparison of three qualitative research methods (Williams, 2007)

Research methods	Key features
Case study	A plan, an event, an activity, a process, or one or more individuals are in depth explored by the researcher. Multiple sources such as direct or participant observations, interviews, archival records or documents, physical artifacts, and audio-visual materials are extensively used for the purpose of data collection for a case study. The researcher must spend time with the people studied on-site interacting. The lessons learned or patterns found that connect with theories should be included in the report.
Grounded theory	Researcher try to use this structured approach to shape and elicit theory grounded in data, through deriving a general, abstract theory of a process, action, or interaction grounded in the views of participants in a study. In a format called constant comparative method, this process includes collecting and analysing the data, and repeating the process. Several sources such as interviewing participants or witnesses, reviewing historical videotapes or records, observations while on-site can be used to obtain data. Five dimensions of describing the research question, literature review, describing the methodology, data analysis explaining the theory, and discussing the implications constitute the GT report structure.
Phenomenological Study	It emphasizes on the participant's perceptions of the event or situation and the study tries to answer the question of the experience. Because of conducting interviews, the method for a phenomenological study is similar to that of GT. In order to understand and interpret a participant's perception on the meaning of an event the method of data collection is conducted through long interviews (1-2 hours). Writing the research questions to explore the meaning of the experience, conducting interviews, analyzing the data to find the clusters of meanings, and ending with a report that furthers the readers understanding of the essential structure of the experience is the procedural format. The study gathers data that leads to identifying common themes in people's perceptions of their experiences.
Content Analysis Study	A process of systematic and detailed review of the content of a particular body of research material with the aim of identifying patterns, themes or biases. The procedural process for the content analysis research designed to achieve the highest objective analysis, which involves identifying the body of the material being studied and defining the characteristics and characteristics of the object being studied. The data collection process is a two-step process. In the first step, it is necessary for the researcher to analyze the materials and place them in a large table that lists the specifications. Secondly, in order to report the results in quantitative format, the researcher has to perform statistical analysis. The description of the materials under study, the properties and qualities studied, a description of the methodology, the statistical analysis showing the frequency table, and drawing conclusions about the patterns, themes, or biases found in the human communications and data collection are the five sections of a research report.

methods, GT, that is a method in which data are systematically collected from multiple sources, has been widely used by management, industrial and organizational researchers. As a neutral, unbiased research frame GT can be used by researchers anywhere with varied epistemologies. The GT usefulness for developing new theory or fresh insights into old theory, generating theory of direct interest and relevance for practitioners, and the ability to uncover micro-management processes in complex and unfolding scenarios are among the reasons of GT popularity in organizational research (Kamasak et al., 2017).

Case studies, GT, phenomenological study, and content analysis are several different methods for conducting a qualitative research that are compared during this chapter:

GT PROCESS

The researcher can develop a theory that is formed by the views of participants to explain a process, action, or interaction by making use of GT process described in this section using description of various GT schools. The approach constitutes a procedure through which theory emerges by employing a continual to-and-fro between data collection, coding, categorizing, memo writing, sorting, validating, and writing. Figure 3 summarily shows the steps of the GT approach.

Figure 3. Steps of grounded theory based on Strauss and Corbin (2008)-Straussian grounded theory (Roman et al., 2017)

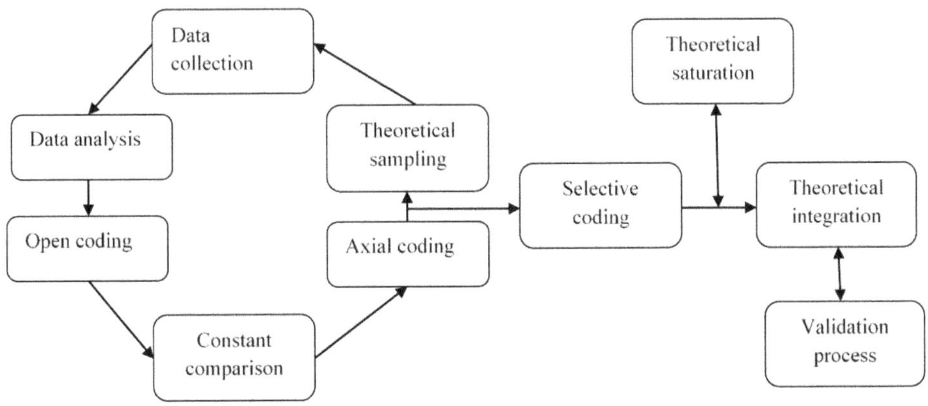

Gathering GT Data

Since the emphasis in the classic GT is on the analysis of actions and process, the first questions to be asked in this way are:

- What's going on here? This question helps develop our vision by asking what happens on two levels:
- What are the fundamental social processes?
- What are the fundamental social psychological processes?

In various types of qualitative research, the intensive interviewing has long been used as a useful method of data collection. Basically, if the interview is a targeted conversation, intensive interviewing allows for an in-depth examination of a particular topic or experience, and is therefore a useful method of interpretation goals. Interviewing is also a contextual and negotiable method.

There may be many commonalities between focus groups and less structured interviews, however, these features are more than just collecting the similar data from many participants at a time. In the focus group approach, a group discussion exists on a specific topic that is organized with specific research goals; a discussion that is purposeful, controlled, and recorded by the researcher (also known as a moderator or facilitator) (Gill et al., 2008).

While a structured format for data collection can be obtained from the interviews, respondents may say one thing in an interview but do something different in practice. Observations are a very useful form of data collection and it is the only way to reveal the dichotomies. A meaning, that is different from the meaning the participants assign to it themselves, may be assigned by the researcher to an action or interaction. Observations should always be supported with interviews and/or documentary evidence because nonverbal behaviors can be easily misinterpreted, especially in the cross-cultural context (Hull, 2013).

Although all the method of qualitative research involves the analysis of texts, some scholars study texts that are partially or completely derived from other sources. For instance, elicited texts can provide us a means to create data, through the research in which participants provide written data in response to a researcher's request. The elicited texts involve research participants in writing the data. On the other hand, the researcher had no hand in shaping the extant texts which are consist of varied documents. The elicited and extant texts can be used as either initial or complementary sources of data.

The next concept is to scrutinize how data is collected and which data you obtain helps to locate them. When coding and categorizing, such scrutiny also helps you since it enables you to place your emerging analysis in its social context. As a result, you can make more accurate comparisons when encoding data.

Coding in GT Practice

The first analytic step, which is the process of defining what the data are about, is qualitative coding. Coding refers to simultaneously categorizing, summarizing, and accounting for each piece of data by naming parts of data with a label. As a first step in moving specific statements in the data to create analytical interpretations, GT coding creates your bones of analysis. These bones are later assembled into a skeleton during theoretical integration. Therefore, coding is not just an initial step, but rather an analytical framework on which you can analyze (Charmaz, 2006). Coding can be considered as an initial phase involving naming each word, line, or segment of data; subsequently, a focused, selective phase is conducted in order to use the most significant or frequent initial codes to sort, synthesize, integrate, and organize large amounts of data. The types of coding as substantive coding and theoretical coding are proposed by Hull (2013). Also, three different types of substantive coding: open, axial, and selective coding are identified by Strauss and Corbin (1990).

The first step, open coding, guides us toward the next decisions about defining conceptual categories. The questions like: "What does the data indicate? Pronounce? From whose point of view? and, what theoretical category does this specific datum indicate?", were asked during the open coding. Line-by-line coding which refers to naming each line of the written data, is the first step in coding for many grounded researchers. Hundreds of codes can be produced during the coding process. The initial codes help researchers to separate data into categories and to see processes. According to Strauss and Corbin (1990), similar codes have to be grouped into categories in order to recognize patterns in the data. A category is code at higher abstraction level and the categorization is obtained by asking and answering the following questions related to each code (Charmaz, 2006):

- What category of the phenomenon does this code belong to?
- What do the phenomena identified with these codes have in common?
- What might this phenomenon (and related code) to be about?

Strauss and Corbin (1990) believe that each category has properties, as the characteristics or attributes of a category and dimensions that refers to the possible locations of properties on some kind of continuum. Since they form the basis of relationships between categories and subcategories, the properties and dimensions of each category need to be recognized and developed.

Performing the initial coding results in the following outputs:

- Concepts including emotions, events, actions, trends and situations that their label should be an action (gerund).
- Categories including concepts grouped by phenomena through a comparison and aggregation of concepts that mostly represent meanings, tacit assumptions, or implicit actions.
- Properties and dimensions including aspects of a category that are mentioned, and their possible values.

Focused coding coding occurs after you have established some strong analytic directions through your initial line-by-line coding. The purpose of focused coding, which refers to use the most significant and / or frequent earlier codes to sift through large amounts of data, is to synthesize and explain larger segments of data. The strength of focused coding in GT is that rather than passively reading your data, you will actively participate in the process (Charmaz, 2006).

As the second phase of coding in Straussian GT, axial coding can specify the properties and dimensions of a category and so, it can relate categories to subcategories. Although this may be occurred in an early stage of development, axial coding follows the development of a major category. Sorting, synthesizing, and organizing large amounts of data and reassemble them in new ways after open coding are among the purposes of axial coding (Charmaz, 2006).

The purpose of the third phase of coding in Straussian GT, selective coding, is conceptually integrating, categorizing, and relating all created categories during axial coding to the core category as one cohesive theory. Thus, the results of axial coding have been further explored, integrated, and validated. In other words, the selective coding is quite similar to the axial coding, but it is done on a more abstract level.

The theoretical coding is related to the concept of how substantive codes may relate to one another as hypotheses integrated into one theory. In short, the possible relationships between the categories you have developed in your axial coding can be identified in theoretical codes (Charmaz, 2006).

Table 2. A series of 18 theoretical coding families (Glaser, 1978; Charmaz, 2006))

Coding families	Concepts
The six Cs	Causes, contexts, contingencies, conditions (… of pain suffering consequences).
Process	Stages, phases, phasings, transitions, careers, chains, sequences (career of a patient with chronic pain passages).
The degree family	Extent, level, intensity, range, amount, statistical average, standard deviation (extent of pain suffering continuum).
Type family	Types, classes, genres, prototypes, styles, kinds (kinds of pain – sharp, piercing, throbbing).
The strategy family	Strategies, tactics, techniques, mechanisms (coping with pain management).
Interactive family	Interaction, mutual effects, interdependence, symmetries, rituals (interaction of pain experience and coping reciprocity).
Identity-self family	Identity, self-image, self-concept, self-evaluation, transformations of self (self-concepts of pain patients social worth).
Cutting-point family	Boundary, critical juncture, cutting point, tolerance levels (point career of pain patient of no return, start of chronification in the medical turning point).
Cultural family	Social norms, social values, social beliefs (social norms and beliefs of pain patients).
Consensus family	Contracts, agreements, definitions of the compliance situation, uniformity, conformity, conflict (conflict of treatment types of pain management).
The unit family	Group, family, organizational, aggregate, territorial, societal, status and role units (status and role of pain patient in pain management).

The causes, contexts, consequences, conditions, etc. that constitute the C-family can be seen as equivalent to the coding paradigm proposed by Böhm (2004). While you are in the early stages of research, coding, as the first step in a journey that enables you to bridge between imaginary events and describing them into insights and theoretical possibilities, routes your work in an analytic direction.

Memo-Writing

Most commonly associated with GT, providing memos is as a methodological strategy that yet all qualitative approaches can be used to improve their procedure. However, with lack or substandard memo-ing as a major shortfall of most qualitative research studies, many researchers fail to capitalize on this valuable tool (Birks et al., 2008). The qualitative researcher is able to engage with their research to a greater degree through the use of memos; a level that would not have been possible without this strategy. By building strong relationships between data, researchers can feel that their sensitivity to the concepts in it has increased.

As a pivotal intermediate step between data collection and writing drafts of papers, memo-writing constitutes a crucial method in GT since it can increase your speed in analyzing your data and codes early in the research process, by applying pauses and analysis of the obtained code you may use at any time and in any way. By increasing your involvement in the analysis and helping to raise the level of abstraction of your ideas, sequential memo writing during the research can help your research process. As you write successive memos, specific codes can be emerged and visualized as theoretical categories. They also help you to clarify what is happening in the field when you use them from the start. According to Strauss and Corbin (1990), the complexity, density, accuracy of memos increases with the researcher's move from data collection to theorization during memes evolution.

Through giving you a non-linear, visual, and flexible technique to understand and organize your material, clustering can help to get start as a shorthand pre-writing technique. This technique can be used to create a tentative and alterable chart or map of your study. Free-writing, that can liberate your thoughts and feelings, refers to put pen to paper or fingers to keyboard and writing for eight minutes to begin, longer with practice; it can also encourage you to: 1) form fresh material and 2) unlearn past immobilizing habits, and 3) write in a natural voice.

Theoretical Sensitivity

According to Strauss and Corbin (1990), theoretical sensitivity is related to the ability to have insight, understand and give meaning to the data, and to detach the relevant from the irrelevant. Also, Glaser (1978) suggests that theoretical sensitivity, or entering the field with an awareness of the subtleties of the data can be used with the initial aim of sensitize the researcher. It is also possible to gain theoretical sensitivity from professional experience and when preliminary review the literature. Of course, it is needed to distinguish between identifying sensitizing concepts that can help to quickly collect data, as well as using these concepts to impose a framework on data.

Theoretical Sampling, Saturation, and Sorting

You seek pertinent data to develop your emerging theory during the theoretical sampling. Through sampling to develop the properties of your category or categories, you conduct theoretical sampling until no new properties emerge.

Thus, in order to integrate your emerging theory, you saturate your categories with data and subsequently sort and/or diagram them. Sampling to develop a researcher's emerging theoretical categories distinguishes theoretical sampling from other forms of sampling. By conducting theoretical sampling, the researcher is encouraged to advance the analysis and thus can improve his research by (Charmaz, 2006):

- determining the relevant properties of the categories
- Increasing the accuracy of the categories
- Providing the substance to move the material from description to analysis
- Increasing level of abstraction and generalization of analysis
- Grounding the conjectures in data
- Specifying the analysis relationships between or among the categories
- Increasing saving on the use of theoretical statements.

In the GT methodology, you start at the initial sampling stage, while the theoretical sampling will guide you. The purpose of theoretical sampling, rather than demographics or increasing the statistical generalizability of your results, is to obtain information to help build your categories. Random samples of individuals with characteristics that represent the population under study are needed in many qualitative studies. Grounded theorists, unlike qualitative researchers who seek to use their data for statistical inference about the target population, are more likely aimed to fit their emerging theories with their obtained data. Also, sometimes the grist is proposed by grounded theorists for the emergent hypotheses that other researchers might pursue, while quantitative researchers test preconceived hypotheses.

When will the data collection end? What criteria are used to stop this process? The standard GT's short answer to this question is: stop working when your categories are saturated. Theoretical saturation is something that should be aimed at grounded theorists. Grounded theorists use the strategies like sorting, diagramming, and integrating your memos as inter-related processes to service the theoretical development of the analysis. It is needed to order memos according to their similarities, connections, and concepts of categories and their properties that are contained in the memos in the sorting phase that cause creating patterns in the memos, and subsequently, shapes the outline of the theory. Also, new ideas can be generated in this phase that should be captured in additional memos as the analyst compares ideas to ideas (Glaser, 1978). Providing a visual representation of categories and the relationship between them is the advantage of diagrams, by which, concrete images of our ideas can be shaped.

Validation

Since validation is one of the most important steps in GT development in order to analyze the relevance and representativeness of the study in terms of the phenomenon, it is suggested to discuss with the participants about the categories obtained from data as well as the representativeness of the theoretical model of the GT. Using data validation, the researcher can pursue information that will help develop more complete explanations and thus allow for further research or appropriate reorientation. Hence, it is possible using validation to analyze whether the theoretical model represents the reality under study, as well as discuss its applicability to other spatial and temporal domains, that enables the modification and addition of new elements to improve the interpretation of the phenomenon under study. The strategy of selecting a conversation circle is adopted in Adamy et al. (2018) among the strategies that could be utilized to validate the data and the theoretical model in GT, with the purpose of co-constructing a theory in collaboration with the participants. As a collective resonance method, the conversation circle consists of creating spaces for dialogue, in which through questioning, sharing information, and reflecting before acting, people can express themselves, listen to others and to themselves, and thus stimulating the construction of the individuals' autonomy.

Table 3. Operationalization of the two conversation circles (Adamy et al., 2018)

Conversation circle 1	Conversation circle 2
Date 1	Date 2
Objective 1: presenting the categories, the diagrams, and the study's theoretical model	Objective 2: validating the theoretical model
Participants 1	Participants 2
Steps 1: · Presenting the objectives of the study and conversation circle · Presenting the methodological approach · Reading and requesting of signing of the informed consent form · Interpreting and validating the data related to codes · providing the phenomenon, categories, and representative diagrams	Steps 2: displaying the phenomenon, categories, and representative diagrams

Through support of critical speaking and sensitive listening, the circles in this dialogical construction provide collective or textual knowledge and hence, lead to the possibility of interaction between the participants and sharing of information that helps to ensure the validity of the theoretical model.

Glaser (1978) in the Glaserian classic GT, reaffirm the criteria by which, it is possible to remain the standards in order to assess the quality of a GT. The four criteria reaffirmed by Glaser include fit, function, relevance, and adaptability (Holton, 2008):

- The fit criterion that refers to extract conceptual codes and categories from the data collected rather than using pre-conceived codes or categories derived from existing theories.
- The function criterion that refers to the GT's ability to describe and interpret behavior in a substantive area in order to predict future behavior.
- The relevance criterion that refers to the focus of theory on a core concern or process emerged in a substantive area. The data conceptual grounding indicates the significance and relevance of this core concern or process that way, it guarantees relevance.
- The adaptability criterion that refers the ability of theory to be continually refined with the emergence of new data to bring new categories, features and dimensions to the theory. This dynamic feature of GT guarantees its perpetual relevance and value in the social world from which it is rooted.

Severe adherence to the complete GT method is vital in order to increase the potential for a rich multivariate conceptual theory. It cannot be said that the GT was used in the wrong or right place, but one only has to check to what extent it is fit, relevant, functional and adaptable. Therefore, GT should be constantly evaluated by readers on the basis of these criteria.

Glaser (1992) also proposed other important requirements relating the quality of GT that should be considered by researchers. First, the importance of the field that make the researcher to understand what is happening; second, the significance of theory which is grounded in reality; third, the nature and importance of experience in the field for the participants and researcher with its gradual evolution; and fourth, the active role played by the people involved in shaping the world around us through symbolic interaction processes.

Other important requirements suggested by Glaser (1992) as denoting the quality of GT also drew the attention of the researcher. These include the following: (1) the significance of the researcher getting out into the field to understand what is going on, (2) the importance of theory which is grounded in reality, (3) the nature and significance of experience in the field for the participants and researcher as continually evolving, (4) the active role of persons in shaping the world they live in through the processes of symbolic interaction.

GT SCHOOLS

Since each of the creators of the different GT approaches use the word theory in a different sense, in this section, it is tried to compare the coding tools used in four different schools (e.g. two versions, status, approach or model exist in the Strauss and Glaser approach). For example, in the Glaser approach, GT is abstract, while it is complex for Strauss; for Charmaz, it is related to theorizing an argument about the world and Clark considers it to be the theory of comparisons. With formal, traditional, classical objective terms, Glaser tries to differentiate the Glaserian approach from other approaches. Whereas Charmaz uses constructivism to differentiate his approach while, Clark's uses the analysis of the situation to distinguish Clarkeian situational approach.

The different approaches presented in GT all have common features as a family that are indicative of a GT approach. That GT is first a process that starts with inductive logic and involves simultaneous collecting, analyzing, and constructing theory, as well as, consistently comparing and writing memo, using theoretical sample and focus on the creation of a GT are the basic features that can be seen in Table 5.

New researchers have difficulties in using GT and selecting between Glaserian GT and Straussian GT (Alammar et al. 2018). According to some scholars, since Glaserian GT assumes that there is an orderly real world that can be objectively observed, it can be regarded based on a positivist realistic ontology approach. While others believe that Glaserian GT is based on the assumption that 'the real world exists but at the same time, acknowledge that it is impossible for humans to understand it', then Glaserian GT is based on post-positivist critical realistic ontology. It is also believed that the purpose of Glaserian GT is the unbiased discovery of new knowledge and is based on an objectivist epistemology that assumes that the researcher is separate from the subject under investigation. According to Glaserian GT researchers, the data can represent a true theory. In the Straussian GT, the philosophical view is based on symbolic and pragmatic foundations and symbolic interactionist do

Table 4. Positions on the nature and purpose of theory in grounded theory (Apramian et al., 2017)

Glaser and Holton (2007)	For Glaser, theory is not expressly descriptive and aimed to do what description cannot do namely transcend person, place, and time. In summary, he refers to produce what sociologists call formal theory which is a theory developed or discovered for a conceptual area of inquiry – such as status passage, social stratification, formal organization, or stigma. Glaser pursues sociological theory at its highest levels of abstraction. Glaserian GT attempts for saving in the coding of data and creation of categories. A more tentative coding and memo-ing process repeats in Glaserian GT, as the researcher returns to the data collection. Glaser's version of the iterative process relies on the presumption of what he calls emergence. Enough iterations of comparison can lead to the construction of a core category that is broadly explanatory and under which almost all observed behaviours and reports fall which is referred to the emergence concept.
Strauss (1987)	The complexity of a theory dominates its level of abstraction in terms of Strauss. As a term used by philosophers of science as a shorthand for the impossibility of discovering linear cause and effect relationships, complexity refers to unpredictability and unreliability that doesn't yield to human understanding for a constitutive. Strauss's emphasis on complexity coaxed the definition of theory toward broader interpretations in the work of others. Strauss wrote that depending on the purposes of the investigator, the final conclusions drawn in the course of the research can vary greatly by level of abstraction rather than focusing purely on formal theory. Strauss is interested in exceptions to his categories in a different way. Strauss argues for the importance of what he calls a 'coding paradigm'. The six 'Cs' are adopted in Strauss's coding paradigm as a coding family. Strauss's coding paradigm, despite this apparent simplification, tends to intense the analysis. Strauss's version of analysis requires that induction, deduction, and verification enter into the research, rather than trusting purely in emergence and induction,
Charmaz (2006)	Charmaz emphasized that the early GT works stress discovering and analyzing a basic social process. The burden of rigor from exacting explications of exceptions is transferred by Charmaz to authentic representations of the words, actions, and stories, the marginalized voices of her participants. According to Charmazian GT, this approach can be used to reveal links between concrete experiences of suffering and social structure, culture, and social practices or policies. Amplifying the importance of gerund-based process coding is her first choice and de-emphasizing the importance of single core categories is her second choice.
Clarke (2003)	GT is being regenerated and updated in order to better address differences and complexities of social life articulated through the postmodernism. The purpose of theory in terms of Clarke, is to attract attention to certain aspects of social life and particular actors and their activities. In this regard, she uses the description of difference as a fundamental principle for her theory building process. According to Clarke, the core activity of a social world changes over time and can be read and experienced differently. She also directs the theory building process toward identifying silenced aspects of work. The pursuit of difference in the Clarkeian GT, comes from an analysis of codes in service to three types of maps including situational maps, social worlds/arenas maps, and positional maps. Each of these maps constitutes one of the missions of Clarke's reformed understanding of the purpose of theory: the description of difference and hidden work. The Clark's maps confirm his broader methodological strategy. The situational maps, as the first group of maps, are strategies for explaining the elements in the situation and examining relationships between them. The most important human, nonhuman, discursive, and symbolic elements of a situation are identified and charted by the situational maps which are essentially descriptive. Pushing the analyst toward looking for the unseen elements of the situation, the Situational maps are a product of a reframed analytic 'forcing'. The social worlds/ arenas and positional maps as the other two maps, both essentially provide an interpretive assumption about social processes. The analyst needs to break from reiterating social power structures to produce these maps. Also, the analyst's focus should be on stripping the positions in a debate from the people who hold them. Positional mapping uses description to create room for the reinterpretation of traditional power structures, by focusing only on describing the positions themselves, and removing questions of hierarchy and the implied value of the positions.

Table 5. Similarities between GT approaches informed by the literature (Rieger, 2018)

Explaining a process	Describes a social process that includes detecting identifiable time steps with a definite beginning and end and criteria in the middle stages.
Getting started with an inductive approach	It starts with no idea to prove or disprove, and important issues come from people's explanations.
Collecting and analyzing data and building theory simultaneously	Analytics in the process of analyzing and collecting data begins with several interviews focused on developing theoretical ideas.
Constant comparison	for the purpose of identifying similarities and differences, developing successively more abstract ideas through comparing data with data, data with code, code with code, code with category, and category with category
Memo-ing	Providing written records of comparisons and analytical thinking about the data analysis process to develop theoretical ideas and direct theoretical sampling
Theoretical sampling	In order to elaborate the developing theoretical categories and address conceptual gaps, concepts derived from the early analysis after developing theoretical ideas, will guide the collection of additional data. It is mostly started with convenience/ purposive sampling and then move to theoretical sampling. When the point is reached at which new data no longer provide theoretical insights, theoretical saturation is achieved as the criteria for stopping data collection.
Building a grounded theory	Theoretical abstractions that are grounded in the data and include the variation of participants' experiences are developed in this phase. Because of explicating delimited phenomenon in a particular area, most grounded theories are substantive theories. The theoretical ideas can be developed into a more formal theory encompassing a higher level of abstraction with broader applicability when they transfer across areas.

not deny the existence of a reality, but rather view it as socially interpretable and believe that to understand human behavior, it is essential understand this construct. According to the Rieger (2018), the philosophical perspectives evolution was occurred in the context of Straussian GT which is based on that GT researchers have an interpretive role rather than seen as blank pages.

The reality, in terms of Charmazian grounded theorists, is a social construction. Charmazian GT researchers are more concerned with the "world created real in the mind and through the words and actions of its members" rather than denying the existence of the objective real world. According to Rieger (2018), the subjective epistemology of Charmazian GT is based on the assumption that researcher and research are not separated and the knowledge is co-created. On the other hand, Clarkeian GT is rooted in postmodernism. Its creator, Clark, sought to develop a kind of GT that departed from its positivist foundations, and because she was a student of Strauss and a fan of his version of GT, and since the Strauss version is rooted in pragmatism, this led to this post-modern approach to GT (Rupsiene and Pranskuniene, 2010).

CONCLUSION

Proper and intelligent selection of a methodology based on the knowledge of the underlying philosophical principles and the unique features of that method is essential for researchers when planning a research. One of the most suitable methods for conducting research in the field of qualitative research is Grounded Theory (GT) approach which provides guidelines for the simultaneous collection and analysis of data in order to develop theories about social processes which is rooted in real-world experiences. Since the GT approach has proven to be an appropriate approach to management research and leads to empirical analysis of policy development related to organizational development, the present chapter will explain this method and its applications in organizational research. Applying GT approach to organizational development can also enable the identification of open and theoretical codes and their relationships as understood in the organizations.

With the increasing evolution of the GT methodology, the applicability of this approach to organizational research is increasing. The distinct background of the GT approach has led to the development of several approaches that, although they have basic similarities, but are based on distinct philosophical assumptions that affect the way of implementation of the GT approach. The Glaserian classic GT, Straussian GT, Charmazian constructivist GT, and Clarkeian situational GT as the four GT schools have been discussed in the present chapter.

Also, the difference of GT process including collecting, coding, sorting, memo-ing, and sorting data has been studied in various GT schools. It is often claimed that academic research is not effective in solving organizational problems. In this regard, the theory, research, development and practical cycle are discussed to overcome this problem. Also, in this chapter, the factors affecting the choice of research methods in organizations, as well as the differentiation of qualitative methods including case studies, GT, phenomenological methodology, and content analysis have been discussed.

REFERENCES

Adamy, E. K., Zocche, D. A. D. A., Vendruscolo, C., Santos, J. L. G. D., & Almeida, M. D. A. (2018). Validation in grounded theory: Conversation circles as a methodological strategy. *Revista Brasileira de Enfermagem*, *71*(6), 3121–3126. doi:10.1590/0034-7167-2017-0488 PMID:30517420

Alammar, F. M., Intezari, A., Cardow, A., & Pauleen, D. J. (2018). Grounded theory in practice: Novice researchers' choice between Straussian and Glaserian. *Journal of Management Inquiry*, *28*(2), 228–245. doi:10.1177/1056492618770743

Apramian, T., Cristancho, S., Watling, C., & Lingard, L. (2017). (Re)Grounding grounded theory: A close reading of theory in four schools. *Qualitative Research*, *17*(4), 359–376. doi:10.1177/1468794116672914

Birks, M., Chapman, Y., & Francis, K. (2008). Memoing in qualitative research Probing data and processes. *Journal of Research in Nursing*, *13*(1), 68–75. doi:10.1177/1744987107081254

Böhm, A. (2004). Theoretical Coding: Text Analysis in Grounded Theory. In U. Flick, E. Kardorff, & I. Steinke (Eds.), *A comparison to qualitative Research* (pp. 270–275). London: SAGE Publications.

Buchanan, D. A., & Bryman, A. (2009). *The SAGE handbook of organizational research methods*. London: SAGE.

Burden, J., & Roodt, G. (2007). Grounded theory and its application in a recent study on organizational redesign: Some reflections and guidelines. *Journal of Human Resource Management*, *5*(3), 11–18. doi:10.4102ajhrm.v5i3.147

Charmaz, K. (2006). *Constructing grounded theory a practical guide through qualitative analysis*. London: SAGE Publications Ltd.

Clarke, A. E. (2003). Situational analyses: Grounded theory mapping after the postmodern turn. *Symbolic Interaction*, *26*(4), 553–576. doi:10.1525i.2003.26.4.553

Draucker, C. B., Al-Khattab, H., Hines, D. D., & Mazurczyk, J. (2014). Racial and ethnic diversity in grounded theory research. *Qualitative Report*, *19*(34), 1–20. PMID:26401523

Fairhurst, G. T., & Putnam, L. L. (2019). An integrative methodology for organizational oppositions: Aligning grounded theory and discourse analysis. *Organizational Research Methods*, *22*(4), 917–940. doi:10.1177/1094428118776771

Gill, P., Stewart, K., Treasure, E., & Chadwick, B. (2008). Methods of data collection in qualitative research: Interviews and focus groups. *British Dental Journal*, *204*(6), 291–295. doi:10.1038/bdj.2008.192 PMID:18356873

Glaser, B. G. (1978). *Theoretical sensitivity*. Mill Valley, CA: The Sociology Press.

Glaser, B. G. (1992). *Emergence vs forcing: Basics of grounded theory analysis*. Mill Valley: The Sociology Press.

Haider, S., Bao, G., Larsen, G. L., & Draz, M. U. (2019). Harnessing sustainable motivation: A grounded theory exploration of public service motivation in local governments of the state of Oregon, United States. *Sustainability*, *11*(11), 3105. doi:10.3390u11113105

Holton, J. A. (2008). Grounded theory as a general research methodology. *The Grounded Theory Review*, *7*(2). http://groundedtheoryreview.com/2008/06/30/grounded-theory-as-a-general-research-methodology/

Hull, S. (2013). *Doing grounded theory notes for the aspiring qualitative analyst*. University of Cape Town: Division of Geomatics.

Kamasak, R., Yavuz, M., Kar, A., & Baykut, S. (2017). Qualitative Methods in Organizational Research: An Example of Grounded Theory Data Analysis. In B. Christiansen & H. C. Chandan (Eds.), *Handbook of research on organizational culture and diversity in the modern workforce* (pp. 23–42). IGI Global. doi:10.4018/978-1-5225-2250-8.ch002

Kenealy, G. J. J. (2008). Management research and grounded theory: A review of grounded theory building approach in organizational and management research. *The Grounded Theory Review*, *7*(2). http://groundedtheoryreview.com/2008/06/28/1004/

Keränen, J., & Oinonen, M. (2019). *Grounded theory studies in industrial marketing: systematic review and implications for future research*. Retrieved August 10, 2019, from https://www.impgroup.org/uploads/papers/8226.pdf

Kwanjai, N. N. (2011). *Cross cultural intelligence amid intricate cultural webs* (Thesis). Maastricht, the Netherlands.

Martin, P. Y., & Turner, B. A. (1986). Grounded theory and organizational research. *The Journal of Applied Behavioral Science*, *22*(2), 141–157. doi:10.1177/002188638602200207

Mohammed, F., & Norman, A. (2017). Understanding information sharing behaviour of millennials in large multinational organizations: Research in progress. *Information Research*, *22*(1). http://www.informationr.net/ir/22-1/isic/isics1605.html

Plessis, E. D., & Marais, P. (2015). A grounded theory perspective on leadership in multicultural schools. *Journal of Asian and African Studies*, *52*(5), 1–16.

Rieger, K.L. (2018). *Discriminating among grounded theory approaches.* doi:10.1111/nin.12261

Rivers, D. L. (2018). *A grounded theory of Millennials job-hopping* (Doctoral thesis). College of Management and Technology, Walden University.

Roman, D. J., Osinski, M., & Erdmann, R. H. (2017). The construction process of grounded theory in administration. *Contaduría y Administración*, *62*(3), 985–1000. doi:10.1016/j.cya.2016.06.012

Rosenbaum, D., More, A. M. E., & Steane, P. (2016). Applying grounded theory investigating change management in the nonprofit sector. *SAGE Open*, *6*(4), 1–11. doi:10.1177/2158244016679209

Rozkwitalska, M., Basińska, B. A., Chmielecki, M., Przytuła, S., & Sułkowski, L. (2016). Intercultual interactions at multinational corporations' workplace: Grounded theory. *Journal of Positive Management.*, *7*(1), 3–31. doi:10.12775/JPM.2016.001

Rupsiene, L., & Pranskuniene, R. (2010). The Variety of Grounded Theory: Different Versions of the Same Method or Different Methods? *Socialiniai mokslai*, *4*(70), 7-19.

Sbaraini, A., Carter, S. M., Evans, R. W., & Blinkhorn, A. (2011). How to do a grounded theory study: A worked example of a study of dental practices. *BMC Medical Research Methodology*, *11*(128), 1–10. doi:10.1186/1471-2288-11-128 PMID:21902844

Shivany, S., & Velnampy, T. (2015). Grounded theory as a methodology for exploring marketing strategies for a special context. *The International Journal Research Publication's Research Journal of Social Science and Management*, *4*(11), 115–126.

Sotiriadou, K., & Shilbury, D. (2008). Using grounded theory in sport management research. *International Journal of Sport Management and Marketing*, *4*(1/2), 125–146.

Strauss, A., & Corbin, J. (1990). *Basics of qualitative research: Techniques and procedures for developing grounded theory.* Newbury Park: Sage Publications.

Susabowska, K. (2016). Application of the grounded theory methodology in HRM research within private and public sector – An attempt at a meta-analysis of articles published on the ISI master journal list between 2010 and 2014. *Problemy ZarzÈdzania, 14*(3), 167–190. doi:10.7172/1644-9584.61.10

Swanson, R. A. (2007). Theory framework for applied disciplines: Boundaries, contributing, core, useful, novel, and irrelevant components. *Human Resource Development Review, 6*(3), 321–339. doi:10.1177/1534484307303770

Swanson, R. A., & Holton, E. F. (2005). *Research in organizations: Foundations and methods of inquiry*. Berrett-Koehler Publishers.

Swanson, R. A., & Holton, E. F. (2008). *Foundations of human resource development*. Berrett-Koehler Publishers.

Tweed, A., & Charmaz, K. (2011). Grounded theory for mental health practitioners. In A. Thompson & D. Harper (Eds.), *Qualitative research methods in mental health and psychotherapy: A guide for students and practitioners* (pp. 131–146). London: Wiley-Blackwell. doi:10.1002/9781119973249.ch10

Williams, C. (2007). Research methods. *Journal of Business & Economics Research, 5*(3), 65–72. PMID:18243945

Ziyatdinova, E. (2017). *The role of cultural intelligence from the perspective of leader* (Thesis). Arcada, Finland.

Chapter 2
The Use of Grounded Theory Methodology in Theory Building

ABSTRACT

The chapter discusses the qualitative analysis method of the grounded theory (GT) and its application in the generation or building theory. The emphasis in the GT approach is on building theory rather than validating the existing theories. The GT methodology has been a topic of interest to management researchers and is intellectually challenging. In order to enhance understanding and skills for continuous professional development and to improve conditions, theory building should be considered a vital activity. In new circumstances where social systems cannot provide a certain predictive power, the need for new theories is felt. The topics discussed in this chapter revolve around theory and theory building; inductive, deductive, and abductive approaches to constructing theory; levels, functions, components, and evaluation of theories; research methods used in theory development; and in particular, the GT method and its application in theoretical coding and the reliability of this approach in serving these purposes.

DOI: 10.4018/978-1-7998-4252-1.ch002

INTRODUCTION

In order to create perspectives and theorize in areas that are theoretically mature, as well as revive and refine existing theoretical frameworks, one can use the grounded theory (GT) approach. Using GT in this context can guarantee that theories are able to adapt the organizational realities they are trying to explain (Locke, 2001).

A few things are important about the GT method. First, the GT method includes the study of qualitative data and, in principle, can be regarded as a key method of confirming the legitimacy of qualitative research in several research areas. Second, building or generating a theory that is preferably new, rather than merely working on existing perspectives, is a central focus of the GT method. Third, empirical analysis is needed to develop a theory with the GT method, and the GT method is actually data-based, and generally large volumes of data is needed for this purpose. Apart from these three issues, there are a number of practices that are generally related to the GT method, including theoretical sampling, memo writing, and development and use of emerging concepts. However, qualitative research, the development of new theory, and empirically grounded induction, as three key areas, have always been found in research using GT approach (Berente and Seidel, 2014).

The GT method can be used in both quantitative and qualitative research, although it is generally used in research with qualitative data. Also, in order to identify patterns and create (rather than test) hypotheses, rich and qualitative data can be investigated inductively. The effectiveness of this approach, however, has been criticized for developing theories regardless of existing theories in order to provide new insights, because this approach can be unrealistic (since people always have theories in mind (and lead to unintended consequences) or address non-important or irrelevant issues (because in the absence of existing literature, researchers may reconstruct existing explanations). In addition, not only qualitative or inductive methods, but also emerging ones can be involved in the GT methodology. Grounded research is developed not based on a pre-prepared plan, but rather organically, and in such research the design have the potential to emerge during the process of research like concepts (Berente and Seidel, 2014).

Accordingly, theory and theory building process, theoretical approaches such as deductive, inductive, and abductive, and levels, functions and components, and how to evaluate theories, research methods for theory development, and in particular, GT methodology and its application to theoretical coding as well as its reliability in meeting this goal are discussed in the present chapter.

THEORY BUILDING

An insight into the paradigm discussion is presented in Milliken's (2001) research, which accordingly, there is a longstanding debate about the most appropriate philosophical position in the social sciences from which research methods need to be extracted. When the attendees in conferences, seminars and workshops share the same thinking, attending and providing papers and therefore, discussing the theory can be reassuring, but it seems unlikely that it will lead to a discussion of theory building. As an intellectual skill, having the ability to think "out of the box", sometimes is an indicative of the individual's knowledge gap.

Of course, a gap in our knowledge is inevitable, and this proves that there are deficiencies and shortcomings in our knowledge that lead researchers to find new solutions to fix them. This implies that there is a need to create new insights into management theory while at the same time, expanding the parameters of management development. By accepting such challenges, management academics prove to be eager to develop new knowledge and impart their findings to a wider audience (Trim and Lee, 2004).

While theory building is a result of and can be the main approach of research, rebellious behaviors lead to the development of new insights and theories. However, to take rebellious actions, appropriate control measures need to be put in place and contradictions and conflicts should not be personalized. Of course, the point is that if a researcher is prepared to think "outside the box" and can deal with the consequences, then he/she should take the necessary precautions and support should be provided for him/her. In this regard, research conducted by Kekale (2001) can identify a researcher's position of self- confidence in the use of different methods of research in theory building. Of course, since the process of theory building is a long process and requires a great deal of effort, and there are many pitfalls to overcome, the researcher's confidence must be high (Lee, 2004).

Different approaches can be taken when dealing with managerial conventional research. Of course, the most important thing when starting a new theory is that the researcher should be aware of the possibility of biases and prejudice about the subject under investigation. After thinking about this, one might argue that the term theory, despite being used in numerous fields, still lacks a clear definition. With confidence, and an open and prepared mind to research, the researcher can adopt a critical theory approach and, therefore, have a more robust research culture in this field can be effective (Trim and Lee, 2004).

APROACHES TO THEORY BUILDING

The use of theory is commonplace in almost all research projects, and it can be explicitly or implicitly included in the design of research project; however, it will usually become explicit in your research findings and conclusion presentation part. Of course, the more specific the theory presented in your research at the beginning of the work, it can lead to important questions about your research project design. Theoretical design can be accomplished through the use of two almost contradictory approaches, namely deductive reasoning and inductive reasoning. In deductive reasoning, the conclusion is the logical consequence of a set of promises, and when all those promises are true, the conclusion will be correct. (Ketokivi and Mantere, 2010).

The research that begins with the theory is often started with academic methods of library review, and then the research strategy is designed to test the theory, which represents a deductive approach. In the inductive approach, instead, research often begins with collecting data to investigate the phenomenon and generate or build a theory (often presented as a conceptual framework). The abductive approach is also when data related to the phenomenon is collected, the themes are identified and patterns are explained, and then, a new or modified theory is finally extracted that should be tested with the collected data.

Performing specific observations are the starting point in the induction approach procedure and the generalization of conclusions is the next step. After correctly selecting a number of observations in the induction method, it is necessary to generalize the conclusions to all or groups of similar situations. After testing, these generalizations may be approved or rejected. Hence, it is possible to counterfeit all principles based on inductive reasoning. As an observer in the induction process, the researcher needs to record what he or she observes honestly, without prejudice and impartiality. Finally, based on these observations, the theories and laws are formed that constitute scientific knowledge. Researchers, who use inductive approach, also believe that

Table 1. Deduction, induction, and abduction (Saunders et al., 2015)

	Deduction	Induction	Abduction
Logic	When the premises are true in a deductive inference, the conclusion should also be true.	Known premises are used in an inductive inference to create untested conclusions.	Known premises are used in an abductive inference to generate tentative conclusions.
Generalizability	Generalization from the general to the specific	Generalization from the specific to the general	Generalization based on the interactions between the specific and the general
Use of data	Using data gathering to evaluate propositions or hypotheses associated with an existing theory	Using data gathering to explore a phenomenon, identify themes and patterns and create a conceptual framework	Using data gathering to explore a phenomenon, identify themes and patterns, locate these in a conceptual framework and test them through subsequent data collection and so forth
Theory	Rejecting or verifying the theory	Generating and building theory	Generating or modifying theory; build new theory or modify existing theory by incorporating existing theory where appropriate.

observations can be reasonably extended to general and inclusive laws in order to validate and confirm scientific assumptions (Zalaghi and Khazaei, 2016).

Theories in the inductive approach are formed at the end of the research and after collecting all observations. Seeking a pattern based on observations and constructing theories for those patterns through hypotheses forms the main basis of the inductive approach. The researcher in inductive research is completely free to determine the direction of research and no theory is required at the outset. In particular, at the beginning of the research, due to the lack of a specific assumption and because the research is not yet completed, the researcher is uncertain about the type and nature of the findings. The researcher during the inductive reasoning uses observations to construct an abstract or describe the conditions under consideration (Zalaghi and Khazaei, 2016).

In the deductive approach, an assumption is developed based on the existing theories and a research plan is created to test the assumption. Using the theory-driven assumption, the deductive approach can be explained; that is, the results are deduced from the premises in the deductive approach. The author develops a set of hypotheses that require experimentation when using a deductive approach in a research project, and then tests this assumption using a relevant approach. The specific features of deductive reasoning are needed to be understood. The conclusion of deductive reasoning is necessarily accepted when its promises are accepted. Due to implicit raising of result content in the premises in a deductive reasoning, this kind of reasoning cannot be expanded.

Even with the addition of new premises to the argument, the conclusion must still be followed. The degree of validity of deductive reasoning makes no sense, and this type of reasoning is either valid or invalid. In making such an argument, no choice, decision, or judgment is involved in achieving the necessary results (Zalaghi and Khazaei, 2016).

In order to determine whether the theory applies under the conditions in question, the deductive research approach tests a particular theory. In the deductive approach, exactly the logical procedure should be followed. As such, the reasoning process begins with a theory and ends with a new assumption. This assumption should be tested via comparison with the observations and finally, it is decided to accept or reject it. Also, deductive reasoning can be regarded as the general to specific (top-down) reasoning, which is the opposite of the inductive approach in this regard. In other words, while inductive studies have nothing to do with hypotheses, the deductive approach involves formulating hypotheses and testing them through the research process (Zalaghi and Khazaei, 2016).

The GT approach, since attempts to resolve the gap between research and theory, is commonly referred to as an inductive method. It is also a systematic generation of theory based on data with both inductive and deductive reasoning. Researchers who adopt the GT approach in their research use it to provide a theoretical explanation applicable to a complex problem. GT directs most researchers to be enthusiastic and to seek the right answers to the right questions, rather than relying on past analysis or assumptions to provide the right answers to the wrong questions (Sepastian, 2019).

In abductive research, unlike inductive and deductive reasoning, the theoretical framework can be explained, developed, or modified before, during, or after research. This means that abductive research has a reciprocal movement between inductive and open-ended research environments on the one hand, and hypothetical and deductive efforts (Dubois and Gadde, 2002). Three reasons have been suggested by Easterby-Smith et al. (2012) to select this approach for the purpose of theory development. Firstly, this approach allows the researcher to make more informed decisions about the research design, and therefore it can be found that this is more than just a technique or procedure for collecting and analyzing data. Second, this approach helps the researcher find appropriate research and methodological strategies for his / her work and exclude those that are not applicable. Third, in this approach, the researcher is able to adapt his research to the constraints by knowing the different research traditions.

MICRO, MACRO, AND MESO THEORIES

In a study (2006), Miner argues that micro theory in organizational research is related to the nature of individual and small groups in organizations. Micro theory is strongly influenced by psychology, and many theorists at this level are first trained in that field. Although theories in some contexts may consist of variables beyond the micro level, topics such as motivation, leadership, and team building are, in essence, micro issues.

In macro theory, we focus on the nature of organizations rather than individuals and groups. Also, parts of the organization may be of interest, and may affect the environment around the organization. As with the important role of psychology in the development of micro theory, sociology has played a very important role in the development of macro theory. Among the theories raised at this level are theories of organizational process and structure that almost represent the macro approach.

Part of the field of organizational research from the early years of its introduction is the distinction between the micro and macro levels. The recent approach, at least in terms of terminology, is the meso theory. The meso approach is defined as the simultaneous study of at least two levels, one level dealing with individual or group processes or variables and the other level relating to organizational processes or variables, and bridging or relating the propositions is used in order to establish a link between two levels.

BUILDING BLOCKS OF THEORY DEVELOPMENT

Four basic elements are needed for a complete theory that will be explained in the following paragraphs (Whetten, 1989).

What: which relates to the question of which logical factors (variables, constructs, and concepts) should be considered as part of explaining social or individual phenomena? Comprehensiveness (that is, the question of whether all relevant factors are included?) and parsimony (that is, should some factors be eliminated because of the little value they add to our understanding?) are the two main criteria for judging the amount. The use of factors is "right".

How: after identifying the set of factors, the researcher's next question should be about how these factors are related. For this purpose, "arrows" is used to connect the "boxes", which is part of the operationalizing this query. This leads to the identification of explicit patterns, and the ordering of conceptualization. It can also determine causality. The researcher may not be able to properly test these links, but the limitations on the methods do not necessarily question the validity of the theory's inherent causal nature. What and how elements together form the domain or subject of the theory.

Why: that to justify the selection of causal factors and proposed relationships, what psychological, economic, or social underlying dynamics is needed?, is the underlying logic in the assumptions of theory that constitute the theoretical glue that links the components of the model together. The question that why colleagues should credit for this particular manifestation of phenomena is the central question that arises here; and the answer lies in the basic logic of this model. The validity of fundamental views on the human nature, organizational needs, or social processes paves the way for judging the rationality of the proposed concept.

According to Whetten (1989), these three elements together provide the "description" (what and how) and "explanation" (why) elements which are the basic components of a simple theory. The boundary of theory is an important issue that, in Whetten's view, is often overlooked.

Who, Where, When: This set of temporal and contextual factors, according to Whetten (1989), forms the domain of theory. Whetten also points out that, unfortunately, a few theorists specify their focus on the contextual framework of the propositions. According to Whetten, in trying to understand the social phenomenon, researchers often tend to consider it only in familiar environments and at a specific time.

THEORY FUNCTIONS

Regarding the practical application of a theory, still there is no agreement between academics and practitioners and endless debate in this area has been formed.

As can be seen in Table 2, the functions of a theory can be coupled with scientific and practical applications. According to their applications, functions and purposes are described below.

THOERIES EVALUATION

Science needs some criteria to evaluate theories and decide on whether or not a theory is good. As is clear from the foregoing discussion, some explanatory

Table 2. Functions of a theory (Koskela, 2005)

Scientific	Practical
Explanation Prediction Validation Research directions (discrepancies between theory and empirical observation)	Basing methods and tools Teaching Communication Knowledge transfer

expressions may not meet the requirements of a scientific theory, and that a theory that was once good may lose its validity in later years as knowledge develops (Miner, 2006).

Criteria: the first criterion is that theories should help to meet scientific goals. Theories should enable and facilitate understanding, prediction, and influence. The more theory meets these goals, the better it is. The broader scope of the theory for covering phenomena is preferable to the finite domain of it. Of course, this criterion alone is not enough. As we can see, some super-theories fail to meet their goals because they cannot really explain the range of phenomena they claim to explain.

Second, the scope of the theory should be clearly defined. The scope of application of the theory and in which situations it is not applicable and not designed for them should be determined.

Thirdly, a good theory is the theory that drives the researcher's efforts to address important research topics. Although research studies that can be done in the world are unlimited, many of them do not yield very statistically significant results, and even though they take a great deal of time and effort, their usefulness is low. Good theory can help us focus our efforts on important variables, identify important relationships, and focus on really important findings, and hence, good theory can help protect the researcher's efforts against wasting time and energy.

Fourth, the best theories are those that lead to some kind of added value in research efforts. By extracting several verified hypotheses from the research, the whole body of theory would be useful and applicable. Therefore, research that is based on theory is useful not just for presenting the separated facts, but also for powerfully explaining and predicting the whole scope of theory. This criterion of good theory is one of the most practical achievements that many theories unfortunately cannot meet it.

Fifth, there should be the possibility to test theories and it should be precisely clear what procedure should be done to adopt or reject the theory. Sometimes, the experiments are done that claim to test the theory properly, but the theorist does not accept them and claim that he meant something else. This problem is rarely seen when a good theory is developed. Ideally the theorists should define their theory variables in the operational language.

Sixth, not only in terms of confirmation by the research formed based on it, but also in terms of its logical internal consistency with known facts, a good theory must be confirmed. When dealing with complex theories, propositions can be developed to predict the diametrically opposite outputs at the same conditions. This is particularly possible when the theorist from different directions and using different concepts and assumptions, addresses the same subject matter. If the theory is to be much of use, such internal and logical inconsistencies must be ironed out. In addition, since theories are not in a vacuum but part of the overall body of knowledge, it must be clear at all times how the theory relates to the larger body of knowledge. It is clear that a theory that fails to establish such relationships from the beginning has some shortcomings. Theories need to be developed on the basis of what is known and have a consistent fit with the broader body of knowledge that exists.

Seventh, the best theories have simple expressions and can express a set of phenomena in a small number of variables, and so theories that have simpler expressions should be preferred to the complex theories with the same level of explanation while having a more complex set of variables and relationships. In the scientific field, complexity is of no value and what surrounds us in nature suffices. The high complexity of the theory often leads to problems in its implementation, and so the ultimate goal should be to replace simple theories rather than complex theories. Inductive theory to refine theory often requires the addition of new structures and variables with the emergence of new unanticipated findings and requiring explanation. Under such circumstances, the theory may lose its value because the difficulty of its implementation overcomes its usefulness.

GT METHODOLOGY AND THEORY BUILDING

Leat (1995) introduced many issues contained in understanding and interpretation. In order to present new theories and research findings from a renewed emphasis on explaining several factors that need to be described, the Grounded theory approach can be used. The GT method has been a topic of interest to management researchers and is intellectually challenging. The GT approach can be used by management academics as a basis for teaching new ways to interpret and evaluate the existing management theory because it forces the researcher to think in both analytical and conceptual ways. Therefore, it can be a well-designed approach to develop emerging theories, and at the same time, using different research tools to achieve greater effectiveness (Trim and Lee, 2004).

The emphasis in the GT approach is more on building theory rather than validating the existing theories. Here we can see different views that illustrate what a theory should be. Theory can be considered as a system of evolutionary explanation, personal thinking, orienting principle, epistemological presupposition, developed argument, craft knowledge, and so on. According to Neal et al., (2009), theory leads to validation of the research, and tests a theory on whether that theory leads to appropriate predictions, explanations, interpretations, and applications. The GT approach has never claimed to be suitable for lean research and its suitability depends on individuals and its applications.

Theory can be described as a coherent description, explanation, and representation of observed or experienced phenomena. Also, theory building is a continuous process of generating, validating, applying, and adapting theory that can be thought of as a deliberate or repetitive cyclic process through which descriptions, explanations, and coherent representations of the phenomena under study and observation are created, validated, and refined. Two types of knowledge come from the construction of theory, which are output knowledge, which is usually explanatory and predictive, and the process knowledge, for example, by increasing understanding of what works and its meaning. Good theory and theory building also represent two important characteristics, namely power and relevance, or in other words, the validity and utility of theory (Lynham, 2002).

Four components are usually considered by academics for a theory (Lynham, 2002; Gay and Weaver, 2011) including: definitions of terms or variables, the application domain of the theory, a set of relationships of variables, and real claims that theory makes about specific predictions. As such, the theoretical definitions are not observable but their existence and properties are stated in order to report what is observable. Theoretical definitions are conceptual in nature and are the domain of the theory, environment, and precise conditions in which the theory is applied. In order to explain why and how the relationships are logically tied so that the theory gives specific predictions, the theories carefully outline the precise definitions in a specific domain. So, a good theory is a finite and relatively accurate picture that takes into account the precision and limitation of the definition of the vocabulary, the scope of the theory, the explanation of the relationships and the specific predictions of the theory. According to the authors, the clear explanation of how and why specific relationships lead to specific events is the goal of 'good' theory. Consequently, these explanations of relationships are critical for 'good' theory-building (Wacker, 1998).

Theory is defined as a set of explanations and principles that describe a set of facts or phenomena. The meta-theory is actually a theory about theories. A meta-theory under certain circumstances may be regarded as assumptions or rules that underpin the particular view that the theory must follow and indicate the high-low generalizability used to guide future work and to describe it prescriptively. According to Onions (2006), the distinction that is made between prescriptive and descriptive use affects the chosen research strategy. For many writers, practitioners are viable theorists who help refine the theory, because they are able to make correct assumptions about their work based on their findings, which can be considered as the basis of contemporary theory (Onions, 2006).

Gooyert (2019) believes that studies to test theory normally use theory in order to formulate hypotheses before using observations to test those hypotheses. Observations that the authors use to generate theory through inductive reasoning are the starting point of studies building theory, and such research generally ends with a set of propositions that summarize the resulting theory. However, there are also many studies that combine the elements of both theory and theory, which often focus on one type of theoretical contributions. Quantitative studies, except in some cases, are used to test the theory, while it is common to use qualitative research generally to build, not to test the theory.

The GT approach is usually used to arrive at middle range theories, of which there are two forms: the substantive and the formal. While substantive theories are 'applied' and associated with the specific field of human interaction, formal theories are conceptual and associated with a number of areas of human interaction. Even though the resulting theory is capable of testing by subsequent researchers, such testing would result in modification rather than rejection because the theory is grounded in the data. The approach is also expected to provide "a theory" rather than "the theory" as a move away from the positivist. The close fit with data, usefulness, conceptual density, durability over time, modifiability, and explanatory power are among the characteristics of the GT approach. However, the preferred test in this area is to test the usefulness of the theory for the practitioners and to apply the outputs by them. This leads to problems in the area of knowledge created by GT.

The ability to develop theory through the use of prescribed, yet flexible, tools for analysis is among the strengths of the GT approach. The analytic guidelines of (a) the constant comparative method, (b) theoretical coding, (c) theoretical sampling, (d) theoretical saturation, and (e) theoretical sensitivity constitute the fundamental principles of GT. It is the nature of these principles and the interplay between them that allows for the development of theory from an epistemological perspective. These features make GT a unique research methodology. While GT is comprised of various analytical principles, it is the collective iterative cycling of these tenets that creates a holistic methodology for theory building. GT procedures allow for systematic and accurate design of theory building (O'Reilly et al., 2012).

Through continuous interpolation between analysis and data collection, the theory is formed during GT. Theory is provisionally verified through a rigorous process of continuous matching of theory against data throughout the research process. Thus, GT is distinctive in its approach to theory building because of its singular commitment to allowing new theoretical understandings to emerge from the data. Through the continuous analysis and comparison of data and emergent theory, theory derived in this way is intended to be closely connected to evidence. In order to verify the resulting hypotheses throughout the course of the theory-building process, rigorous matching of data with theory is pursued. For this purpose, GT tries for authenticity which refers to faithfulness to the data that closely reflects the meanings and understandings of people participated in the phenomenon that is modeled by the theory. Using this theory-building approach, one can come to a new theoretical understanding and testable hypotheses about the phenomenon under investigation. Also, when there is no need for empirical confirmation (or disconfirmation) of preexisting conceptions by the type of theoretical knowledge, GT is valuable (Torraco, 2002).

Building theory based on data that automatically grounds the theory in empirical data, is one of the most important strengths in GT. Hence, the ability to trace data, categories, and theory is well established which means that there are good possibilities for a transparent process which increases the credibility of the study. Some techniques have been proposed by researchers to increase the transparency of data during the analysis of theoretical results (Goldkuhl and Cronholm, 2010).

When the built theory authenticity is paramount to the researcher, GT is of particular value. The reason for GT's distinctive approach to theory building is its commitment to achieving a new theoretical understanding of the data. The same fidelity to the substantive data as GT's special feature enables it to be more consistent between theory and data. When no empirical confirmation (or disconfirmation) of preexisting conceptions is needed in the type of theoretical knowledge, GT is of particular value. When it comes to creating new insights and tentative assumptions, this approach is best, regardless of existing theoretical explanations of the phenomenon of interest. The knowledge obtained may or may not have been anticipated by the researchers since GT allows specific elements of research design to be shaped after starting the research process, For that reason, it is possible to obtain really new findings about the phenomenon during GT (Torraco, 2002).

The warning that GT users should get rid themselves of presumptions to achieve the true nature of the field under study will come through is one problem and controversy in this regard. In this regard, GT researchers need to refrain from reading relevant literature until the end of the study. The warning also goes a step further, referring to the formulation of originator's earlier writings: Ignoring the literature of theory and reality under study is the first step and an effective strategy in implementing this approach to ensure that the emergence of categories has nothing to do with concepts derived from other domains. The issue of the impact of existing literature on the GT researcher has been much discussed so far and if this warning is ignored, it may lead to reinventing the wheel. Since researchers often develop new knowledge based on existing knowledge, the development of the theory in quarantine may lead to its incoherent development. From our point of view, relating the evolving theory to established research during the process of theory building is important; because existing knowledge can serve as a basis for supporting empirical data that will shape emerging theory (Goldkuhl and Cronholm, 2010).

Because existing knowledge can serve as a basis for supporting empirical data that will shape emerging theory (Eisenhart, 2007). Whether the research question is answered by constructing a better theory or testing a hypothesis is a subject that should be justified by the researcher (Eisenhart, 2007). The nature of the research question, lack of existing plausible theory and the significance of the phenomenon being researched are the factors that can justify the theory building (Eisenhart, 2007). Thus, case studies in order to build a theory generally answer questions about how and why about un-explored subjects (Eisenhart, 2007). The logical connection at the beginning of the theory construction is the result of pattern matching between data and theory (Eisenhart, 2007).

According to Bendassolli (2013;2), due to the risk of forcing data into previous conceptual categories (low level of inductivity) and the risk of producing such a large volume of data threat hinders categorization and theoretical development (low level of deductivity), GT methodology rest in state of tension. The conventional idea that qualitative research is a cycle of induction and deduction reasoning, and that coding (finding a concept or category fitted with certain incidents in the data) is the inductive part of that cycle are assumed in the generic analytical cycle (Bendassoli, 2013). Findings related to a category are not purely inductive, but also include a deductive approach, where the deductive component creates a mental lip that links previously unrelated entities (Bendassoli, 2013).

As a result of the accumulation of knowledge during research activities including sense-making, interaction of role players, structure- agent relationship, cultural historical context, etc. theories are created which would indicate the significance of the phenomenon under investigation. Theories usually discuss the conceptualization of empirical data. Theory construction expresses the meaning and importance of social phenomena as well as for work, practice and thinking.

In his research in 2014, Charmaz believes that theorizing is a practice including practical activities for engaging the world while creating abstract understanding about it. The GT approach's main contribution in this area is the interpretative theoretical practical guide, and besides, a blueprint for theoretical products (Charmaz, 2014a). Hence, social constructivist assumptions derived from individual, collective, and institutional conditions based on the symbolic interaction between active actors form the interpretative theorizing in the GT approach (Alasuutaari, 1996). According to Charmaz (2014), in order to build theory in GT, we need to pause, think, and reflect. In this way, the grounded theorists are able to see possibilities, establish relationships or ask questions once the data analysis is completed. It should be noted, however, that even after completing the data analysis and constructing all the categories and properties, the theory building is still ongoing and a continuous process, since GT pursues an abductive argument that continues even during the writing-up that unexpected insights may be found at any point (Gasson, 2004).

In addition, the use of gerunds for the purpose of coding can lead to the theoretical sensitivity of the categories because they cause enacting processes rather than restricting data to pre-conceived subjects (Charmaz, 2006). Highly descriptive GT studies that can lead to a limited analytic momentum, can be formed in case of relying on preconceived topics (Thornberg, 2012). The categories that best represent the most analytical data are grouped together. The researcher implementing the GT approach should be able to make an informed decision about which categories have high analytical value and which are of low value. By making this decision, the categories are grouped and their attributes and relationships to other categories are identified (Charmaz, 2014). By designing categories as the main categories, the process of theoretical construction continues. At this point, the categories need to be subjected to more analytical refinement so that their relationships can be clearly specified (Charmaz, 2014). The core categories for an objectivist represent the main variables with explanatory and predictive power, whereas for a constructivist, they provide an abstract understanding of relationships (Alasuutari, 1996).

RESEARCH METHODS FOR THEORY BUILDING

Various paradigmatic approaches have been used by researchers and theorists, utilizing preferred strategies and methods to develop new theoretical knowledge. Despite the variety of methods available for constructing theory, theorists tend to do so in a way that reflects deeply held values and assumptions about what constitutes knowledge (epistemology), the nature or existence (ontology) of what constitutes value (axiology) and other philosophical and ideological approaches; approaches that play a key role in the researcher's choice of purpose, subject and method. Not surprisingly, in terms of the intention and personal choice of theorists, some methods are preferred over others for the specific purposes of theory building.

To simplify the variety of theories and due to the variety and complexity of existing definitions of the theory, scholars and theorists have used many typologies and classification systems, including purposed, functions, ranges, and goals. Five types of theory were identified based on the Torraco's (2002) taxonomy including: 1) Dubin's hypothetico-deductive method, (2) inductive GT, (3) meta-analytic theory, (4) social constructionist theory, and (5) case study approach.

- Theory building using Dubin's method; the method developed by Dubin's (1978) for theory building follows the quantitative research tradition based on a hypothetico-deductive approach to create knowledge. The underlying assumption of this approach is that knowledge is created to explain, predict, and control the phenomenon under investigation; satisfying the technical / utilitarian interests of the relevant goals and purposes is achieved through this new knowledge (theory); and the desirable and possible goal of Dubin's theory-building method, is

Table 3. Contributions of research methods to theory building (Torraco, 2002)

	Research type		Driving rationale		General theory building phase				
	Quantitative	**Qualitative**	**Deductive Driven**	**Inductive Driven**	**Conceptual Development**	**Operationalization**	**Confirmation or Disconfirmation**	**Application**	**Continuous Refinement and Development**
General method of theory building (Lynham)	X	X	X	X	X	X	X	X	X
Quantitative research/ Dubin (Lynham)	X		X		X	X	X	X	X
GT research (Egan)		X		X	X			X	
Meta-analysis (Yang)	X		X		X	X	X		X
Social constructionist (Turnbull)		X		X	X	O		X	
Case study research (Dooley)	X	X	X	X	X	X	X	X	X

Note: X = definite role; O = limited role.

the discovery of generalizable laws and explanations of human and organizational phenomena.

- Theory building with a meta-analysis approach; utilizing statistical methods to aggregate separated but similar studies, the meta-analysis approach is used to synthesize and organize existing empirical findings on a topic with a coherent pattern. As a basis for theory development, the meta-analysis method draws general conclusions from numerous studies.
- Theory building with social constructivism approach; for the social constructionist, theory building is not performed to discover the theoretical truth or reality but also to model our understanding of the meaning people give to the social world around them. How to create and make meaning of social experience are the issues that constructivism theory addresses.
- Using case study research to build theory. The focus of the case study is on understanding the dynamics of a single environment. Although studying the phenomenon in the study environment is the main focus of research and theory building in the case study, research activities with this approach also contribute to the creation of new knowledge.

Due to robust hypotheses testing, thereby yielding greater explanatory power and predictability, quantitative contributions to theory, which in terms of theory testing and nomothetic, tends to be more generalizable. Though more narrow in scope, qualitative contribution to theory is equally as important, particularly when exploring topics that are difficult to quantify, in the situation that we try to make sense of complex social situations (especially those populations closed to outsider observation) and answer the broader question. In behavioral and social domains, the qualitative methods have the potential to make fundamental contributions to the development of the basic knowledge (Gay and Weaver, 2011).

THEORETICAL CODING

What is of particular importance for the purpose of theory formation is to develop relationships between the axial categories and the concepts related to them in terms of their formal and content aspects. Temporal and spatial relationships, relationships of cause and effect, means–ends relationships and terms of argumentative and motivational connections are the context in which the axial category is developed. It is needed to repeatedly check the relationships in axial coding in a deductive procedure, using new data material. The Strauss's coding paradigm that is proved to be of value for this purpose was used to explain the relationships between categories that relate to partial aspects of social action (Figure 1).

Figure 1. Coding paradigm for social science research questions (Böhm, 2004)

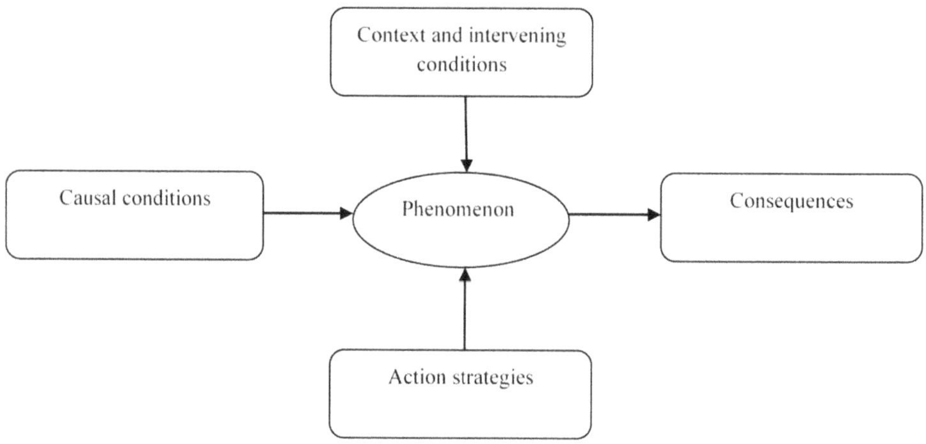

Suppose an event or a fact is identified as a phenomenon referred to as a axial category in which the actions of an individual as well as the interaction between different individuals form around this phenomenon. Asking the following questions will make it easier to choose a category: What does my data refer to? What items do the actions and interactions relate to? Causes or causal conditions play a role in the occurrence or development of the phenomenon in question. It is important here to identify the attributes of the cause.

Causes sometimes make a distinction between the subjective perspectives because they may, for example, represent the speaker's perspective on the context of the interview and the researcher's perspective. There is only a specific set of conditions that the causes are valid, and here it is important to form a theory of action that is conducive to promote or limit the possibility of action or interaction. Specific time, place, and duration are contextual conditions, and social, political, cultural, and individual biographies are among the intervening conditions. There are two characteristics of action and reaction including: 1) as these concepts are process, they have sequence, so it is important to ask about the sequence and time course of action; 2) These concepts are goal-oriented and are often done for specific reasons that one must refer to (interactive) strategies or tactics for this reasoning.

The concept of goal-oriented should not be confused with intention. A functional mode of observation for preferred analysis purposes is to ignore the intentions. Actions and interactions lead to certain consequences. Researchers in using encryption patterns for linguistic features in data should consider keywords like 'because', 'since', or 'owing to' as indicators of causal conditions. Usually the consequences of actions are frequently shown by using words like 'as a result of', 'and so', 'with the result that', 'the consequence was', 'consequently'.

Instead of looking at all kinds of relationships, grounded theorists focus on causal relations simply to simplify the process and adapt things to the basic framework of generic relations. The following elements are included in a framework:

Table 4. Elements of coding paradigm

Element	Description
Phenomenon	This group is what is called a research scheme or research framework. This concept puts the components together, and in the GT it sometimes comes as a desirable output or it can be the subject.
Causal conditions	These are the set of events or variables that lead to the occurrence or development of a phenomenon and include their causes and characteristics.
Context	It is difficult to distinguish it from causal conditions; specific places (values) which are contextual variables; set of conditions that influence action / strategy. Researchers often distinguish between active variables (causes) and contextual variables (context). Studying what the researcher finds interesting (causes) and less interesting (context) is more important than distinctions they made in nature.
Intervening conditions	Like context; the content can be identified with mediating variables and intervention conditions along with mediating variables. But the distinction between the two is not well understood by grounded theorists.
Action strategies	Targeted and goal-oriented activities performed by agents in response to confounding phenomena and conditions.

TRUSTINESS IN GT METHODOLOGY

Trustiness in GT methodology in the areas of internal validity, external validity, reliability, and objectivity has been examined from the point of view of quantitative-positivist researchers. In this regard, credibility is consistent with internal validity, transferability with external validity, and dependability with reliability. Of course, it should be noted that there are two different paradigms in this regard and therefore this adaptation cannot be fully established (Sikolia et al., 2013).

- **Credibility:** Credibility is a concept related to trustiness and almost equivalent to internal validity. Internal validity in positivist research is the elimination of competing hypotheses whose constructs may be real or reliable and the tool measures the correct content. This concept refers to the accuracy of the collected data in representing multiple facts of the phenomenon. Long time participation with informants, triangulation of data or gathering data from a variety of sources (interviews, documents, etc.), sharing the verbatim transcript of the individual interviews with each participant, and the emerging concepts and categories or respondent validation or participant checks can be used to establish credibility. Based on the findings and emerging concepts, the interview qucstions guide will be updated for the participants. Emerging concepts and categories of raw data are confirmed by negative analysis, which examines cases that are inconsistent with the original findings, and also peer debriefs that allows another person to verify the validity.
- **Transferability**: This concept is related to trustiness and it is equivalent to external validity and. In positivist research, external validity refers to the degree of generalization by a tool or its consistency in different constituencies. It also means the usability of a set of findings to another setting and can be improved through specific descriptions of research, participants' views and experiences, methodology, interpretation of results, and peer debriefers. Also, transferability can be enhanced through information about the researcher as an instrument in the process, the relationships between the researcher and participants. To this end, an audit trial should be provided to allow other researchers to repeat the same questions in the same environment in as much detail as possible.
- **Dependability:** This concept is related to trustiness and it is closely matches reliability. Reliability, within the positivist research, refers to the extent to which a variable or set of variables is compatible with something that it intends to measure multiple times. This concept also refers to the confirmation that the data reflect the changing conditions of the phenomenon under study and should be consistent over time, by different researchers, and by the application of different analysis methods. This is done by other people who verify and validate GT

methodology procedures. Detailed chronology of research activities or audit trial to determine the reliability of findings can be performed by paired researchers, student advisors, or colleagues.

- **Verifiability/ Confirmability**: Verification in GT methodology implies that another researcher confirms that similar findings are obtained with the same data. The material needed to confirm the research is obtained through an audit trial.

CONCLUSION

The usefulness of Grounded Theory (GT) methodology in understanding the social system involved in theory building has been discussed in the present chapter. First, we propose the definition of theory and theory building because there is a high degree of uncertainty around the areas of managerial decision making and processes without having a clear definition. Subsequently, deductive, inductive, and abductive approaches to the development of theory are discussed. Although the GT methodology usually has an inductive approach, but based on the literature of the subject, all three reasoning approaches can be used in GT-based theory building.

Introducing the functions, levels, components, and how to evaluate theories, issues such as research methods for theory development, in particular GT and theoretical coding, as well as the reliability of the GT method were discussed in this chapter. It is important to note that in developing GT theory, the development of relationships between categories and concepts is central.

The Strauss's coding paradigm as one of the most valuable paradigms in this regard, was used here to explain the relationships between categories that link partial aspects to social practice. When a wave of criticism of fundamentalist and constructivist theories with a deductive and speculative approach arises, a new theory usually emerges. In this regard, the introduction of GT two decades ago has been a great help, especially in the fields of psychology and sociology, in terms of explicit and systematic conceptualization of theory.

REFERENCES

Alasuutaari, P. (1996). Theorizing in qualitative research: A cultural studies perspective. *Qualitative Inquiry*, *2*(4), 371–384. doi:10.1177/107780049600200401

Bendassolli, F. (2013). Theory building in qualitative research: Reconsidering the problem of Induction. Forum. *Forum Qualitative Social Research, 14*(1), 25.

Berente, N., & Seidel, S. (2014). Big data and inductive theory development: Towards computational grounded theory? *Twentieth Americas Conference on Information Systems*, Savannah, GA.

Böhm, A. (2004). Theoretical coding: text analysis in grounded theory. In U. Flick, E. Kardorff, & I. Steinke (Eds.), *A comparison to qualitative research* (pp. 270–275). London: SAGE Publications.

Briggs, A. R. J. (2007). The use of modelling for theory building in qualitative analysis. *British Educational Research Journal, 33*(4), 589–603. doi:10.1080/01411920701434102

Charmaz, K. (2006). *Constructing grounded theory – a practical guide through qualitative analysis*. London: SAGE Publications.

Charmaz, K. (2014a). *Constructing grounded theory* (2nd ed.). London: SAGE Publications.

Dubois, A., & Gadde, L. E. (2002). Systematic combining: An abductive approach to case research. *Journal of Business Research, 55*(7), 553–560. doi:10.1016/S0148-2963(00)00195-8

Easterby-Smith, M., Thorpe, R., Jackson, P., & Lowe, A. (2012). Management research (4th ed.). London: Sage.

Eisenhardt, K. M., & Graebner, M. E. (2007). Theory building from cases: Opportunities and challenges. *Academy of Management Journal, 50*(1), 25–32. doi:10.5465/amj.2007.24160888

Gasson, S. (2004). Rigor in grounded theory research: an interpretive perspective on grounded theory from qualitative field studies. In M. E. Whitman & A. B. Woszczynski (Eds.), *Handbook of Information Systems Research* (pp. 79–102). Hershey, PA: Idea Group Publishing. doi:10.4018/978-1-59140-144-5.ch006

Gay, B., & Weaver, S. (2011). Theory building and paradigms: A primer on the nuances of theory construction. *American International Journal of Contemporary Research, 1*(2), 24–32.

Goldkuhl, G., & Cronholm, S. (2010). Adding theoretical grounding to grounded theory: Toward Multi-Grounded Theory. *International Journal of Qualitative Methods*, *9*(2), 187–205. doi:10.1177/160940691000900205

Gooyert, V. D. (2019). Developing dynamic organizational theories; three system dynamics based research strategies. *Quality & Quantity*, *53*(2), 653–666. doi:10.100711135-018-0781-y

Koskela, L. J. and M. Kagioglou (2005). On the Metaphysics of Production. *IGLC 2005*.

Locke, K. (2001). *Grounded theory in management research*. London: SAGE Publications Ltd.

Lynham, S. A. (2002). The general method of theory-building research in applied disciplines. *Advances in Developing Human Resources*, *4*(3), 221–241. doi:10.1177/1523422302043002

Miner, J. B. (2006). *Theory building and kinds of theories. In Organizational behavior 3: Historical origins, theoretical foundations, and the Future*. ME Sharpe.

Neal, L. (2009). Researching Coaching: Some dilemmas of a novice grounded theorist. *International Journal of Evidence Based Coaching and Mentoring*, *3*, 1–10.

O'Reilly, K., Paper, D., & Marx, S. (2012). Demystifying grounded theory for business research. *Organizational Research Methods*, *15*(2), 247–262. doi:10.1177/1094428111434559

Onions, P. E. W. (2006). *Grounded theory applications in reviewing knowledge management literature. Leeds Metropolitan University Innovation North Research Conference*, Leeds, UK.

Saunders, M. N. K., Lewis, P., Thornhill, A., & Bristow, A. (2015). Understanding research philosophy and approaches to theory development. In M. N. K. Saunders, P. Lewis, & A. Thornhill (Eds.), *Research methods for business students* (pp. 122–161). Harlow: Pearson Education.

Sebastian, K. (2019). Distinguishing between the types of grounded theory: Classical, interpretive and constructivist. *Journal for Social Thought*, *3*(1), 1–9.

Sikolia, D., Biros, D., Mason, M., Weiser, M. (2013). Trustworthiness of grounded theory methodology research in information systems. *MWAIS 2013 Proceedings.*

Thornberg, R. (2012). Informed grounded theory. *Scandinavian Journal of Educational Research, 56*(3), 243–259. doi:10.1080/00313831.2011.581686

Torraco, R. J. (2002). Research methods for theory building in applied disciplines: A comparative analysis. *Advances in Developing Human Resources, 4*(3), 355–376. doi:10.1177/1523422302043008

Trim, P. R. J., & Lee, Y. L. (2004). A reflection on theory building and the development of management knowledge. *Management Decision, 42*(3/4), 473–480. doi:10.1108/00251740410518930

Wacker, G. (1998). A definition of theory: Research guidelines for different theory-building research methods in operations management. *Journal of Operations Management, 16*(4), 361–385. doi:10.1016/S0272-6963(98)00019-9

Whetten, D. A. (1989). What constitutes a theoretical contribution? *Academy of Management Review, 14*(4), 490–495. doi:10.5465/amr.1989.4308371

Zalaghi, H., & Khazaei, M. (2016). The role of deductive and inductive reasoning in accounting research and standard setting. *Asian Journal of Finance & Accounting, 8*(1), 23–37. doi:10.5296/ajfa.v8i1.8148

Chapter 3
Exploratory Analysis in Information Systems Area:
Using Grounded Theory Methodology

ABSTRACT

Providing an overview of grounded theory (GT)'s approaches to information systems (IS) research to IS researchers who are now interested in applying GT is the goal of the chapter. Also, research contributions about the application of GT in IS, qualitative perspectives on IS research, the types of GT approaches used in IS research, and the GT study guidelines in IS are presented in this chapter. Examples of GT in IS research, which provide a description of the methodology and references to more detailed presentations, are also included, especially from the field of software engineering and system development. It should be noted that using the GT methodology is time consuming and requires high accuracy, and it starts with a phenomenon that the researcher finds is not well explained by existing theories. In such research, data sampling should provide a broad, in-depth, and pluralist view of the phenomenon under study, and a literature review on the phenomenon should be provided.

DOI: 10.4018/978-1-7998-4252-1.ch003

INTRODUCTION

As a practical approach to professional research in every social context and context of current debate, information systems (IS) are increasingly expanding and adopting the application of socio-technical theories that are often adapted from other fields such as sociology. Also, due to the fact that events are studied quantitatively, qualitatively, or in combination in their natural environment, IS can be considered practical. According to Mkhomazi and Iyamu (2013), Grounded Theory (GT) can be used in IS studies in real-life contexts, particularly when the boundaries between the phenomenon and its contexts were not clear, nor were they thought to be clearly defined between the information and communications technology (ICT) practices and the organization.

For the Management Information System (MIS), which is a relatively new field and therefore welcomes the development of practical theories, the GT methodology can be very useful. Of course, instead of being used as a way to build theory by consistently comparing data samples until achieving the theoretical saturation, the GT approach has so far been used as a coding method in MIS. Perhaps the reason for this is the predominance of objectivist and the scientific method criteria for rigorous evaluation in MIS studies; the criteria that caused rejection of many GT studies, or post-rationalized in ways that make them appear to be based on extant theory. However, as a critical issue as the field widens to embrace constructivist, situated, and community-oriented theories of action, it is clear that the approach generates original theory in MIS research. Gasson (2009) believes that GT seems increasingly popular as a research approach in MIS since MIS journals become more open to qualitative and interpretive studies.

Since IS researchers often do not seek to use qualitative research methods in their studies, we are encouraged to conduct research in this field and, to this end, subjects like an overview of GT approaches in the IS research including application of GT in IS research, qualitative research perspective in IS, types of GT approaches used in IS research, guidelines for GT studies in IS, and examples of GT in IS research especially in software engineering are presented.

GROUNDED THEORY AND INFORMATION SYSTEMS

Since qualitative research is often dependent on the use of qualitative data from interviews, documents, and observations from participants to understand and explain social phenomena, the focus of IS research also shifts from technical issues to managerial and organizational issues, and qualitative research methods have become increasingly important in this field (Myers, 1997). Because the methodology is extremely useful in developing context-based, process-oriented descriptions and explanations of the phenomenon, GT approaches are becoming increasingly common in the IS research literature.

For researchers who want to use qualitative research for the first time, GT is attractive because of its specific procedures and more importantly, in its analytical style, it is not dependent on particular disciplinary perspectives and can be viewed from the perspective of IS field research as a hybrid discipline. GT analysis, because of being based on theory at various levels for a deep understanding of social phenomena, seems appropriate for the purpose of examining the way of achieving agreement between system analysts and their clients (Urquhart, 1997).

The widespread use of GT in the social sciences, nursing and psychology since its introduction in the 1960s is due to its interpretative emphasis and ability to explain socio-cultural phenomena. Later, however, in order to clarify the intentions, actions, and ideas related to management, change, and professional interactions, GT also came to the business and IS field.

To be rational, qualitative research in IS must be grounded in theories that have emerged in interpretive and phenomenological places. According to Myers (1997), GT has been increasingly accepted in IS research because it is a very effective way of developing context-based and also process-oriented explanations of the phenomena studied.

Of course, IS research has not fully exploited the GT methodology for two reasons. One is that many studies do not develop the theory, which is intended to support the GT methodology. Although each form of GT methodology results makes a theoretical contribution, there is a formal distinction between developing new theory and developing models and rich descriptions of new phenomena. Also, there is ambiguity regarding how GT methodology should be used in IS research (Wiesche et al., 2017).

Although the main purpose of the GT methodology is to develop the theory, GT methodology studies in IS do not exclusively develop the theory. Instead, these studies include three research contributions, theories, models, and rich explanations as shown in Table 1.

Table 1. Three forms of research contribution (Wiesche et al., 2017)

Research contribution forms	Description
Theory	Descriptions statements, variables definitions, determinations of their relationships in addition to justifications for those relationships, and the boundaries of the theory
Model	Defining abstract variables and their relationships
Rich description	Narratives of empirical observations without abstraction

The abstract variables, their relationships, the justification for those relationships, and the boundaries that constrain the scope of the theory, form the theory, and the models are, in fact, the definitions of the abstract variables and their relationships. These variables and relationships are based on data generalization. Critically, the models do not provide an explanation for the relationships. Rich descriptions are narratives on the basis of empirical observations without abstraction. They include objects, people, systems, activities, and events that occur in a particular area of study. These narratives identify patterns and clusters among the attributes in the data (Wiesche et al., 2017).

The role of theory in IS has recently been highly regarded. GT is capable of producing a theory that exists in all of these categories because it contains the basic building blocks of each theory - constructs in the form of categories and the relationships between the constructs in the form of theoretical coding. What is certain is that because GT emphasizes constructs and relationships, it is easy to generate statements about IS phenomena that may - or may not - be tested. A well-known feature of IS research is the use of many theories borrowed from other disciplines. Although it is often valuable to import theories from outside the field, it is suggested that GT be used to build theories from within. GT may be useful in developing theories concerning such phenomena (Urquhart et al., 2010).

Lanamäki and Haj-Bolouri (2019) argued that Wiesche et al. (2017) did not discuss paradigmatic issues such as ontology and epistemology and represented a single paradigm mindset. According to their viewpoints, the GT approaches classification of Wiesche et al. into three categories: Glaserian, Straussian, and Second-Generation is problematic. In this way, they tried to propose a pluralistic GT methodology in IS research.

A qualitative perspective on IS research using GT, personal construction theory and narrative research has been explained by Hunter (2004).

Table 2. Qualitative theories (Hunter, 2004)

Theory	Approach	Technique
Grounded Theory	Theory discovery Analysis of data	Categories emerge from data Property: attribute of a category
Personal Construct Theory	Personalized system for past experiences interpretation	Elicited using the RepGrid: Elements Constructs Elicitation Laddering
Narrative Inquiry	Recounting of personal experiences	Rich in context (first-hand experience) Time constraint (start, sequence of events, end) Long interview technique (big tour questions, scheduled questions, floating queries)

Personal Construct Theory: Designed to help evaluate patients' interpersonal relationships. Individuals construct personal constructs based on their own interpretations of past experiences to cope with present or future situations. A person's personal structure system may be registered using a technique known as the Role Construct Repertory or RepGrid. It has two main components including elements and constructs. There are elements as entities in the research area that help the research participant to form an opinion. Constructs are, in fact, the interpretation of research participants about the elements in the same field of research. The RepGrid technique has been used in a number of IS research projects.

Narrative Inquiry: Includes documentary stories that are contextually rich and temporally limited. It is temporally bounded means that narratives must have a beginning and an end, along with a timely description of the intervening events to identify the main impacts on the career path of IS specialists.

The progress of interpretive research from insignificance in the 1980s to its current mainstream status in the IS community is evident in terms of using GT methodology in IS studies. GT research has been published in major IS journals, and this methodology has gained sufficient support to acquire its special interest group in the IS Association (Urquhart and Fernández, 2016).

There are a number of key misconceptions about the GT methodology that act as an important obstacle to using the theoretical building potential of the GT methodology in IS research (Urquhart and Fernández, 2016).

Misconception 1: The researcher is considered as a blank page who enters the data collection without looking at the literature: This misconception about the GT methodology is probably harmful because understanding the role of literature in the GT methodology for production good grounded theories is essential.

Misconception 2: Because of the complex nature and contradictory guidance on how to use this methodology, GT is inflexible; the GT methodology is sometimes as inflexible and hard to apply.

Misconception 3: The GT methodology produces low-level theories that don't work much: founded in the view that GT methodology's, this issue concerns with a limited substantive field prevents the development of theories with greater appeal with regard to usability or generalizability.

Misconception 4: GT methodology is Positivist/Interpretivist/Critical: There have long been discussions about the basic philosophical position in GT, a good example in IS.

Several models and theories have gained wide acceptance, such as the Theory of Reasoned Action (TRA), the Technology Acceptance Model (TAM), the Unified Theory of Acceptance and Use of Technology (UTAUT), the Delone and Mclean IS success model, and the Diffusion of Innovation (DOI) model are provided in the field of IS. They have been widely accepted in IS research to investigate, discover and measure the factors affecting the adoption and use of IS. However, for some researchers, research problems using existing theories or models cannot be addressed. This is especially the case when examining new phenomena or topics that do not exist in existing literature. Therefore, there is a need for qualitative exploration to generate and create new meaning that helps to understand the phenomenon (Alfarraj et al., 2005).

The four alternative GT approaches they consider are: the Glaserian, or traditional method of Glaser; the Straussian GT approach; the use of GT as a part of a mixed methodology; and the use of GT techniques for data analysis (Alfarraj et al., 2005).

In order to develop a theory of data collected rather than experimenting with a theory or hypothesis, the Glaserian approach is used which requires several rounds of interviewing, and the analysis must consist of two basic coding steps of 1) open coding and, 2) selective coding.

Table 3. Four GT approaches used in IS research (Alfarraj et al., 2005)

Typical Refs	Glaser & (1967); Strauss Glaser (1992)	Strauss & Corbin (1990, 1998)	Variety	Mingers (2001)
Paradigm model	Viewed as family of codes	Greater emphasis	Sometimes applied	Sometimes applied
A priori theory	No	No	Maybe applied	Maybe applied
Coding	Open, selective	Open, axial, selective	Any or all applied	Any or all applied
Principles	Required	Required (Glaser disputed adherence)	Not necessarily	Not necessarily
Approach	Glaserian	Straussian	Analytical	Mixed

The theory behind the Straussian approach is to build a theory that clarifies the field of study. It provides guidelines for techniques and methods for new and inexperienced researchers to develop a theory on how to encrypt data and make more use of it. This approach is required for several rounds of interviews and the analysis should be free of the three basic coding steps: (1) open coding, (2) axial coding, and (3) selective coding.

In the analytical approach, the techniques and procedures of data analysis in GT methodolgy are used to create meaning for the field under study. The techniques in GT for coding can be used for any one or all three coding steps. Using this approach, which requires neither multiple interviews nor the need to stick with any specific formulation of GT, the researchers define the relationships between categories and concepts generated by the codes to create meaningful categories and present this information in templates to provide diagrams explaining the situations, events, people, and activities under investigation.

As discussed in Table 1 above, the fourth approach is a mixed approach, which means using the GT or its techniques in combination with other research methods.

The capacity of the method to interpret complex phenomena, fit into social issues, its relevance to social experiences, its vital importance to theories emergence, the absence of prior knowledge constraints, and its ability to fit a variety of research are some of the advantages offered by GT for IS research. A thorough conceptual understanding of the complex and multifaceted environment of IS entails dealing with many intertwined themes. Because research provides a strong descriptive interpretive research, it helps to separate conceptual relevance. This is of value to those who benefit from its product by presenting meaningful emergent concepts. A GT study goes beyond deep explanations to provide substantive theory. When literature cannot support the theoretical evolution of the phenomenon, GT can create surplus value (Jones & Allison, 2011).

An important way to study topics of social nature is GT. Discussions with professionals involved in the IS environment also have social and technical aspects. Researchers must apply a new methodology in order to investigate the importance of emerging social and technical areas. In this regard, a new methodological alternative has been proposed: GT building research in which emerging theory helps unfold what is happening in the substantive field of research. Other methods may have the effect of imposing presumption through the transmission of false theoretical assumptions on emerging phenomena. By providing views that do not cause default bias, GT can overcome these problems by eliminating a selection of predetermined theories that the researcher must explain in social and technical phenomena (Jones and Alony, 2011).

The constructive nature of the phenomena is another consequence of the social aspect of IS. An interpretive approach to research requires social structural knowledge in IS, which is a subjective and valuable interpretation. Therefore, the data are obtained as researcher composite social constructs along with the socially constructed perspectives of those being studied. This composite is divided into first and second order concepts. The first-order components are the artifacts presented by the research subject - these are taken as fact. The second-order components are research structures - these lead to theories that the researcher develops to explain the phenomena studied. Simply put: first-order concepts are interpretations, second-order concepts are interpretations. GT provides a tool for assembling and sorting first order concepts by looking for patterns and saturation as well as a tool for drawing second order concepts through abstraction processes (Jones and Alony, 2011).

Urquhart et al. (2010) sought to answer the basic question about the way of using GT to construct theory in IS by providing guidelines for conducting and evaluating GT studies in IS. These guidelines are oriented towards building theory in our field and are summarized in Table 4. The guidelines are built on the two axes of the framework outlined in Section IV, Conceptualization and Theory Domain. The first three guidelines address how the researcher achieves the level of conceptualization needed to build a good theory through analytical mechanisms, such as continuous comparison. These guidelines can also be related to the process of theory building. The final two guidelines help address the issue of theory by providing guidance on the level of theory

Table 4. Guidelines for GT studies in IS (Urquhart et al., 2010)

Constant comparison	Continuous comparison is the process continuously comparing labelled data samples as a special category with other data samples in the same category that helps to develop the theory by placing analytical properties of codes and categories in close examination. This guideline for data analysis encourages researchers to be rigorous and theoretical.
Iterative conceptualization	According to this guide, researchers should increase the level of abstraction through a process of repeated conceptualization and relate categories to one another. In grounded theory, this is done using theoretical encryption. Relationships between categories can have many different types, not just causal. Theoretical coding helps to understand the relationships between the concepts or factors of a theory. Theoretical memos are also very essential for the development of theoretical coding and the whole iteration process.
Theoretical sampling	This guide emphasizes the importance of making analytical decisions that you will take at a later stage of the study. Theoretical sampling helps to make sure the comprehensive nature of this theory and ensures that the theory building is in fact grounded in the data.
Scaling up	This guide illustrates how a researcher might deal with what is said to be a usual problem in grounded theory. The production of a low-level theory, which can hardly be linked to the broader literature. It is the process of grouping higher level categories into broader themes. Scaling up helps to generalize the theory.
Theoretical integration	This guide helps the researcher counter what he thinks is a theoretical underpinning - theoretical integration. Theoretical integration is defined as linking theory to other theories in the same or similar context. This is a process of comparing the substantive theory produced with other previously developed theories. This principle contributes to theoretical integration in the field and can help generate formal theories.

and how to integrate it with existing literature, a significant aspect of theory. Therefore, the last two guidelines are about the theory that is the result of the first three steps.

GT AND SOFTWARE ENGINEERING

The necessity to consider the social, cultural and human aspects of software development in software engineering (SE) research is a growing awareness. As a result of this awareness, researchers have adopted a variety of social science research methods. Qualitative research methods are increasingly used in SE research. According to Lee and Liebenau (1997), qualitative research in IS is needed, because while there has been a great deal of success in applying natural science and engineering models to computer technology research, they have been unsuitable in the explanation of human, group, organizational, and social matters that surround the application of IS.

GT, as a methodology that attracts particular attention, has been used by several researchers in the field of IS whose experiences provide useful guidance for prospective GT researchers (Stol et al., 2016). Software development areas pose several unusual challenges in GT research. Most GT research relies on interviews and documents. However, software texts provide a variety of data sources including source code, test suites as a collection of test cases, code commit logs, task data through project management software, design diagrams (e.g. wireframes, class diagrams), design documents, domain models as a conceptual model of the domain (such as scenarios, personas, user stories, use cases), project management documents (e.g. backlogs as a set of tasks that must be finished before code release, burn down charts as graphical representation of remaining tasks to do versus time), performance data, data of issue[1] tracker, temporary photo charts (e.g. in whiteboards), online communities and discussions (e.g. at Internet Relay Chat (IRC) or Slack), and contracts and financial statements (Stol et al., 2016). However, a growing number of GT projects deal with development processes, engineering requirements, software tools, and development practices. Such work is usually published in journals that are not relevant to empirical studies (Badreddin, 2013).

The lack of integrated theories in the literature concerning a number of areas in SE practices indicates the need for an inductive approach to assist the emergence of theories based on pragmatic reports of experts. There are good guidelines for conducting inductive research and producing theory in GT. Since software development is a human activity and development processes are heavily reliant on human adaptation with an emphasis on the human aspects of software engineering, GT is renowned for its application in human behavior analysis (Badreddin, 2013).

Orlikowski (1993) study is the most notable use of GT in IS research in which findings of a study into the adoption and use of CASE tools are provided. The contradictory results evident in the CASE literature obtained using the GT in this study reflect the fact that differences in intentions, processes, and contexts around the adoption and use of CASE tools have largely been overlooked in research that sought to derive constant results from CASE tools.

GT has been used by a number of researchers in a range of socio-cultural activities in IS. In addition to studying how IT works, new combinations of action research and GT have been developed to create grounded action research methodology. Also, this methodology have been used to study the use of systems thinking practices, and software inspections (Carver and Basili, 2004, Seaman and Basili, 1997), process modelling (Carvalho et al., 2005), requirements documentation (Power, 2002) and virtual team development

(Sarke et al., 2001; Qureshi et al.,2005). GT has been also used by Hansen and Kautz (2005) to study the use of development practices in a Danish software company and it is concluded that it was an appropriate methodology to use in the IS sector.

A GT-based methodology is developed by Carver and Basili (2004) for literature review as a basis for study of variables that were not the primary goal in prior studies. This methodology is illustrated throughout the study, with a specific example focusing on searching for variables that deal with the individual variations among software inspectors that affect their performance during an inspection. The purpose of software inspection, which is a static software artifact analysis (requirements, design, code, etc.) is to ensure that certain quality features are present.

An empirical study is described by Seaman and Basili (1997) to investigate the issue of members communication in a software development organization. In particular, data was collected concerning code inspections in one software development project. The purpose is to answer the questions of whether or not organizational structure (the network of relationships between developers) has an effect on the amount of effort expended on communication between developers and both quantitative and qualitative methods were used to this end. An exploratory study is developed by Carvalho et al. (2005) to investigate two descriptive software process models derived from the same process data using two different techniques. For this purpose, the qualitative methods, particularly GT and its techniques, were described and then, the nature of the differences in the two models produced was explored.

The GT is to analyze data on virtual teams in a study by Qureshi et al. (2005). The effects relate to coordination, communication and adaptation to distributed electronic work environments are uncovered in the analysis in the way distributed projects are managed. A model for distributed project management is presented following an analysis of the e-Collaboration effects. A GT approach is followed including the discovery of theory from data systematically collected and analyzed from the research process. Three main categories emerged from the open coding. When setting up distributed projects, sourcing strategies would have to consider these episodes. Outsourcing challenges facing distributed project management are investigated using a GT. How the GT methodology was adapted to develop a process model of collaboration in virtual teams is outlined by Sarker et al. (2001).

Attempting to explain the diversity of styles of requirements documents found in practice a GT is provided by Power (2002) in relation to the different software products and systems development situation. This approach identifies the factors affecting the situations categorization from the requirements documentation perspective.

GT is also used to construct theories at various levels, such as the development of descriptive theories of a substantive domain, such as software architecture, as well as more complex explanatory and causal theories such as the factors surrounding software inspection, and the adoption of CASE tools in software engineering research (Seaman and Basili, 1997). How to use GT to study whether and how system developers use IS Development methodologies in practice is also reported by Hansen et al. (2005).

For a variety of reasons, requirements engineering is attractive for GT methodology. As applications and systems move towards more complexity and more users and stakeholders, GT can help uncover patterns from stakeholder perspectives of the system under development and increase knowledge about the needs of users and understanding of the new system, like the organization impact of the new system and changes in business tasks and activities. Due to thc naturc of continuous change raised by the various stakeholders, requirements engineering is inherently dynamic. IS contexts are mainly characterized by qualitative data as it is argued that it is soft and ambiguous. Such characteristics make GT an appropriate methodology for research in the requirements engineering discipline (Badreddin, 2013).

The use of GT as an alternative socio-technical approach is rationalized by Mohanad (2012) to requirement analysis. As GT solves some problems of the existing traditional and socio-technical system design methods, it will establish theoretically that applying GT procedures and techniques will support and add value to the analysis phase. Furthermore, a case study applying GT on a real project is conducted to validate this proposal that demonstrates its applicability and success for requirement analysis.

GT is used by Dagenais et al. (2010) to explore the important features of the project landscape, new team members' orientation barriers and guidance aids that can help new marketers are used in a new project landscape. The research is based on qualitative data collected from 18 participants in 8 countries, most of whom were developers with less than one year's experience. According to the findings of the study, newcomers often face unfamiliar and unfriendly project landscapes, while residents with a helpful perspective help newcomers settle in the city. Having a guide or a human coach was very helpful compared to manuals. .

Aimed to create a model to test best practice in the telecommunications industry using a qualitative research methodology, Hendrick (2013) developed a GT that could be used to guide testing within a large telecommunications company. An important part of the software development process is software testing regardless of the development method it follows. Based on previous research, qualitative research methods can be used successfully when conducting research in software engineering. In particular, GT was very appropriate for research in this field.

The results of a GT study of how software process and software process improvement (SPI) is applied in the practice of software development in a study by Coleman and O'Connor (2007). The focus of this study is on what is actually happening in the software industry. SE is a purely social activity that attempts to study human behavior and the social contexts in which it operates and in which the researcher moves to qualitative techniques. In search of a suitable approach for examining aspects of the SE software process, GT has been selected as a suitable candidate and describes the successful implementation of GT in the SPI study.

GT's is an inductive and pragmatic approach that offers a very robust approach. When using GT in the field of IS, the task is to develop a theory of holistic data collected through naturalistic research, understanding the interaction between software engineers and their environments, and the effects, and consequences of these interactions. GT can also be used by researchers to test theories of their practice, and the relationships between action and effects can lead researchers to the experimental world to find out whether they really think they are the essence of the experimental world. GT is a suitable and valuable way for the SE researcher, specifically to explore and understand the performance and interaction between professionals and their environments, in relation to the software process and SPI.

The GT method is applied in this research and its results provide an image of software process utilization, the result of which is a theory based on field data, which explains how software processes are shaped, evolve, and when and why SPI is performed. GT is based on two conceptual themes, process formation and process evolution, and a core category, processing cost.

Table 5 shows the final list of themes, core category and main categories identified by the study. Each category and code can be linked to interviews and used to provide rich support and descriptions for the results. The saturated categories and various relationships were then combined to shape a theoretical framework.

Table 5. Themes, Core Categories and Main Categories (Coleman and O'Connor, 2007)

Theme	Category
Process formation	Software development manager's background Founder background Management style Process matching Market needs
Process evolution	Process erosion Minimum process Business event Trigger of software process improvement Employee buy-in to process Hiring knowledge and skills Process inertia
Core Category	Category
Processing cost	Bureaucracy Documentation Communication Tacit knowledge Creativity Flexibility

PRACTICAL APPLICATIONS OF GT IN IS RESEARCH

Safari Mehr et al. (2018) aimed to identify key issues in developing health information technology innovation by using GT method. The case study involved the use of information technology in health care (e.g. computerized medical records to share patient care among physicians in different services).

The focus of the study conducted by Lawrence (2002) is on deep understanding of the factors that influence small and medium sized enterprises (SMEs)' decision to adopt and use the Internet in business. This study aimed to describe, interpret, analyze, and understand the use of the Internet from the perspective of SMEs.

The study involved seven SMEs that met the criteria, all of which were seven separate field studies that were conducted in a broad tradition of interpretive case study. The case study included extensive interviews of key stakeholders (e.g. company owner or manager in each SME), along with documentary evidence, such as company reporting. The detailed writing of the records and all data from the interviews and documentation focused on the factors influencing acceptance were reviewed and coded. This technique uses open coding in which data is read and divided into concepts that are classified by evidence rather than by external force.

Some of the initial codes obtained from the open coding process were promotional and advertising, communication medium to enhance organizational efficiency, simple entering into new markets, and the Internet generates new business opportunities, all these codes contributed to the category: benefits of using the Internet. By reviewing all the evidence, the codes were organized with frequent themes, such as the benefits of Internet use, cost-effectiveness, compatibility, and perceived usefulness. These themes became the main candidates for a series of stable and common categories that linked a number of related codes. This is known as axial coding and relies on making relationships between subcategories to core categories to build a more comprehensive design based on a synthetic technique. The benefits of Internet use, cost-effectiveness, compatibility, and perceived usefulness are transformed into technology subcategories (Internet features). The first SME case data were then re-examined and coded using this proposal, aiming to cover as many categories and concepts as possible. This repeated examination yielded a set of broad categories and related concepts that explain the conditions, events, experiences, and consequences of using and adopting the Internet in the first case of SME.

The process of data collection, coding and purposeful analysis is based on the initial concepts guiding the rest of the field study. The rest of the remaining SMEs were systematically compared to the original SME, systematically, using a continuous comparative analysis approach. Theoretical saturation occurs when the relevant categories and concepts are defined and the factors that influence SMEs' decision to adopt or use the Internet in business are explained, with other SME data related to the development or addition of a set of concepts and categories. Since the unique data from each case study as well as the generalization of patterns among the cases are obtained, the theoretical model achieved is practically valid. Study participants provided their comments, corrections, and descriptions of the draft findings and the theoretical model.

The GT method is used in the study Esteves et al. (2002) to analyze several key issues in four case studies. The purpose of the first case study is to identify and define the critical success factors (CFSs) for intranets integration in organizations from technological, organizational, and social perspectives. The explicitly emergent resulting theories as what most differentiates GT method from other research methods and it is not testing a hypothesis and also, that the analysis is undertaken concurrently with the data collection in the GT method, are the relevant issues for the application of GT in this case study. Therefore, since sampling is associated with the study findings after the initial selection and where the findings lead the researcher, predetermined sample sizes are not appropriate.

Identification and definition of CFSs in the Enterprise Resource Planning (ERP) implementation project is the purpose of the second case study which has two stages. The first stage is the definition of the research topic and scope, through the analysis of relevant articles on ERP systems and identifying knowledge gaps in ERP implementation in the organization. Consequently, identifying and defining CFSs for ERP implementation is the purpose of this study. The second stage involves collecting and analysis of relevant literature.

Ten papers related to CSFs models, that describe case studies related with CSFs were used in Phase II (data collection stage) as initial research documents. The process of dividing, conceptualizing, and organizing data is performed in a new way in step 3 (data analysis step) that only the open coding process is performed here. Several sources of information where triangulated and inconsistencies where clarified with extra documentation (namely with documents published in the trade press) to increase validity and reliability of the resulting unified model. During the last phase (comparison phase), a comparative analysis of the resulting model is conducted with other studies related to the subject.

The main themes of the coding process for this case were one of the most important steps in using the GT methodology started by CSFs pre-defined lists and the purpose was to summarize these lists. The major concern was the concepts associated with CSFs, and they found different meanings for the same terminology or the same meaning associated with different terms. This aspect is related to what has been identified in the GT methodology as theoretical coding, namely comparing, linking and reducing categories. In addition, the experience and knowledge of the field of ERP was one of the most important aspects in bringing together concepts and understanding of documents. The GT methodology should include research techniques, quantitative or quantitative techniques, which can improve the accuracy and explanation of the results obtained.

Two case studies were conducted to evaluate the satisfaction level of organizational actors with computer-based systems used to support their business processes. In both cases, the goal was to understand how the organization's actors interact with the system, how they interpret the interaction, and how they integrate the system into a task that those actors are simultaneously responsible and constrained.

Informal interviewing and observation methods, review of managerial and technical documentation, participatory observation of system use, and daily tasks and semi-structured interviews with some organizational actors were used to collect data. Transcripts of interviews and notes from observations are coded in line, identifying key ideas (concepts) about how people interact with the system and how they interact. Explanations of the concepts mentioned form the themes. The concepts and themes were then grouped into categories. Inconsistencies and contradictions in the themes or concepts of later stages guide data collection and analysis. This process stopped when inconsistencies and contradictions were resolved, and no new concepts or themes emerged from the new data.

The final theory which describes the reasons supporting the satisfaction level within the system emerged through the interpretation of the grouped themes that explained the structural, social, political and symbolic aspects of satisfaction/dissatisfaction. With the research participants, the organizational implications of the emerging theory were discussed. In each study, the developed theory provides an opportunity to express several perspectives determined.

Participants discussed the organizational implications of emerging theory and came up with several views.

The main uses of the GT methodology in two case studies were:

Different criteria were used to select participants to observe and interview. A broad literature view on organizational theory and user satisfaction also facilitated the coding process. The data were collected and analyzed through a dynamic process. Although the three main stages of document review, participant observation, and interviewing were defined, in practice, two additional steps were performed informally during each phase. This led to field notes to identify conflicting perspectives from the data. Ethics plays a central role in such research, in which researchers seek to reach rapport and empathy with participants.

Some recommendations were achieved based on the findings from the experience of implementing this methodology as follows:

- Since the GT methodology does not start with hypotheses or research questions like deductive methods but starts with a phenomenon that is not well described in the existing literature in terms of the researcher, researchers should be cautious about using the GT methodology. To this end, regardless of the GT version used, either the original Glaser and Strauss (1967) version, the Strauss and Corbin (1990) version, or the version corresponding to Glaser's (1978, 1992), the GT approach must be precisely defined and the interpretation must be related to the methodological and philosophical assumptions that are taken into account at the time of selecting and using a particular approach.

- In order to gain a deep, broad, and collectivistic (constructivist approach) to the phenomenon under study, accurate data sampling should be undertaken and additional documentation related to the phenomenon collected so that the theory derived from the phenomenon data be more generalizable.
- In order to better define codes and encode documents, a literature review of the subject should be conducted to help understand the relationships between the categories. At the same time, these a priori categories may limit the researcher's interpretation that because of this, the researcher must search for local categories that ultimately conflict the previous categories.
- Since one of the time-consuming tasks is to write memos that take more time than observations, researchers must be prepared for these time-consuming tasks. We may, of course, think that all the techniques and procedures must be followed to achieve a valuable new GT-based theory. Several issues such as statement of the phenomenon, purpose, method, sampling, data collection and analysis, empirical grounding of the study (i.e., findings), and define procedures for theory validation should be described by GT report. Researchers should also provide recommendations for further validating the theory using formal deductive methods in addition to proposing a theory.

Apart from qualitative/ quantitative differences, there are other differences, such as qualitative and quantitative research in IS following the social science model of research, while design research or design science research follow the research engineering model. The latter usually involves the design of an artifact, something that is not usually taken into consideration. However, some kind of qualitative or quantitative research may be applied to contribute to design or evaluate the artifact.

Overall, interpretive studies attempt to interpret phenomena through the meanings that people give them. The purpose of interpretive methods of IS research is to produce an understanding of the information system context, the processes by which influence the information system and are affected by the context (Walsham, 1993).

OTHER INTERPRETIVE METHODOLOGIES AND IS RESEARCH

The article by Susman and Evered (1988) is briefly overviewed here. In their view, action research implies system development, and the process of action research encourages the development of a system's capacity to facilitate, maintain and regulate the cyclic process of detection, action planning, action, evaluation and identification of learning. The purpose of this research is to build appropriate structures, create the system and the necessary competencies and change the relationship of the system with the relevant environment. The focus is on producing the essential communications and problem-solving techniques. The system infrastructure, from which it operates, is the primary tool for (1) reducing problematic urgency and (2) producing new knowledge about system processes. Action research creates the theory that has been put into practice. In action research, the theory provides guidance on what should be considered in identifying the organization as well as producing possible practical courses to deal with the problems of the members of the organization. In addition, action research contributes to the development of the theory by taking measures to guide the theory and assess its implications for the problem that members of the organization are facing; then the theory can be supported or revised based on the evaluation.

Baskerville and Wood-Harper (1996) provides a good introduction to how action research might be used by IS researchers. They describe different frameworks, assumptions, and goals for analyzing different types of action research. A more comprehensive action research paradigm has been defined that provides the basis for validating a wider range of IS research. Accepting a wide range of different types of action research may make the IS context more explicit about its research methodology, thus improving the criteria and applying it to a wider range of IS research.

Baskerville and Myers (2004) about action research published in a special issue of MIS quarterly. Their research methods provide a potential way to improve the practical relevance of IS research. Action research has been described as the cornerstone of best organizational development practices and is a key way to practice organizational development. There is no reason to accept action research in the field of IS.

The purpose of interpretive endeavor is to attempt to establish the concept of organization as text-analogue if hermeneutical analysis is used in an IS study. In an organization, people (e.g. different stakeholders) can have erroneous, flawed, cloudy, and contradictory views on many issues. The purpose of hermeneutical analysis is to attempt to rationalize the whole and the relationship between individuals, organizations, and information technology.

CONCLUSION

Topics covered in this chapter include grounded theory (GT) approaches to information systems (IS) research including GT research contributions to IS research, the qualitative perspective for IS research, the types of GT approaches used in IS research, and guidelines for GT studies in IS, and also, examples of GT in IS. Research is provided especially on software engineering. One of the main focuses of this work is to explain how the GT approach is used in IS research.

Over the years, the GT has been modified to meet the scientific demands of the IS field. The GT methodology flexibility makes it useful in the social and technical areas of IS, where the nature of data changes with technological advances. GT is a rigorous approach that can and should be adapted to the specific needs of IS research. While this methodology is more than 40 years old and its procedural development seems generally sustainable, subsequent innovations in GT stem from its application to new types of data and new social structures. The GT not only permits and encourages the use of different types of data, but also combines well with other methodological approaches.

REFERENCES

Alfarraj, O., Alkhalaf, S., Nielsen, S., & Alghamdi, R. (2015). The use of grounded theory techniques in IS research. *International Journal of Computers*, *9*, 115–124.

Badreddin, O. (2013). Thematic review and analysis of grounded theory application in software engineering. *Advances in Software Engineering*. doi:10.1155/2013/468021

Baskerville, R., & Myers, M. D. (2004). Special issue on action research in information systems: Making IS research relevant to practice-foreword. *Management Information Systems Quarterly*, *28*(3), 329–335. doi:10.2307/25148642

Baskerville, R. L., & Wood-Harper, A. T. (1998). Diversity in information systems action research methods. *European Journal of Information Systems*, *7*(2), 90–107. doi:10.1057/palgrave.ejis.3000298

Carvalho, L., Scott, L., & Jeffery, R. (2005). An exploratory study into the use of qualitative research methods in descriptive process modeling. *Information and Software Technology*, *47*(2), 113–127. doi:10.1016/j.infsof.2004.06.005

Carver, J., & Basili, V. (2004). Identifying implicit process variables to support future empirical work. *Journal of the Brazilian Computer Society*, *9*(2), 1–10.

Coleman, G., & O'Connor, R. (2007). Using grounded theory to understand software process improvement: A study of Irish software product companies. *Information and Software Technology Journal.*, *49*(6), 654–667. doi:10.1016/j.infsof.2007.02.011

Dagenais, B., Ossher, H., Bellamy, R. K. E., Robillard, M. P., & de Vries, J. P. (2010) Moving into a new software project landscape. In *ICSE '10: Proceedings of the 32nd ACM/IEEE international conference on software engineering*. ACM. 10.1145/1806799.1806842

Esteves, J., Ramos, I., & Carvalho, J. (2002). *Use of grounded theory in information systems area: An exploratory analysis*. Retrieved September 10, 2019, from https://repositorium.sdum.uminho.pt/bitstream/1822/346/1/Ecrm.pdf

Gasson, S. (2009). Employing a grounded theory approach for MIS research. In Y. K. Dwivedi, B. Lal, M. D. Williams, S. L. Schneberger, & M. Wade (Eds.), *Handbook of Research on Contemporary Theoretical Models in Information Systems*. IGI Global. doi:10.4018/978-1-60566-659-4.ch003

Hansen, B., & Kautz, K. (2005). Grounded theory applied –studying information systems development methodologies in practice. *Proceedings of 38th Annual Hawaiian International Conference on Systems Sciences*. 10.1109/HICSS.2005.289

Hendrick, D. (2013). Using grounded theory to develop a framework for software testing best practice in a Telecommunications Company (MSc dissertation). Dublin Institute of Technology.

Hunter, M. G. (2004). Qualitative research in information systems: consideration of selected theories. In M. Whitman & A. Woszczynski (Eds.), *The Handbook of Information Systems Research* (pp. 291–304). IGI Global. doi:10.4018/978-1-59140-144-5.ch016

Jones, M., & Alony, I. (2011). Guiding the use of grounded theory in doctoral studies – an example from the Australian film industry. *International Journal of Doctoral Studies*, *6*, 95-114.

Lanamäki, A., & Haj-Bolouri, A. (2019). Grounded theory methodology as resource for pluralist information systems research. *Proceedings of the 27th European Conference on Information Systems (ECIS).*

Lawrence, J. E. (2002). *The Use of Internet in Small to Medium-Sized Enterprises* (PhD thesis). University of Salford.

Lee, A. S., & Liebenau, J. (1997). Information systems and qualitative research. In A. Lee, J. Liebenau, & J. I. DeGross (Eds.), *Proceedings of Information Systems and Qualitative Research.* Boston, MA: Kluwer Academic. doi:10.1007/978-0-387-35309-8_1

Mkhomazi, S., & Iyamu, T. (2013). A guide to selecting theory to underpin information systems studies. *International Working Conference on Transfer and Diffusion of IT (TDIT)*, 525-537. 10.1007/978-3-642-38862-0_33

Mohanad, H. (2012). Using grounded theory as a method for system requirements analysis. *Journal of Information Systems and Technology Management*, *9*(1), 23–38. doi:10.4301/S1807-17752012000100002

Myers, M. D. (1997). Qualitative research in information systems. *Management Information Systems Quarterly*, *21*(2), 241. doi:10.2307/249422

Orlikowski, W. J. (1993). CASE tools as organizational change: Investigating incremental and radical changes in systems development. *Management Information Systems Quarterly*, *17*(3), 309–340. doi:10.2307/249774

Power, N. (2002). *A grounded theory of requirements documentation in the practice of software development* (PhD Thesis). Dublin City University.

Qureshi, S., Liu, M., & Vogel, D. (2005). A grounded theory analysis of e-collaboration effects for distributed project management. *Proceedings of 38th Annual Hawaiian International Conference on Systems Sciences*. 10.1109/HICSS.2005.18

Safari Mehr, E., Carswell, P., & Day, K. (2018). An adaptation of grounded theory using a modified convergent interviewing technique. *Qualitative Report*, *23*(6), 1456–1469.

Sarker, S., Lau, F., & Sahay, S. (2001). Using an adapted grounded theory approach for inductive theory building about virtual team development. *The Data Base for Advances in Information Systems*, *32*(1), 38–56. doi:10.1145/506740.506745

Seaman, C., & Basili, V. (1997). An empirical study of communication in code inspections. *Proceedings of the 19th International Conference on Software Engineering*, 96-106. 10.1145/253228.253248

Stol, K. J., Ralph, P., & Fitzgerald, B. (2016). Grounded theory in software engineering research: a critical review and guidelines. ICSE '16, Austin, TX. doi:10.1145/2884781.2884833

Susman, G. I., & Evered, R. D. (1978). An assessment of the scientific merits of action research. *Administrative Science Quarterly*, *23*(4), 582–603. doi:10.2307/2392581

Urquhart, C. (1997). Exploring analyst-client communication: Using grounded theory techniques to investigate interaction in informal requirements gathering. In A. S. Lee, J. Liebenau, & J. I. DeGross (Eds.), *Information Systems and Qualitative Research* (pp. 149–181). London: Chapman and Hall. doi:10.1007/978-0-387-35309-8_10

Urquhart, C., & Fernández, W. (2016). Using grounded theory method in information systems: The researcher as blank slate and other myths. Enacting Research Methods in Information Systems, 1, 129-156.

Urquhart, C., Lehmann, H., & Myers, M. D. (2010). Putting the 'theory' back into grounded theory: Guidelines for grounded theory studies in information systems. *Information Systems Journal*, *20*(4), 357–381. doi:10.1111/j.1365-2575.2009.00328.x

Walsham, G. (1993). *Interpreting Information Systems in Organizations.* Chichester: Wiley.

Wiesche, M., Jurisch, M. C., Yetton, P. W., & Krcmar, H. (2017). Grounded theory methodology in information systems research. *Management Information Systems Quarterly, 41*(3), 85–701. doi:10.25300/MISQ/2017/41.3.02

ENDNOTE

1 A bug, a requested feature, task, missing documentation, etc.

Chapter 4
Grounded Theory in Practices of Technology Management

ABSTRACT

The present study explores the application of grounded theory (GT) methodology in various aspects of technology management (TM) including technology commercialization, adoption, and transfer. These processes, resulting from the actions of different actors and organizations, are recognized as key factors in promoting innovative capabilities in organizations. In order to facilitate the successful implementation of TM measures, specific mechanisms need to be designed, the first of which is to identify the drivers and obstacles. As one of the most common methods in the field of management research for qualitative theory building instead of quantitative hypothesis validation, GT's application in this regard is to analyze the drivers and barriers and develop a conceptual model relevant to each function. This chapter discusses the GT application in theory building in the field of TM research.

INTRODUCTION

Today, the total number of products being launched is increasing, while at the same time the time for new products to come to market has been reduced in many industries. These changes are driven by the ever-increasing customer demand and competitive pressure in today's markets. Under such circumstances, companies can maintain their advantage and continue to optimize their operational processes to balance product innovation and

DOI: 10.4018/978-1-7998-4252-1.ch004

process. According to Siemens (2009), effective technology management (TM) requires supporting the strategic needs of the company which are mapped to the marketplace requirements. TM is a set of concepts, skills, techniques and practices that help in decision-making and implementation in the technology development and use by firms, aimed at succeeding in innovation and increasing firm's competitiveness. According to Kropsu-Vehkapera et al., (2009), creating synergy among all the factors (i.e. research, development, planning, engineering, machines, software, production, and communication) to make them work together in the most efficient way to produce profit for the company in the long-term is the ultimate goal of TM. TM covers all aspects of organizing technology knowledge, technology forecasting, technology development, technology commercialization and technology usage through the technology life-cycle.

Because of their complexity, TM studies need an in-depth understanding of different domains, and therefore, a qualitative research approach is an appropriate approach for this study. To conduct qualitative research, the researcher observes and collects data through interviewing, taking notes, and interpreting the phenomena in their actual dimensions. The opportunity to deepen research is one of the main advantages of a qualitative research approach. According to the literature review, qualitative research significantly facilitates research in new areas. Furthermore, the qualitative research might be a suitable research approach because of the (a) uncertainty about the concepts, factors and phases under consideration, (b) the need for interpretation of factors and phases, (c) the need for understanding the nature and complexity of the phenomenon under consideration, and (d) the need for understanding the interaction of key factors and phases (Basias and Pollalis, 2018).

According to Glaser and Strauss (1967), as a powerful research method, through their grounding in empirical observations, GT seeks to develop a new understanding of the patterns of relationships among social actors in the real environment, and to develop the theory and explanation of these interactions in the natural environment (Corbin and Strauss, 2008). Also, as it allows the researcher to delve deep into the lived experience and incidents of the management world, it is especially useful in discovering rich insights from social interactions and developing context-based, process-oriented descriptions and explanations of complex managerial processes in a specific real-life setting. As key issues in TM, such as complex decision-making processes and interactions in relationships and social networks require often deep analysis of the empirical data from a real-life setting, the characteristics of GT make it specifically suited to examine them. Accordingly, GT offers valuable research possibilities for TM research.

This chapter examines the type of qualitative research that has been implemented using the GT approach in the TM domain. Aspects covered in TM in this study are: Technology commercialization, technology transfer, and technology adoption.

TECHNOLOGY COMMERIALIZATION AND GT

Commercialization refers to turn research results into products, services, and processes that can be the subject of business transactions (Downie, 2006) and emphasizes the applicability of research results and their economic value creation. Many countries have realized its role in development and placed it at the core of their scientific programs and policies.

The technology commercialization process is not a straightforward process, but rather a complex one with multiple actors playing different capacities. This process requires skills such as product development, market evaluation, market strategies, financial resource management, engineering and production management, accounting, etc. (Bandarian, 2007). Studies on the commercialization process and its related infrastructure are mainly concerned with defining business concepts and conceptualizing the process (Sohn and Moon, 2003).

According to Wan et al. (2013), technology commercialization is the process of fulfilling the potential tasks of technology innovation and product concepts with specific business activities and achieving technical value and value utilization by breaking down constraints and removing political, economic, cultural barriers and enhancing market value added and creating the necessary profits for survival and corporate development. Technology commercialization specifically refers to the process of transferring technology and generating profits in the form of products and technologies. Therefore, technology commercialization is a complex innovation process and different classifications of the technology process, commercialization for different purposes, and mainly involving two-stage, three-stage, four-stage, and five-stage theory has been proposed by several scholars.

A systematic and conceptual model of the factors affecting the mechatronic technology commercialization process in small businesses is provided in the study by Mohammadkhah and Hejazis (2014). In their research, mechatronics technology commercialization process is investigated in seven small enterprises using GT for analyzing the effective factors. Finally, a conceptual model is derived based on in-depth interviews with managers of successful companies in the technology commercialization. According to pattern obtained from this study, mechatronics technology is a major issue that is affected by the specialized knowledge, experience and collaboration between engineers from various disciplines of engineering. Also, it was found that obtaining more financial profits is the final goal of technology commercialization. Various skills can be used by engineers to sell technology to the manufacturers in various situations and different factors underlying medium and different qualifications.

In a study by Namdarian and Naimi-Sadigh (2018), it is tried to extract research commercialization drivers from the Iranian researchers' perspective and develop a model based on institutional and local contexts. Studying the performance of Iranian universities and research centers, it is evident that despite their research and development (R&D) capacities, most have fallen short in research commercialization, leaving them dependent on government funding. Therefore, to facilitate successful research commercialization in Iran, specific mechanisms are needed beginning with the identification of its drivers. This study uses a three-stage interpretive-qualitative approach: documentary research, interviews and GT. In the first step, a comprehensive review of the existing literature was carried out to determine the research commercialization drivers mentioned in previous studies. Subsequently, a theoretical saturation index was used and a total of 30 researchers were selected and interviewed through a purposive sampling procedure among the researchers were familiar with the concepts of commercialization. Then the list of drivers extracted from the literature was completed based on the opinions of these experts. Subsequently, in order to analyze the drivers and develop the conceptual model in the third stage, the GT approach was used. According to the research results, designing managerial mechanisms; creating strategic alliances; modifying the educational system; improving the research structure; modifying contextual factors; creating supportive infrastructure; and strengthening researchers' positive characteristics are the most important drivers of research commercialization in Iran.

The technology commercialization phenomenon is analyzed by Byeongmun et al. (2018) using the GT approach in the field of agro-food. Due to the lack of research with this approach, this study was conducted in which 98 concepts, 22 subcategories, and 9 categories were derived by open and axial coding of interview data. Accordingly, the core category of technology commercialization in the agro-food sector was determined as the influencing factors of technology commercialization based on the results of open coding and axial coding. The predicted factors affecting the technology commercialization include threats and opportunities based on the industrial characteristics, corporate factors, and corporate environment factors, while the actual factors obtained from the finding are technological support and protection and business development capability factors.

A literature review on commercialization indicates that most of the research in this field has either focused on commercialization in general or on one of the branches of the natural sciences, and no research was conducted specifically focusing on commercialization of the Humanities. Consulting, patent registration, licensing and start-up companies owned by students and professors, and training courses for applicants (Jacob et al., 2003), research contracts with industry (Landry et al., 2006), start-up of technology-based companies through the efforts of researchers, affiliates, university and industry communication (Debackere and Veugelers, 2005), research contracts, R&D unions and cooperatives (Bozeman, 2000) are among the mechanisms proposed for commercialization. The same methods can be used considering the specifics and characteristics of the Humanities and the specific conditions of each of its subsets, together with other proprietary methods for commercializing Humanities research.

The results of the researches can be transmitted by different mechanisms. Although transferring the research results to industry has been widely acknowledged as a key factor in industry competitiveness, there is no best mechanism to transfer knowledge and technology. Given the different types of knowledge transfer mechanisms, there are some different ways in which the business sector can access and benefit from university research results:

- Free dissemination and exchange of ideas and information through seminars and other forms of informal communication (Shinn and Lamy, 2006),
- Effective university-industry relationship through the establishment of industry and university liaison offices,
- Transfer of people, including recruitment of students, researchers and staff by corporations and transfer of staff in and out of the science base (Shinn and Lamy, 2006),
- Formation of consulting and contract research teams with the industry (Shinn and Lamy, 2006),
- Exploiting intellectual property through various methods including establishing companies based on university licensing activities,

establishing joint venture companies and startups by staff and graduate students,

- Establishing high-tech incubator centers and science and technology parks at universities: as a process of support for businesses with growth potential, business incubation can be targeted at one or a combination of support to (United Kingdom Science Park Association, 2015):
- Start-ups,
- Early stage businesses,
- Established businesses with new products/ new directions.

Survival and growth of growth centers during the startup period, which is the most vulnerable phase can be reinforced with nurturing the development of entrepreneurial companies. Such programs lead to the provision of business support services and resources tailored to young companies. Creating jobs in a community, enhancing a community's entrepreneurial climate, retaining businesses in a community, building or accelerating growth in a local industry and diversifying local economies are the most common goals of incubation programs. The most common forms of support include (infoDev, 2009):

- Infrastructure, such as office space;
- Business services, such as administration and information services;
- Financing, such as providing information and support for the incubator's client businesses to help them access appropriate sources of finance; and
- People connectivity, which includes mentoring and coaching services, and access to networks.

According to the definition of International Association of Science Parks (IASP) (2018), ESCAP (2019) mentioned the following items as the park characteristics:

- A property-based initiative with formal and operational links with universities or other higher educational institution, or major centers of research;
- Designed to encourage the formation and growth of knowledge-based industries or high value-added firms, normally resident on site; and
- Having a steady management team actively engaged in nurturing the technology transfer and business skills to tenant organizations.

Also referred to as technology or research parks or innovation and science centers, the term technology park usually indicates a focus on technology innovation and tenant company involvement in applied science.

- The technology market: technology market is one of the mechanisms that has recently emerged to facilitate and enhance technology development activities. The market has been set up in various countries with the support of international unions and organizations, and even in many industrial areas and science and technology parks. It called with different named in each of these areas such as: "Techno Mart", "Tech Market" that depending on their mission, they have key differences in terms of structure, function, location, boundary of activity, etc. and different characteristics. The main plan of technology market is to help resolve the problem of projects commercialization. Unlike international exhibitions where products have been displayed, in the technology market, technology or marketed, research output ready for the production marketed for sailing, not merely finished products.

The GT approach was also used by Hassangholipour et al. (2010) as a research method to design a model of knowledge commercialization in Management schools.

Open Coding: As a process of categorizing several separate phenomena, the categorized concepts are clustered around a related theme to structure more abstract categories in open coding. In order to form categories and properties in this process, incidents or events are labeled and assembled together through constant comparison. By creating categories in open coding, categories are developed based on features and dimensions. Properties are common attributes in all concepts of a category or the characteristics of a category, the depiction of which describes and gives it meaning. Dimensions indicate the position of a property along a continuum or range. Properties and dimensions lead to the richness of the abstract category (Moghaddam, 2006).

Axial Coding: The next stage is to reduce the number of codes and to collect them together in a way that shows a relationship among them through systematic analysis and constant comparison of data. The characteristics of a concept are defined precisely and ranked in terms of strengths and weaknesses. Finally, data is organized as a core category that researcher has

Table 1. Open coding (HassanGholipour et al., 2010)

Sub-categories	Categories
The supportive role of senior managers in transformation Providing facilities The role of human resource management	**Management mechanisms**
Management of revenues and expenses Financial support for research ideas Fair distribution of benefits	**Financial mechanisms**
Changing the teaching method of research method Providing research-based training Being problem-centric of research Change the educational system Creating a strategic research document The relationship between science production and commercialization	**Educational and research mechanisms**
Improving the evaluation system Product quality improvement Correction of defective structure	**Mechanisms of structure modification**
The rule of values Eliminate political unrest Presenting a positive image of the faculty	**Culture reform mechanisms**
Redesigning internal processes Creation of knowledge sharing process Transparency of regulations	**Legal mechanisms**
University-industry interaction Achieve the benefits of commercialization Creating a customer network Understanding marketing practices Understand the need for commercialization Creating a competitive environment and thinking	**Design and deployment of the commercialization process**

to justify as the basis for the emergent theory. The core category, which is the principal phenomenon around which all the other categories are related, unites all the strands in order to provide an explanation of the under study. It represents the description of hypothetical relationships between categories and subcategories. Axial coding is the realization of concepts with regard to their dynamic interrelationships (Moghaddam, 2006).

A grounded theorist relates other categories to it, after selecting one core category and positioning it at the center of the process being explored. These categories that are the causal conditions, strategies, contextual conditions, and consequences, are identified to show the context (structure) and the process of a phenomenon. Causal conditions refer to factors that lead to the occurrence of a phenomenon, subject under study, or main idea. Strategies are specific actions or interactions that are the result of the core phenomenon. The specified set of conditions (patterns of conditions) that intersect dimensionally at this time and place to make a set of positions or issues to which individuals

Figure 1. Axial coding (HassanGholipour et al., 2010)

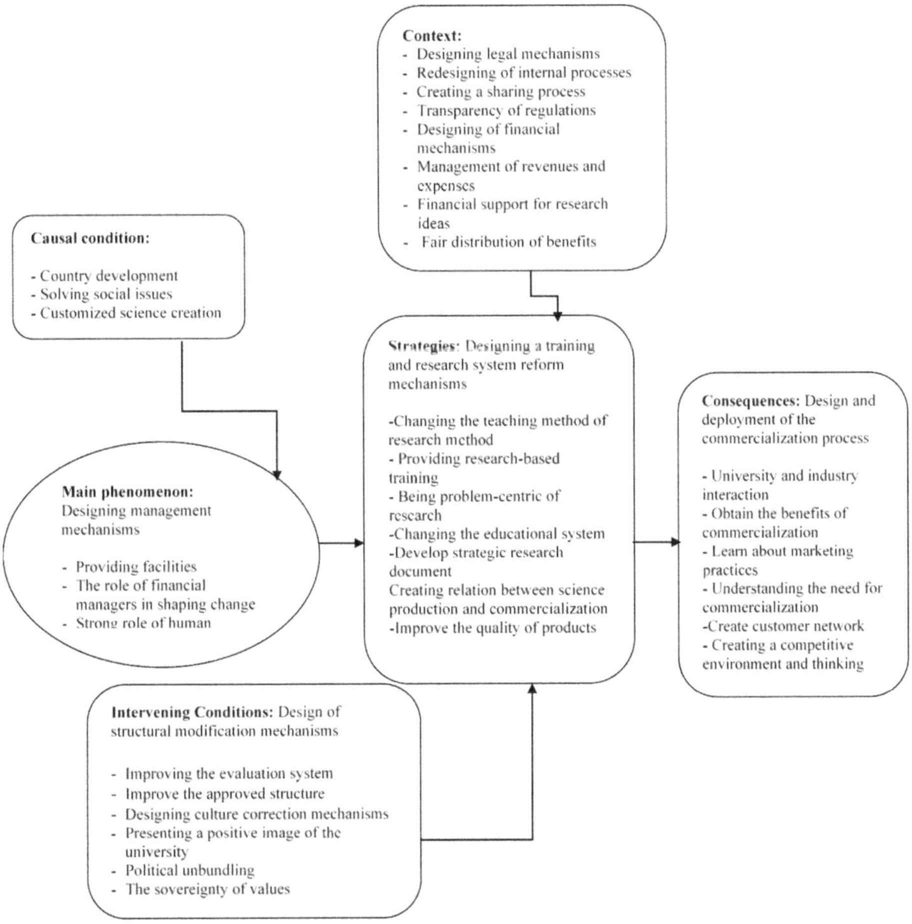

respond via actions/interactions are contextual conditions. Consequences are the outcome of the phenomena as they are engaged by way of action and interaction. The causal conditions have an effect on the core category, the core category and the contextual conditions have an effect on the strategies, and the strategies have an effect on the consequences (Moghaddam, 2006).

Selective Coding: Selective coding is the final stage of data analysis that can be defined as the process by which relates the categories to the core category to finally form the basis for the GT. Selective coding is the process of selecting the central/ core category, relating it to other categories in a systematic way, validating those relationships, and filling in categories that require more refinement and development (Moghaddam, 2006).

Figure 2. Knowledge commercialization mechanism model (HassanGholipour et al., 2010)

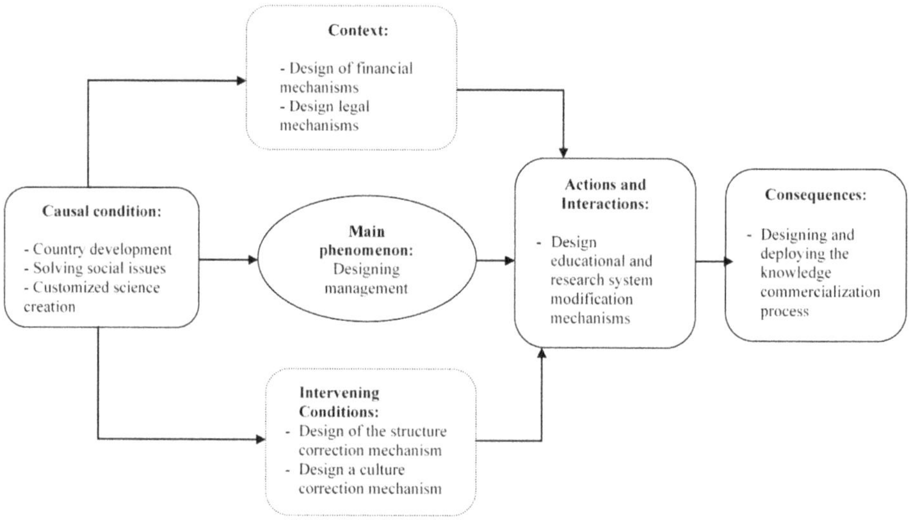

Mohammadpour et al. (2012) used the GT approach to analyze the challenges facing the commercialization of the Humanities research. For this purpose, at the open coding stage in order to achieve more certainty and accuracy, coding of basic concepts has been done in two stages. In the first phase, 36 concepts were extracted from interviews with Humanities researchers. These concepts were then coded at the second step of open coding for more coherence in the form of 11 more abstract concepts. In the next step, axial coding, the basic concepts extracted in the previous step (open coding) were classified into 5 major categories. These major categories, that are more abstract at a higher level than the concepts of the preceding stage include: 1) scientific identity 2) policy making 3) incapability of researcher 4) bad impression of commercialization 5) research structure. The category of scientific identity was extracted as a core category at this stage. The literal similarity between some concepts and the categories obtained from the methodological perspective of the GT is not problematic. In many cases some concepts may be used in the production of a major category or at a higher level the core category may have a literal similarity with one or more major categories. These core concepts and categories are discussed separately in Table 2 which a GT in the form of a paradigm model is presented in the third step of coding, i.e., selective coding based on these categories. We will briefly explain each of these categories and compare them with the research literature.

Scientific Identity: Many of the obstacles and challenges that Humanities researchers pointed in the research commercialization are due to the nature and complexity of the Humanities, the uncertainty of their function and application in society. It has long been a subject of debate among philosophers and thinkers whether the Humanities are really science. Can they, like the natural sciences, play a role in the well-being of society? Accordingly, the place of the Humanities among the human knowledge is vague and lack of understanding of its importance has caused the public unawareness of its function. The attitude towards Humanities is poor compared to other areas of human knowledge. The weakness of the education system and the Humanities literature is another problem facing the Humanities in Iran and, naturally, in the research commercialization.

Policy-making: The challenges that lie with this category are mainly due to the existing policies and contexts in the country's academic and research centers, which indicate that the policies and infrastructure aligned with the research approach to commercialization have not been changed significantly and they practice according the same traditional values and duties. Although the relationship between industry and university has long been the focus of policymaking and action has been taken in this regard, this relationship has not yet been properly established. There is no system of communication between knowledge creators and centers of exploitation.

The researchers' incapability is a part of the challenges facing the commercialization of Humanities research due to the lack of researchers' incentives and skills in commercialization of research results. Based on the findings of this study, most researchers in the field of Humanities have stated that they do not have the skills to market and identify community needs and commercialize research. On the other hand, the lack of need and motivation by the researcher, the weakness of entrepreneurship culture and the spirit of symbolizing among the researchers are some of the challenges in the field of commercialization.

Poor impression of commercialization: Contrasting the commercialization of research with academic freedom, the emergence of the contradiction between

Table 2. The concepts, categories and core category extracted from the raw data (Mohammadpour et al., 2012)

<table>
<tr><th>Concepts (basic coding)</th><th>Concepts (Secondary Coding)</th><th>Main categories</th><th>Core category</th></tr>
<tr><td>Nature and quiddity, position, function, application</td><td>Natural obstacles</td><td rowspan="3">Humanities identity</td><td rowspan="12">Scientific identity</td></tr>
<tr><td>Lack of understanding, public unawareness</td><td>Attitudinal barriers</td></tr>
<tr><td>Education, translation</td><td>Academic obstacles</td></tr>
<tr><td>Promotion and scoring system, resource allocation, university-industry relations, more value to education instead of research, number of articles</td><td>Incentive policies</td><td rowspan="2">policy making</td></tr>
<tr><td>Weak communication system, funding by the government</td><td>Infrastructure</td></tr>
<tr><td>Marketing skills, identifying needs</td><td>Skill barriers</td><td rowspan="2">incapability of researcher</td></tr>
<tr><td>Lack of feeling needs, lack of entrepreneurial culture, lack of motivation, self-esteem and symbolism</td><td>Motivational barriers</td></tr>
<tr><td>Scientific freedom, conflicts of duties, scientific development, opposition to entrepreneurial thinking in scientific centers</td><td>Intellectual barriers</td><td rowspan="2">bad impression of commercialization</td></tr>
<tr><td>Intellectual property rights, researcher share and income</td><td>Legal barriers</td></tr>
<tr><td>Problems and complexity of research, quality of implementation, variability of results, extent of implementation</td><td>Obstacles to research in the Humanities</td><td rowspan="2">research structure</td></tr>
<tr><td>Lack of confidence in the transferability and credibility to the results, gap between theory and practice, ornamental research, research work, the nature of human technology</td><td>Technology barriers in the Humanities</td></tr>
</table>

commercialization with traditional university teaching and research tasks, the challenge of scientific development in universities, the opposition to the establishment of corporate thinking in science centers, and the Humanities as enlightened science are of the major ideological and intellectual barriers against research commercialization. On the other hand, even turning to the research commercialization by researchers presents them with the challenges of intellectual property and the uncertainty of the researcher's share of its income, which narrows the arena of researchers' desire for commercialization.

Research Structure: The concept of research refers to a different way of doing things and to the different results of Humanities research. Problems and complexities of research, quality of implementation, variability of research results, extent to which research findings are implemented are major barriers to research in the Humanities. On the other hand, the lack of confidence in the results, the gap between theory and practice in the Humanities, decorative and hypocritical research, and different and soft nature of human technology are technological barriers to the Humanities.

Commercialization obstacles of Agricultural Research, Education and Promotion Organization is investigated by Khosravipour et al. (2011) identified using the GT in which, they classified obstacle into four categories of strategic, structural, human, and market.

The ICT commercialization risk factor model is constructed by Wan et al. (2013) using GT focusing on implied relationship between the core category, the main category, and subcategory. In this regard, 21 risk factors

Figure 3. A paradigmatic model of the challenges facing the commercialization of Humanities research (Mohammadpour et al., 2012)

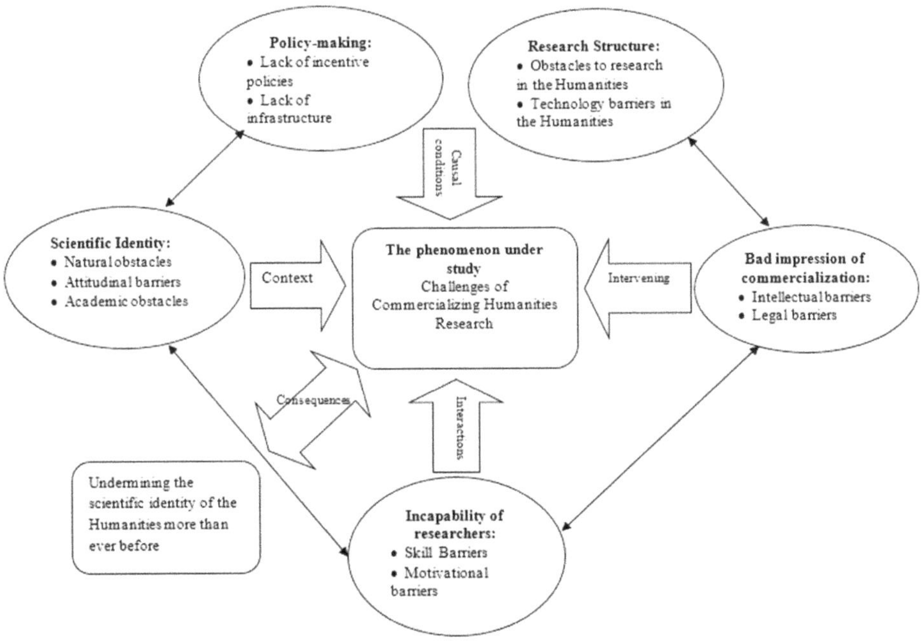

are identified and analytic hierarchy process (AHP) method was used to rank the risk factors and 10 key risk factors were selected, including outdated supporting facilities, unclear strategic goal, technology life cycle, weak intellectual property protection, slow technology update, insufficient ability for product improvement, lack of system training, difficult market positioning, unscientific evaluation and incentive mechanism, and single sales channel. Finally, interpretive structural modeling (ISM) method was used to construct an interpretive structural model of the key risk factors, and the three root risk factors respectively are weak intellectual property protection, technology life cycle and lack of systematic training.

An integrated model for developing the level of innovation and commercialization of knowledge-based companies is developed by Mirghafuri et al. (2017). According to their findings, research findings commercialization

Table 3. Core category, main category, and subcategory of ICT commercialization risk factors (Wan et al., 2013)

Paradigm Model	Subcategory	Main category
Action/interaction strategy	Selecting the technology: · Outdated supporting facilities · Technology life cycle Utilization of technology: · low technology update · Insufficient ability for product improvement · Disorder in the process of technology application · Technology protection · Weak intellectual property protection	**Technology management**
Context	Strategic positioning: · Ambiguous strategic goal · Hard market positioning HR management: · Project managers with low level of capability and experience · Unscientific evaluation and incentive mechanism · Staff shortages Marketing: · Single sales channel · limited ways of promotion	**Project management**
Causal conditions	Organizational learning: · Shortage of system training · Technologists' blind optimism about the future of technology Organizational agility: · Failure to adapt to rapid changes in market demand · Failure to respond quickly to changing internal issues · Highly centralized decision-making · Resources allocation and integration · Difficult financial resource allocation · Difficult to establish a strategic cooperative relations · Unclear division of labour and poor communication.	**Dynamic capability**

and transmission to the industry and marketing are certainly one of the most complex stages of innovation process. Based on the experiences of different countries, small and medium-sized enterprises (SMEs) play a key role in technology development, economic prosperity and employment that are the basis of knowledge-based economy according to the most of the scholars.

A conceptual model for knowledge commercialization in the higher education system is developed by Hafezi (2015) using GT. for this purpose, they implement open coding process to identify the 133 concepts (the initial

Figure 4. Axial coding (Mirghafuri et al., 2017)

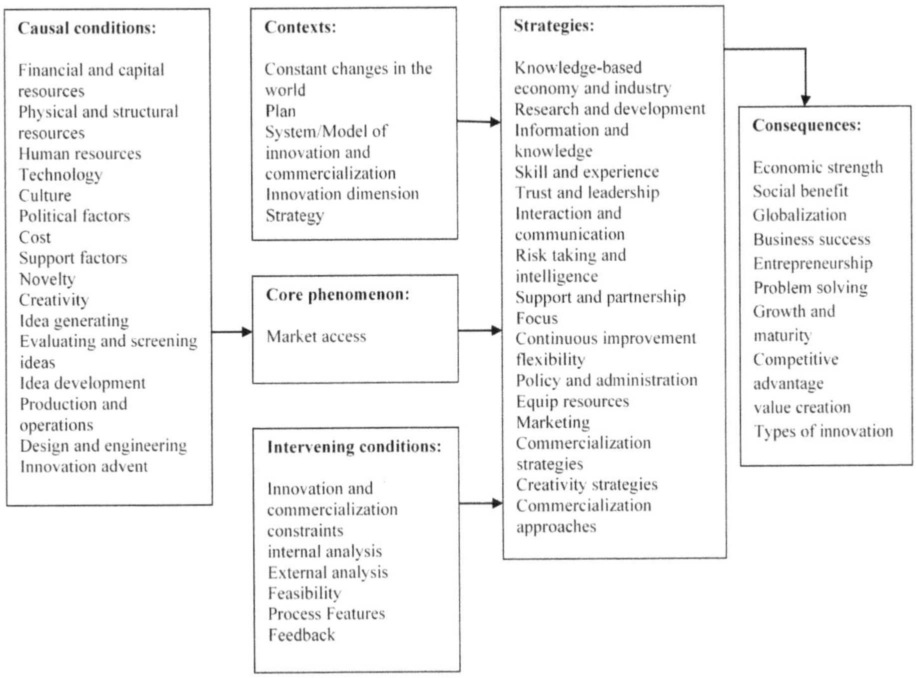

open codes) and summarize them in the form of 8 main categories with 33 subcategories (the secondary open codes). Then, they attempted to define the paradigm model based on the axial coding process in the form of the causal conditions (environmental capabilities), the contextual conditions (organizational capabilities), the intervening conditions (individual knowledge builder features, characteristics of productive knowledge and knowledge customers), the core phenomenon (knowledge commercialization), strategies (designing and implementation of facilitating mechanisms) and consequences (society of knowledge-based).

TECHNOLOGY ADOPTION

The prerequisite for using technology is its adoption. The technology adoption refers to the acceptance, integration, and use of new technologies in the community for which several models have been proposed so far that predominantly look at the behavior aspects leading to adoption (Gururajan, 2010). Technology adoption theory examines individuals or business leaders' decisions to accept or not to accept a given technology for integration of that technology into the whole organization.

A theoretical foundation is developed by Wang et al. (2018) for the process of older adults' technology adoption, based on their perspectives. For this purpose, an inductive content analysis method and GT were used to collect and analyze data from 16 older adults in Taiwan. According to their results, technology adoption behavior could be divided into 3 stages and 8 factors: pre-adoption (including self-management, self-compensation, self-image, and negative perception of technological products), adoption (including technology adoption obstacles and technology adoption and usage), and post-adoption (including denial to change to new technological products and technology value seeking).

The factors affecting the timing and assimilation of technology adoption was investigated by Gaddam (2019) through comparing institutions that were successful with those that were not. Another purpose of this study was to understand individual motivations, organizational readiness, external environmental factors, and the timing of adoption. In the qualitative part, the study is essentially based on semi-structured interviews to develop GT. This study proposes that the factors affecting the timing of technology adoption and successful deployment are different among organizations. Findings also show the details of where and how these differences occur. Consequently, the basis for emergent findings is sequencing and ordering of events.

- **New Resonant Leaders:** the data provide strong evidence that resonant leaders bring new ideas, fresh perspectives, and a greater ability in

Figure 5. The factors that influence the timing and assimilation of technology adoption (Gaddam, 2019)

Event-driven: the technology adoption timing:	Developing new technology	Technology adoption advantages:	The customer's desired state
Resonant leader vision: New leadership Retire legacy technologies: obsolete and disintegrated Competitive pressure: technology disruption and low cost Vendor, peer or tradeshow effect Government rules and incentives	Organizational alignment: shared vision, stakeholder, team and employee buy-in Organizational readiness: preparing, planning, right talent, communication and training Advanced technology: cloud automation, technology fit, systems and data integration	Single view of the customer data: one patient, one record Operational efficiencies: reduced human touch points and cost mitigation	Customer-centric organization: Ease of use, improvement of health care, safer practice, reduced errors or delays in timing

affecting others toward the successful adoption of new technologies. According to the evidences, approximately 52% of new technology adoption decisions were made when new resonant leaders were introduced to the organization.

- **Retiring Legacy Technologies:** improving operational efficiencies, reducing costs, integrating digital systems, gaining a competitive advantage, and becoming a customer-centric organization are the primary reason for retiring legacy systems and adopting new technology. Based on the obtained data, 64% of healthcare organizations that adopted new technology had either obsolete or disintegrated legacy systems.
- **Competitive Pressure:** According to data obtained in the healthcare industry, competition forces companies to cope with the pressures of technological innovation, price reductions, government regulation, customer acquisition and maintenance costs. Accordingly, 33% of organizations have adopted new technology because of reduced margins, regulations, or the hope of getting competitive advantage.
- **Vendor, Peer or Tradeshow Influence**: based on the data, 13 percent of the organizations in healthcare are forced by software vendors or peers in the industry to adopt new technology. Most of this adoption

comes from learning improved practices from peers and software vendors, as well as from tradeshows or industry publications.

- **Government Regulations and Incentives:** as data shows, the reason of adopting new technology by 24% of healthcare organizations is due to the mandatory government regulations or incentives.
- **Organizational Alignment:** based on the obtained data, although expectations as well as goals and objectives were clear in 90% of the successful technology deployment teams, 71% of the failed technology adoptions lacked team buy-in and overall organizational alignment.
- **Organizational Readiness:** according to the obtained data, taking initiatives towards organizational readiness including preparation, resource planning, change management, and training to ensure that their organizations are prepared to adopt new technology is the reason for the success of 90% of firms in the technology deployment.
- **Advanced Technology:** According to the data, 52 percent of companies choose advanced technologics such as digital cloud and integrated systems to comply with government regulations and take advantage of incentives.
- **Single View of Customer Data:** According to evidence from the data, 43% of a companies' decision to adopt new technology is to obtain a single view of customer data, i.e., "One Patient, One Record." Also, obtained data show that multiple disintegrated legacy systems that are isolated and do not communicate with each other are created as a result of substantial consolidation in the healthcare industry. The operational inefficiencies and a decline in patient satisfaction are also expected as the result of inability to access a patient's up-to date information across hospital systems.
- **Operational Efficiencies**: According to evidence from the data, 50% of a companies' decision to adopt new technology is based on achieving desired operational efficiencies. Also, it is found that the firms are looking to build the more automated integrated systems with less human touch points in the operational aspects, e.g., patient, physician, and hospital management.
- **Customer-centric Organization**: 86% of a companies' decision to adopt new technology is based on becoming a customer-centric organization according to evidence from the data. Also, it was found that these organizations mostly emphasize on patient experience and believe that organizational success relies primarily on being patient-centric. As a result, providing improved healthcare, safer practice, less

errors or delays, and patient care while offering an easily available platform for patients, physicians, nurses and other stakeholders within the organization are important for a firm.

TECHNOLOGY TRANSFER

The variety of definitions and concepts of technology transfer have been used based on the research field and according to the research purposes. Technology transfer is usually a chaotic, turbulent process with the participation of many groups and individuals with different views on the value and potential use of technology. The value or meaning of technology transfer is usually not very clear, and different researchers may have a different understanding of technology. But what is clear from the literature is that the technology transfer is a complex and difficult process that occurs among functions in a single product segment in a single company and this complex process takes time to evolve (Wahab et al., 2012).

In a study by Lavoie and Daim (2017), the way of helping the Technology Readiness Levels (TRL) to organizations and the potential implications of using it to the betterment of R&D management were studied. As a method developed by NASA nearly 40 years ago, TRL has been proven to help organizations to manage their technologies. Because it is important to measure technology readiness and management, organizations need to make better decisions about technology. In this regard, the research mentioned, interviews with managers and researchers and GT approach to data analysis is used. Based on the findings of this study, TRLs can improve R&D management.

The difficulties caused by international technology transfer process for example in cases of foreign direct investment where companies set-up existing manufacturing lines in new locations, and in situations of international outsourcing where a new supplier receives product and/or production process information was discussed by Steenhuis and Bruijn (2005). For this purpose, a GT approach was used to describe the process of international production technology transfer. They carried on four case studies in the aircraft industry and analyzed the problems that occurred. According to their findings, technology transfer includes three phases of preparation, installation and utilization which are influenced by three types of technological, organizational and environmental factors. Combining the activities with factors enables an integrated view on international technology transfer. Also, according to their findings, the technology level, the information accuracy, and the extent of organizational and environmental differences have a huge effect on the efficiency of the technology transfer process.

A conceptualization of factors affecting technology transfer capability is provided by Huynh (2018). In this study, the factors affecting the technology transfer by GT perceived by experts were used to classify the concepts and model conceptualization. The organizational, departmental and environmental factors affecting technology transfer capability were provided in the study results. The three main themes obtained include: 1) new technology identification, acquisition and implementation ability; 2) research and development (R&D) ability; and 3) external environment. The data also show how these factors work together in the food industry environment and provide a basis for developing a theoretical framework.

The underlying mechanism influencing the patent behavior and activities in the public health sector in South Africa (SA) is investigated by Maart (2015). The study will offer a new plausible theory through action research methodology using GT, which can assist health organizations in SA to exploit patenting in alignment with the public health strategic vision. From the phase one and two of action research, the categories were merged using axial coding according to table 4. Theoretical saturation is also achieved through the use of literature to create categories (Table 4) to subsumed phase three –action research categories through selective coding.

Table 4 shows the findings of the phase two -action cycle that were coded and categorized. Noteworthy findings include: 1) public managers were more inclined to the economic viability-ROI than defensive patenting; 2) some pragmatic policy decision already is emerging when dealing with ad hoc crisis of ownership; 3) a feasible option is to enter into a partnership agreement with universities, with the aim to share their patent expertise and TTO; 4) labor negations will need to precede any changes in employment conditions change (IP clause insert); 5) an innovation hub is needed parallel to government department to support innovation and innovators; 6) there is a need to change management to assist in hanging the culture of the public health sector; 7) an incentive scheme to reward public entrepreneurs is needed. A part of incentive scheme is shared benefits with partners and inventors. Also, the lack of clarity regarding the strategic objective of patenting is as an unexpected finding. In order to merged categories and themes from phase one and two action cycles the axial coding was used according to Table 4.

Table 4. Axial coding and selective coding (Maart, 2015)

Merged categories	Themes	Sub-category
Strategic vision	Lack of strategic vision and regulatory framework causes ambiguity and legal uncertainty which negatively has an impact on the innovation culture (dependent on intellectual property rights (IPR) protection) and leads to employee and employer IPR ownership conflict.	Strategic vision Strategic mission Macro-policy Legal framework Leading government departments (cluster) Avoiding commitment conflict Strategic and complementary partnership /agreements Clarity Strategic objective: knowledge transfer, statutory obligation, potential revenue flow, economic development, jobs creation, increased GDP, improved human condition and good price control, knowledge monopoly, persistent problem, reputation and prestige, attract talent
Dynamic capabilities and organizational design	The required organisational capacity (intangible and tangible resources) depends on the strategic objective of public sector, type of patent value chain constructed (shared vs total outsource vs in-house model) and expected volume of patentable new inventions	Patent value chain construct dependent Out-source In-house Shared or complimentary value chain Development of patent technical expertise Shortage of capacity Independent innovation entity /hub Cooperate partnership Volume dependent Policies or Standard Operating Procedure (SOP) Source of invention Future trends
Creating innovative culture	Creating an innovation entity in state sector to help continuous collaboration of complimentary converging fields and stakeholder in safe space, access to latest technology and free from red tape bureaucracy will increase patent and innovation activity	Support –finance, legal, networking opportunities, lowering operating cost, access to technology and information, legal services and access to venture capital Independent Innovation hub Reducing red tape Creating public entrepreneur Less bureaucracy Education –marketing Incentives –bonuses, equity in spin-off entities, recognition, profit sharing in royalties Leadership driven
Profitable or financial sustainable Technology Transfer Office (TTO)	Reducing the cost of patenting through shared patent value chain with partners, meticulous adjudication process to assess economic feasibility (focus on practical applicability and commercialization potential) of new inventions and pipelining venture capital will ensure that the state decreases loss of investment.	Reducing the cost of value chain: outsource services, partnership agreements, complimentary agreement, rigorous adjudication process and screening High and moderate value invention patented Exponential growth Champion inventor TTO struggling word wide Business incubator Spin-off companies Inventor equity in spin-off Commitment conflict

CONCLUSION

The purpose of technology management (TM) is to support and improve the competitive positioning of enterprise technology. This chapter provides an overview of the application of grounded theory (GT) in the TM specific concepts such as research and technology commercialization, technology adoption, and technology readiness and transfer. In order to facilitate successful practices of TM, certain mechanisms should be designed beginning with the identification of its drivers and barriers. To that end, approaches like the GT can be used to analyze the drivers and obstacles and develop a conceptual model related to each function. As one of the most frequently used methods in the field of management research, GT is used for qualitative theory building instead of quantitative hypothesis validation. The purpose of this chapter is to discuss about the way of using GT for theory building in the field of technology management research.

Bridging the gap between basic research and commercialization is an inherent challenge in commercialization of public and academic research processes. According to the studies in this area, four categories of policies, organization, people, and market are determined as critical factors playing as causal conditions, context, and intervening conditions. Also, the strategies are designing and implementation of facilitating mechanisms related to these factors which lead to related consequences.

Despite a track record of adoption research, there is still a demand for a new approach to adoption. There are various stakeholders and contexts to consider, ranged from the organizational to the individual, when examining the technology adoption. Hence, choosing an appropriate approach and method is a critical issue when conducting any research. The present chapter reviews studies which applied GT to identify affecting factors and build theoretical foundation for the technology adoption process.

The application of GT in the technology transfer literature which is typically about factors and difficulties influencing technology transfer capability is reviewed in this chapter. As one of the most critical factors to enhance innovative capabilities within firms, technology transfer results from measures performed by various actors and organizations.

REFERENCES

Basias, N., & Pollalis, Y. (2018). Quantitative and qualitative research in business & technology: Justifying a suitable research methodology. *Review of Integrative Business and Economics Research*, *7*(1), 91–105.

Bozeman, B. (2000). Technology transfer and public policy: A review of research and theory. *Research Policy*, *29*(4-5), 627–655. doi:10.1016/S0048-7333(99)00093-1

Byeongmun, S., Jongbog, B., & Yeong-geol, J. (2018). Exploratory study on the phenomenon of technology commercialization in Agro-food sector based on the grounded theory approach. *Innovation Studies*, *13*(3), 147-174.

Corbin, J., & Strauss, A. L. (2009). *Basics of qualitative research: Techniques and procedures for developing grounded theory* (3rd ed.). Newbury Park, CA: Sage.

Debackere, K., & Veugelers, R. (2005). The role of academic technology transfer organizations in improving industry science links. *Research Policy*, *34*(3), 321–342. doi:10.1016/j.respol.2004.12.003

Downie, J. (2006). The Power of Money: Commercialization of Research Conducted in Public Institutions. *Journal of Otago Law Review*, *11*(2), 305–324.

Economical and Social Commission for Asia and the Pacific (ESCAP). (2019). *Establishing science and technology parks: A reference guidebook for policymakers in Asia and the Pacific*. United Nations Publication.

Gaddam, S. R. (2019). Timing and assimilation of new technology adoption in healthcare. *Journal of Health & Medical Informatics*, *10*(3), 1–8.

Gholipour, H., Gholipour, A., GhaziMahale, M., & RoshandelArbatani, T. (2010). The requirements, needs, and mechanisms of knowledge commercialization in Management schools. *Business Management*, *2*(6), 41–60.

Glaser, B., & Strauss, A. (1967). *The discovery of grounded theory*. Aldine.

Gururajan, R. (2010). Organizational factors and technological barriers are determinants for the intention to use wireless handheld technology in healthcare environment: An Indian case study. In Handbook of Research on Advances in Health Informatics and Electronic Healthcare Applications: Global Adoption and Impact of Information Communication Technologies. IGI Global.

Hafezi, H. (2015). Designing a conceptual pattern of knowledge commercialization in distance higher education system: The case of Payame Noor University. *Journal of Educational Sciences*, *22*(1), 215–240.

Huynh, T. T. (2018). Exploring factors influencing technology transfer capability: Constructing a model through grounded theory. *International Journal of Technology Management & Sustainable Development*, *17*(1), 49–64. doi:10.1386/tmsd.17.1.49_1

InfoDev. (2009). *Business incubation definitions and principles*. Washington, DC: World Bank Group.

Jacob, M., Lundqvist, M., & Hellsmark, H. (2003). Entrepreneurial transformations in the Swedish University system: The case of Chalmers University of Technology. *Research Policy*, *32*(9), 1555–1568. doi:10.1016/S0048-7333(03)00024-6

Khosravipour, B., Nosrati, S., & Yaghoubi, J. (2011). Identifying commercialization obstacles of Agricultural Research, Education and Promotion Organization with the use of grounded theory. *Journal of Agricultural Promotion and Education Research*, *3*(43), 11–20.

Kropsu-Vehkapera, H., Haapasalo, H., & Rusanen, J. P. (2009). Analysis of technology management functions in Finnish high tech companies. *The Open Management Journal*, *2*(1), 1–10. doi:10.2174/1874948800902010001

Landry, R., Amara, N., & Rherrad, I. (2006). Why are some university researchers more likely to create spinoffs than others? Evidence from Canadian universities. *Research Policy*, *35*(10), 1599–1615. doi:10.1016/j.respol.2006.09.020

Lavoie, J. R., & Daim, T. U. (2017). Technology readiness levels improving R&D management: A grounded theory analysis. *Portland International Conference on Management of Engineering and Technology (PICMET)*. 10.23919/PICMET.2017.8125383

Maart, K. (2015). *Why does government not exploit patent activity in the public health sector? Towards designing a patent-sensitive public health organization that will exploit patenting in the public health sector of South Africa*. Graduate School of Business, University of Cape Town. Retrieved October 13, 2019, from: http://passthrough.fw-notify.net/download/325878/ http://gsblibrary.uct.ac.za/researchreports/EMBA16/Maart.pdf

Mirghafuri, S.H.A., SharifAbadi, A.M., & Zahedi, A.E. (2018). Designing an integrated model for developing the level of innovation and commercialization of knowledge based companies of Iran. *Journal of Innovation and Creativity in the Humanities*, *7*(4), 107–142.

Moghaddam, A. (2006). Coding issues in grounded theory. *Issues in Educational Research*, *16*, http://www.iier.org.au/iier16/moghaddam.html

Mohammadkhah, M., & Hejazis, R. (2014). Mechatronic technology commercialization in small and medium enterprises: Based on grounded theory. *Journal of Economic and Business Research*, *5*(7), 85–101.

Namdarian, L., & Naimi-Sadigh, A. (2018). Towards an understanding of the commercialization drivers of research findings in Iran. *African Journal of Science, Technology, Innovation and Development*, *10*(4), 389–399. doi: 10.1080/20421338.2018.1463644

Reza, B. (2007). Evaluation of Commercial Potential of A New Technology at The Early Stage of Developement With Fuzzy Logic. *Journal of Technology Management & Innovation*, *2*(4), 73–85.

Shinn, T., & Lamy, E. (2006). Paths of commercial knowledge: Forms and consequences of university–enterprise synergy in scientist-sponsored firms. *Research Policy*, *35*(10), 1465–1476. doi:10.1016/j.respol.2006.09.024

Siemens. (2009). *Research, development and technology management*. Retrieved October 14, 2019, from https://www.plm.automation.siemens.com/zh_cn/Images/7915_tcm78-4603.pdf

Sohn, Y., & Moon, T. (2003). Structural equation model for predicting technology commercialization success index (TCSI). *Technological Forecasting and Social Change*, *70*(9), 885–899. doi:10.1016/S0040-1625(03)00004-0

Steenhuis, H. J., & de Bruijn, E. J. (2005). International technology transfer: building theory from a multiple case-study in the aircraft industry. *A New Vision of Management in the 21st Century: Proceedings of the Academy of Management Annual Meeting*.

United Kingdom Science Park Association. (2015). *A brief introduction to business incubation*. Saffron Walden, UK: Chesterford Research Park, Little Chesterford.

Wahab, S. A., Rose, R. C., & Osman, S. I. W. (2012). Defining the Concepts of Technology and Technology Transfer: A Literature Analysis. *International Business Research*, *5*(1), 61–171.

Wan, J., Liang, L., & Wan, D. (2013). Research on risk factors of ICT commercialization with grounded theory. *Journal of Computers*, *8*(9), 2356–2365. doi:10.4304/jcp.8.9.2356-2365

Wang, K. H., Chen, G., & Chen, H.-G. (2018). Understanding technology adoption behavior by older adults. *Social Behavior and Personality*, *46*(5), 801–814. doi:10.2224bp.6483

Chapter 5
Grounded Theory in Sustainable Energy Initiatives

ABSTRACT

The purpose of this chapter is to raise awareness by introducing ideas that are generally based on transition studies and grounded theory (GT). In addition, to support us to understand phenomena such as green building investment decision making, changing energy saving behavior, and diffusion of smart grids and energy systems, these ideas also help developing interventions to reduce climate change through renewable energy technologies. Since energy systems are important determinants of social structure and complexity, and also because little attention has been paid to the social dynamics of energy transition in a social setting, the use of GT as a qualitative research methodology suitable to study this social phenomena can be helpful in this regard.

INTRODUCTION

At the core of most countries' policies, research on transition to cleaner and renewable energies is not merely technological but requires a holistic view of a combination of economic, political, institutional and socio-cultural change (Berkhout et al., 2012). In order to overcome dependency on imported energy, the European Union (EU) has taken the lead in developing approaches for the development of new and low-carbon energy, and in this respect has formulated the European Strategic Energy Technology Plan (SET plan). This plan includes the areas such as energy efficiency, smart grids and energy

DOI: 10.4018/978-1-7998-4252-1.ch005

systems, and renewables integration. Significant improvement in energy efficiency will undoubtedly continue as a challenge in all sectors including energy production, distribution and consumption in industry, buildings, transportation, agriculture and services for years to come. There is a growing tendency towards a network of different networks and even different types of energy (electric, heat) that are interconnected and need to communicate with each other to provide an optimal solution, to ensure resistance. The transition to a low-carbon society largely depends on the successful integration of energy from low-carbon renewables (EUA, 2017).

In response to global warming and its impact on the environment, industries are now trying to be greener. It also makes global consumers aware of the need to protect the environment. Consequently, green electronics and electrical products have become a trend. When a plant produces toxic, recyclable and energy-saving green products, it must coordinate its supply chain with all companies, including supplier, customer, and specialist sales distributors. A green supply chain management coordinates the concept of green in order to produce, supply and recycle products in coordination with the manufacturing process. The green supply chain management practices were investigated by Chien et al. (2012) in the Taiwanese industry using the grounded theory (GT). According to the obtained results, Taiwan's electronics and electrical industry is using green theory worldwide to support material analysis. As an inductive and exploratory research method in subject areas, GT can be used by researchers to formulate the theory using it without relying on existing theories. The researcher began working with a specific study area instead of starting with a pre-conceived theory, allowing the theory to emerge from the heart of the data. The process of conducting research on the GT involves: research questions, notes and data collection, analysis, theoretical sampling and theoretical saturation, writing and formulating theory, and comparing texts. The analysis process begins with open coding and ideally ends with selective coding (Corbin and Strauss, 2008). According to Osarumwense Asemota (2013) stated on power consumption theories in Namibia, GT is useful when current theories are either inappropriate or lacking.

This chapter reviews the applications of GT in the field of energy transition. Transitions studies concerning energy efficiency in building industry and relevant behaviors through which people try to reduce overall energy, diffusion of smart grids and energy systems, and mitigating climate change with renewable-energy technologies are discussed in this chapter.

GREEN BUILDING

Green building, in terms of Singh et al. (2010), is a concept containing a wide range of solution and best practices which is a result of design philosophy that emphasizes on optimum utilization of resources and increases the resource utilization efficiency. Green building also referred as sustainable building which considers the construction of structures and the use of environmentally responsible and energy-efficient processes throughout the building life cycle from sitting to design, construction, operation, maintenance, renovation, and deconstruction. This practice leads to the development and completion of the classical building design concerns of economy, utility, durability and comfort. Efficient use of energy, water and other resources, protecting occupant health and improving employee productivity, reducing waste, pollution, environmental degradation, and better waste management are among the basic objectives of these kinds of buildings.

As the key to achieve sustainability in green building, energy efficiency causes lowering the energy consumption in construction to create a significant improvement chance for many organizations. International Energy Agency (IEA) (2015) defines energy efficiency as the lesser energy usage to provide the same quality of service. Green building is a kind of sustainable building or "high performance" building. Sustainable building is implemented throughout the whole phases of building, from preconstruction to removal of the construction, lower the dangerous or toxic effect on the environment of building, which is similar with green building in terms of the development of constructing and building structures, and utilizing procedure that are environmental and resource efficient in a construction's activities. Generally, green building is expected to decrease the environment impacts of the construction activities and it is sustainable. Some benefits to the community arise from energy efficiency, which is a key to achieve sustainability in green buildings and organizations. Also, energy efficiency can help to manage of increasing energy costs, decrease environmental impacts such as lower the greenhouse gas emission, and added the value and to increase competitiveness of green buildings. Showing a really green buildings or construction is effortless using energy efficiency (Ann and Abualrejal, 2015).

The way real estate developers experience change in the improvement of the built environment through changing demand for more "green" building products is investigated in a study by Hoffer (2015) studied. This change is realized in three aspects of "Discovering Opportunity" - when potential

Figure 1. GT Category 1 – Discovering opportunity (Hoffer, 2015)

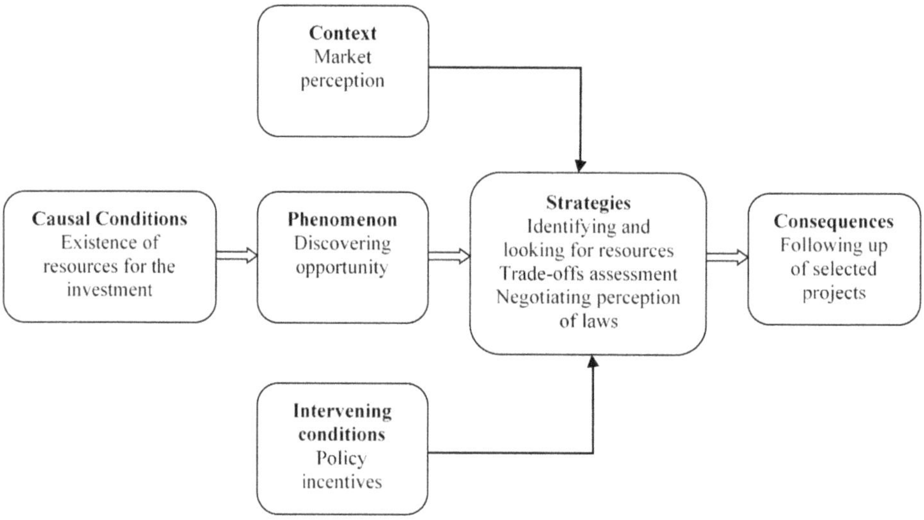

projects are determined and prioritized, "Experiencing Difficulty" - when projects hit barriers, and "Changing Practices" - the timeline over which rules are internalized in a company via new processes and methods.

When interviewees described the process of becoming initially engaged with projects, the "discovering opportunity" phenomenon emerged.

- **Causal Conditions:** A key issue with a real estate development business model is having the resources to invest and the need for stakeholders which is aligned with the drive of the real estate developer to produce economic value through a unique skillset.
- **Context**: Due to the capability of identifying promising sites and then assessing the feasibility of project development, the real estate marketplace is the context for opportunity discovery and these are considered as a core competency for companies in real estate development, involving a range of social, market, financial and technical skillsets.
- **Intervening Conditions**: Awareness of policy changes and opportunities is one of these skills. Interviewees mentioned the prospect of so-called "green" financial incentives associated among factors which can positively affect project feasibility. Simultaneously, policy requirements can affect the opportunities attractiveness.

- **Adopted Strategies**: Seeking information and identifying resources to assist in resolving the question of feasibility are the strategies in this regard.
- **Consequences**: The projects assessment and prioritization is the final result of employing strategies in the situation of "discovering opportunity".

Figure 2. GT Category 2 – Experiencing difficulty (Hoffer, 2015)

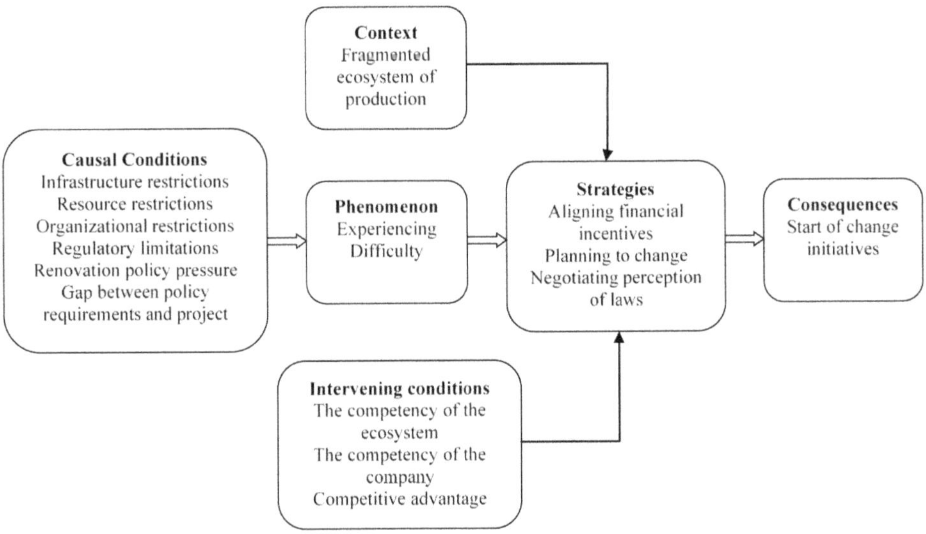

Several observations achieved on the challenges inherent in the real estate development process when coding instances of cause and effect in the data:

- **Causal Conditions:** Challenging sources in the real estate sector range from economic conditions to resource constraints and organizational and physical complexities of the urban environment. The need for large volumes of resources, including financial, organizational and technical resources, to build and manage large commercial assets in the metropolitan area is at stake here, with huge risks even for experienced and qualified organizations. Political factors were also cited as contributors to difficult circumstances. Also, the interviewees stated that they were aware of the changes taking place and remain closely connected to the agencies which govern projects increases the sense that the process is reasonable.

- **Context:** The challenges and perceptions in terms of the fragmented ecosystem of professionals which completes the work of entitlement, financing, design, and construction for building projects were mentioned repeatedly by interviewees. According to the third party rating standard, such as the (U.S. Green Building Council) USGBC's LEED, green building policy, specifically the requirement to achieve or demonstrate a degree of sustainability, has had an impact on the interactions and responsibilities within the ecosystem.
- **Intervening Conditions:** The competency of the ecosystem provides a moderating influence by contributing expertise, although the production ecosystem and its fragmentation form the context for the category of "Experiencing Difficulty". For instance, according to interviewees, design teams play a role in leading the effort to identify innovative solutions and to negotiate compliance strategies with enforcement agencies. The topic of competitive advantage has been addressed in terms of competencies, experience, and communication by interviewees. Besides, focusing on green building has been suggested by specific individuals as a competitive advantage who predicted increasingly stringent green building policy requirements in their marketplaces.
- **Strategies:** Interviewees expressed a number of strategies to face with difficulties including risk management as a core competency in real estate development, managing and tracking risk factors as a normal course of business. Also, the use of financial incentives as an important source, including building policy incentives provided by utilities, incentives offered by utilities, tax incentives offered by jurisdictions, and incentives for conversion of brownfields is of interest to real estate developers. Finally, interviewees perceive that these challenges can be overcome by maintaining a level of competence in the economic, organizational and technical environment with the help of consultants in the manufacturing ecosystem. Interviewees are aware that the real estate marketplace is exposed to economic volatility, and that the entitlement environment in which they operate goes through change as policymakers make new regulations to positively impact the city. Agility, which translates into the willingness to change practices, innovate, or adopt new ways of working, is a paramount strategy in this context. At the same time, interviewees also know that regulations are not zero and one. An important strategy in this regard is the ability to bring together legislators and other key stakeholders to negotiate

approvals for final results which might be different in some ways from a requirement of a policy, but which achieve the objectives.

- **Consequences:** The interviewees mentioned their companies increase willingness to change practices, and prepare to launch initiatives or engage in new ways of working as the consequence of applying these strategies to the difficulty experienced.

Figure 3. GT Category 3 – Changing practices (Hoffer, 2015)

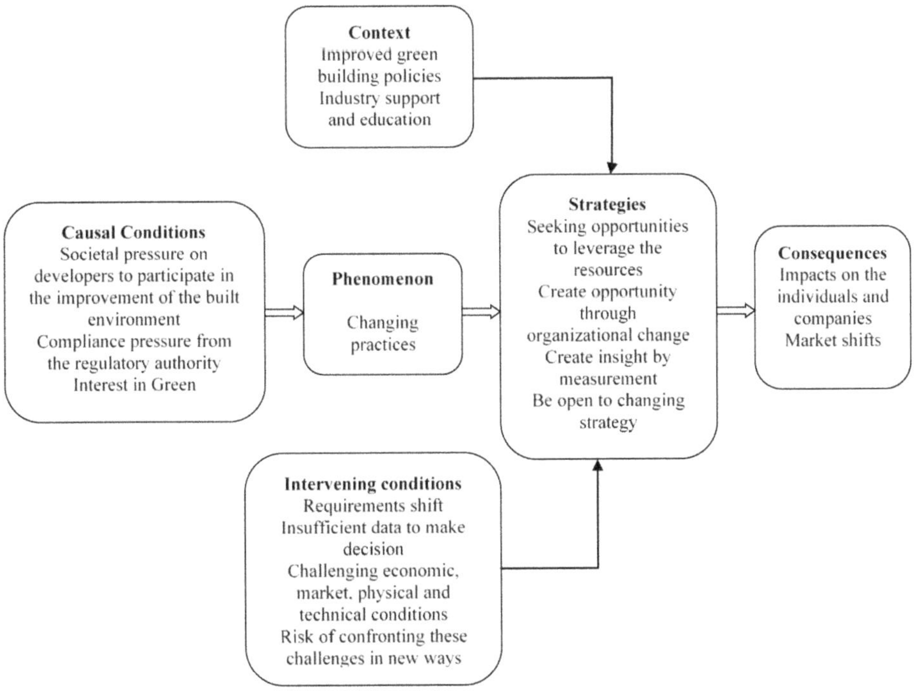

- **Causal Conditions:** There are pressures for community developers to contribute by shifting the demand for more "green" building materials to improve the environment. However, the society interest in "green" in terms of health or fashion does not always mean that customers willingness to pay more or translate into profitability. In this regard, real estate developers are forced by the compliance pressure from the regulatory authority to change their practices, to push their consultants in the professional ecosystem to implement sustainable design and construction approaches.

- **Context:** Developers are mindful of the context for new ways of work as they experience the condition of practice change. Jurisdictions continue to modify and improve green building policies. Furthermore, there are interactions among the policies to encourage green buildings with other policies driving accessibility, historic preservation, and a number of other community objectives. Policies can provide support for practice change by providing incentives which increase project feasibility or reduce risk.
- **Intervening Conditions:** The fact that requirements shift, and new policies or practices put individuals in a position to make decisions without data from past experience result in the conditions which intervene to moderate or counteract the condition of changing practice. Although professional norms for decision-making are flexible, these types of practice changes may be difficult to measure, plan or execute with traditional quantitative assessment approaches, such as cost-benefit or pro-forma analyses. The real estate field requires interviewees to execute projects and manage risk in challenging economic, market, physical and technical conditions. Since confronting these challenges in new ways, without the experience from past project, represents an increase in risk, all of these factors interfere with the ability to change practices.
- **Strategies:** A number of strategies to deal with the condition of practice change are described by interviewees. Even companies which specialize in affordable housing that produce similar projects, interviewees observe that each real estate project is a unique situation requiring an ability to devise new solutions and solve unexpected problems. Openness to changing strategy, at a fundamental level, is a part of the professional role of interviewees. They are required to continually evaluate and ameliorate risk, anticipate economic impacts, and to look for opportunities to leverage the resources available to complete successful projects. Some risk associated with practice change will be inevitably transferred by developer to the professional consultants in the production ecosystem. In fact, without the participation of these allied firms, including specialists with government connections who can streamline the process of gaining approvals, no practice change can be realized.
- **Consequences**: Finally, the impacts on the individuals and companies experiencing it, and the transformation it imparts on the urban fabric are the consequences of practice change. Some expressed satisfaction

in having successfully navigated changes, and described feeling that they were well positioned to be knowledgeable and competitive in a valuable skillset going forward in their careers are mentioned by interviewees,.

Social acceptance is an important necessity to the successful adoption of any technology (Mosly and Makki, 2018). There are a number of limitations in terms of acceptance rates for renewable / sustainable energy technologies (Luthra et al., 2015). In fact, social phenomena allow us to recognize who we are, why we act the way we do, and perhaps some of the consequences of these actions and behaviors toward others in the community and the environment and systems around us (Pulla, 2014). Although not a methodology with a long history compared to other methods, GT qualitative method is the most appropriate method for studying social phenomena. GT involves a process of collecting data and analyzing it in a cyclic motion to produce concepts from which a theory evolves, producing the end result embedded in the data from which it is extracted. Perhaps this is what makes GT more suitable for studying social phenomena, a theory that is not initially assumed by the researcher to evolve from data given by a sample of people and then to be used for working with similar people.

Trevarthen (2011) selected GT methodology to study the topic of stakeholder perceived barriers to the use of solar energy has not been fully explored in Thailand. The use of GT enabled exploratory exploration of participants' views on the topic without being limited to existing theories. Despite the tropical climate in Thailand, there is little adoption of either passive solar design strategies or solar energy technologies. For the purpose of this study, 30 interviews were conducted with stakeholders in the Thai building industry and analyzed using GT methodology to determine what stakeholders perceive as the barriers of using solar energy in buildings in Thailand. In addition to analyzing the transcript of the interview, the participants also conducted a 20-item Likert-scale survey to gauge their views on known barriers to solar energy use in buildings. The study identifies 25 barriers that stakeholders in the building industry know as barriers to using solar energy in Thai buildings.

- Financial and economic barriers: solar energy cost in buildings, payback periods and return on investment, responsibility for ongoing cost, access to financial instruments;
- Institutional and regulatory barriers: constraints of the building design process and a lack of applicable standards and laws;

- Technical barriers: increased complexity, solar system performance, required maintenance, access in Thailand;
- Market barriers: economic climate encouraging more low end developments, low cost of electricity in Thailand, unwillingness of electricity generating companies to support the use of solar because of the potential loss of profit, high import duties, no continuous use of standards and regulations and costs being increased for high end developments;
- Awareness and information barriers: shortage of awareness, knowledge, understanding and experience;
- Behavioral barriers: a person's mindset, aesthetics, or look towards solar energy, the concept of whether the use of two languages, Thai and English as a barrier to use solar energy.

The difference between the concepts of awareness and knowledge perceived by stakeholders and a lack of awareness and a lack of knowledge is the primary reason solar energy is not used more often are the research core concept. The primary way to encourage consideration of solar energy in Thailand's building projects is increasing both awareness and knowledge of solar energy.

Unuigbe et al. (2020) investigated the understandings and experiences of building professionals in adopting renewable energy in commercial buildings in Nigeria by the principles of the GT. This study demonstrated the importance of contextual (cultural) characteristics and the role of identity in realizing of renewable energy acceptance.

ENERGY SAVING BEHAVIOR

Many consumers today are aware of the need to reduce resource consumption, including energy, due to financial pressures and environmental concerns. People's behavior toward trying to reduce total energy consumption (electricity) can be considered energy saving behaviors (Sweeney et al., 2013). As the energy efficiency is considered as a key strategy for the sustainable growth of our planet by the EU knows, some clear objective were set for it: for example, the consumption of traditional energy and greenhouse emissions should be reduced by 20% in 2020. In order to achieve a global awareness of the problem, energy saving and energy efficiency policies must also be applied at all levels and sectors within this broad framework (García et al., 2017).

In 2015, one of the sectors in which proposals for the energy consumption optimization have a wide impact are households: have consumed 33% of total energy. By recognizing this issue, EU recognized determined around 650 action measures in the residential sector including the use of smart meters, information campaigns or the encouragement to change user behavior. Currently, household energy consumption in the EU accounts for about 25% of total consumption, and although there has been a 1.8% annual decline since 2000 in this sector, there is still much room for improvement. Since much of this reduction in consumption has been driven both by technical improvements in equipment and by rising energy prices, the effectiveness of policies that seek to influence and change consumer behavior should not be overlooked (García et al., 2017).

The occupant energy behavior research grounded its root in the field of social and behavioral sciences according to Zhao (2014). Many researchers have recognized that Occupant Energy Behavior (OEB), play a vital role in reducing energy use. From the previous research on the field of occupants' energy behavior, it is possible to mention two categories regarding their methodological approaches. Most research in this area has been conducted using a quantitative approach, the results of which have been collected through large, structured questionnaires and several factors have been identified in relation to the energy consumption behavior agreed by the researchers (e.g. age, housing characteristics, set point temperature, etc.). Of course, only a few of these studies have used qualitative and mixed methods, which demonstrates the capacity to work in this field to gain a better understanding of people's daily lives and the nature of energy consumption, which serves as firmer grounding to march towards energy efficiency. In terms of discussing the fundamental properties of the subject matter, and discovering specific aspects of energy behavior which these different approaches could bring to the field, conducting comparisons between these two main research methods in the same field is particularly interesting.

Although GT has gained popularity in the social and behavioral sciences, it has rarely been used in energy research for the past 10 years. The GT features that made it appropriate for this research are as follows (Zhao, 2014):

- Firstly, in new fields, which will lead to new perspectives in the areas that have been studied so far GT can be of great help.
- Secondly, GT can provides relations with broader contextual issues to the phenomenon and thus create a thorough framework from microscopic details that were previously being neglected. A qualitative approach

is appropriate to engage a more complete picture of the comparison between occupants, to study the social side of each households and their ideology in purchasing/building, operating, revising the low-energy housing.

- Thirdly, as GT includes theory development, and is unique due to a concurrent approach in both collecting and analyzing data, the data analysis in the research process will be taken at the same time as data collection, to ensure that the area of interest and the method suit each other. So, as long as data collection continues, researchers can have an open-ended conceptual framework and supplement relevant aspects/ concepts until no further information emerges to generate a theory. By unfolding the central framework, both technical literature and data collection started to contribute in more and wider aspects of the frame. It is also desirable to study the social aspect of the phenomenon as fully and comprehensively as possible in order to identify the themes overlooked in previous research.

It is generally thought that the qualitative method is essentially a deductive method for testing the theory, whereas the qualitative method is a useful process for the creation of theories. The GT framework, in which 'the concepts and relationships among them are not only generated but they are also provisionally tested' (Strauss and Corbin, 1990), naturally a ground is provided for quantitative and qualitative methods to work together.

The construct of electricity energy-saving behaviors was revisit qualitatively by Sony and Mekoth (2018) to expand our scope of understanding. For this purpose, they seek to answer the research question why customers don't care about electricity energy- saving behaviors. Utilizing the GT methodology, a qualitative study is undertaken in Western, India consisting coding data, combining the codes into broader categories and themes, and interpreting the results according to basic steps in the analysis of qualitative data. The seven master themes unearthed in this study are:

- Lack of reward and motivation: low cost of electricity energy, high cost of energy- saving measures, higher pay back time for the use of energy-saving measures or equipment;
- Lack of environmental concern: lack of belief in environmental issues, ignorance about environmental problems, environmental issues- this is not my problem;

- Lack of information: lack of specified and conscience information about energy-saving measures;
- Lack of communication;
- Lack of policy and legislation;
- Lack of social norms;
- Lack of user friendly technology.

According to the obtained results, great opportunities exist for policy makers to design the energy saving policies based on the results.

Much work has been published on using technological interventions to motivate reductions in home energy consumption according to Foster (2011). Promising results were achieved by these interventions, which are generally focused on emphasizing the financial benefits of consumption reductions to users. As employees are typically not responsible for energy costs, motivating them to reduce their energy consumption in the workplace is more problematic. So far, little research has been done on energy interventions in the workplace and in fact there are many challenges in this regard.

An overview analysis, using the GT method, of a series of organizational energy workshops investigating perceptions and behaviors of energy usage, as well as both positive and negative implications for intervention design was conducted by Foster et al. (2010). The first phase of the GT, namely open coding includes manually trawling for conceptual labels (codes) relating to energy usage. Six identified key axial categories are as follows:

- **Incentives:** Employees want to be incentivized by negotiable rewards. This comprises the question 'What's in it for me?'
- **Openness**: An atmosphere of trust and acceptance of the reasons why trying to save on a lack of cynicism about saving jobs is essential for staff participation in energy interventions. The most important factor in this regard is the trust of employees in the organization.
- **Engagement:** With particular emphasis on negotiated targets being achievable, competition and negotiated targets were favored to engage with an intervention. Unrealistic targets, inability to set targets and unfair competition were highly cited for bringing about potential disengagement.
- **Communication:** Communication, encompassed workshops for educating employees on energy as a finite resource to effective marketing campaigns for recruitment, along the lines of selling the idea of a green intervention as a product, was seen as critical at all stages of

an intervention. As an important factor, lines of communication should be open up and down in an organization with quality of the message, not the mode of communication.

- **Visualization**: There is no 'silver bullet' or 'one size fits all' method. Instead, having a choice of visualizations that embed the attributes of the other five key categories in the GT would be the most engaging. Energy data granularity was considered important with the office or department level preferred. Comparison feedback was favored just when presented fairly, i.e. like for like or compared to self.
- **Management buy-in**: A thread involved throughout most of the data analyzed, is senior management buy-in, without which, staff felt disempowered and frustrated that their attempts would be trivial with interventions destined to fizzle out. As the most motivating factors in employees engagement, charismatic leadership and leading change from the top were cited causes adhering to an intervention, with change trickling down thc organization.

Corporate responsibility', as the selected core category, is a theme that integrates and links our key categories and generates the developed theory's whole story. Trust, ethical values and transparency in an organization's activities can be promoted by corporate responsibility and it acts as the main driver for key categories identified in the GT such as openness, communication and management buy-in. Corporate responsibility means that the whole organizational structure from top to bottom conveying the message that all levels of employees have to engage to realize a positive effect when deploying interventions.

DIFFUSION OF RENEWABLE ENERGIES

Recently, in many parts of the world, various energy technology options have been adopted and implemented as a solution to sustainable energy sources, which can be reviewed through literature review. By studying the factors that hinder or impede investment decisions on alternative energy technologies, the diffusion of alternative technologies can be investigated. In this context, comparing different studies in various environments reveals the strengths and weaknesses of the models used and provides insights into the barriers or drivers of alternative energy technologies adoption (Iskin et al., 2013).

The diffusion of renewable energy technologies is studied by Elahi et al. (2005) using GT methodology on valid and relevant texts. According to the results of the study, a model is developed that illustrates the existence of four main categories of factors: science's push, demand elasticity, investment attractiveness, and infrastructure. At the step of axial coding, main categories were identified, and then the other categories were linked. The main categories and their relationships with the other categories in this phase are:

- The diffusion of renewable energy technologies is strongly dependent on the willingness to invest and compatibility of the private sector.
- Although the push for science to use renewable energy technologies is essential, is not enough.
- The demand elasticity for renewable energy consumption is required, but not enough.
- The financial attraction for generating energy using renewable energy technologies is needed but not enough to diffuse renewable energy technologies.
- The required infrastructure and regulations as government supports for energy consumption from renewable sources are needed, but not sufficient for the diffusion of renewable energy technologies.
- Increasing specialized skills and knowledge is essential to increase the pressure of science on the application of renewable technologies that are affected by learning conditions, the degree of industry-university communication, and the level of specialized education.
- In order to increase the elasticity of demand for renewable energy, which is influenced by public knowledge of these resources and technologies, it is needed to reduce the fear of changing consumption patterns and improving attitudes towards renewable energies.
- Given the cost of investing in many renewable energy technologies, increasing the cost-benefit ratio and reducing business risk are two key variables to improve their financial attractiveness, which are influenced by their pricing mechanism, subsidies and facilitating financial mechanisms, and political instability.
- Increasing influential and coalition interest groups to support renewable energy, along with reducing the problem of dependence on traditional energy paths, are important factors in improving infrastructure and regulatory support for renewable energies that are influenced by strategies such as increased public knowledge and support.

At the selective coding step, they put the axial codes in a unified framework. The relationships between the axial categories are represented in Figure 4.

Figure 4. Relationships between the axial categories (Elahi et al., 2005)

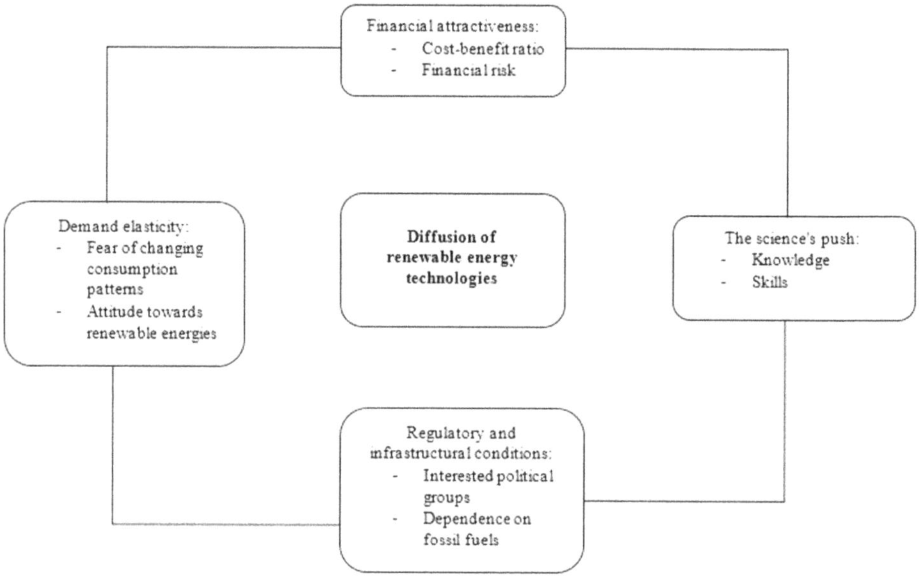

The simultaneous existence of these four factors is essential for the diffusion of renewable energy technologies. On the one hand, development of science and technology as the mechanism of science's push to apply these technologies and the need to use cleaner energy, on the other hand, drives the diffusion of renewable energy technologies as the mechanism of elasticity of demand for renewable energy. The success of the diffusion also depends on two other key factors: the financial attractiveness of renewable energies that drives private sector entry into the field, and government support for the creation of appropriate infrastructure and regulation appropriate for renewable energy.

The theory produced in this study can be efficient because it can "predict" relying on Iran's future fossil fuel sources; for example, it will have a negative impact on the diffusion of renewable energy technologies and can also offer problem-solving solutions; for example, designing appropriate financial mechanisms can affect the cost-benefit analysis of investors, reduce the relative advantage of fossil fuels, or informing and educating can reduce the fear of changing consumption patterns by consumers. Finally, this theory is modifiable, that is, with the emergence of new data, it can change and evolve in any of the causes, underlying conditions, classifications, etc.

The factors affecting the adoption and diffusion of smart grid technology from user's perspective are investigated by Joo and Kim (2013) to provide strategic guidelines of diffusing smart grids. For this purpose, the data were analyzed using procedures of GT and 19 categories representing as factors of diffusing smart grids, were identified through open coding. Finally, a paradigm model as proposed for diffusing smart grid and total of seven propositions as strategic guidelines for government and providers and some implications were provided.

Figure 5. A paradigm model for adopting and diffusing of smart grids (Joo and Kim, 2013)

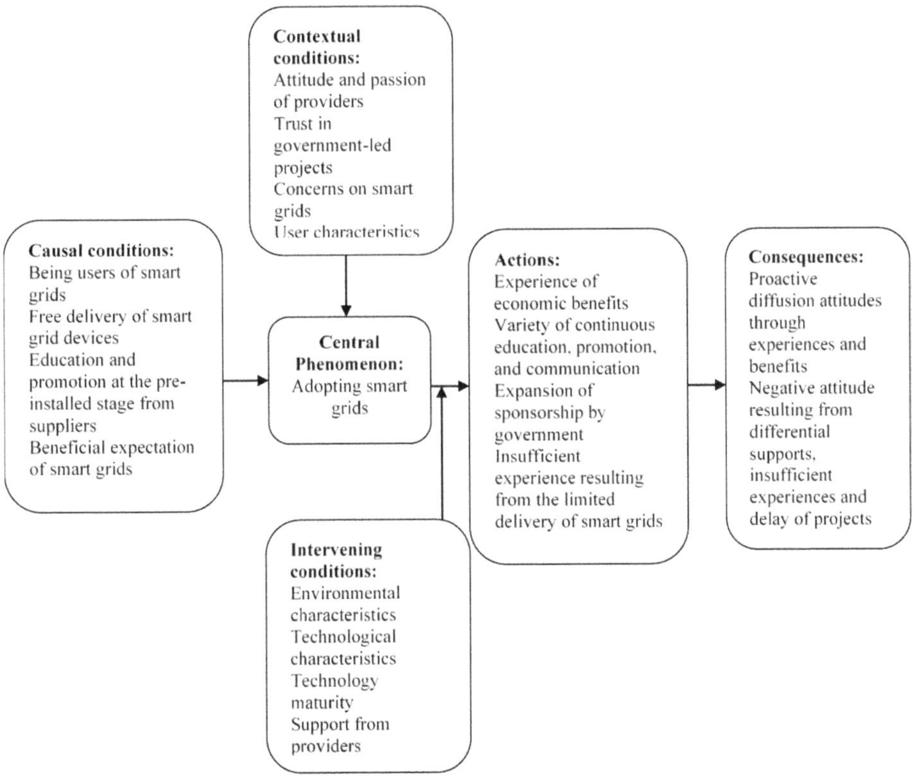

Dehkordi at al. (2018) analyzed barriers of using renewable energies in villages with the susceptibility to use renewable energies in Chaharmahal and Bakhtiari Province. GT methodology was used in this study for data analysis. According to the obtained results, informational-cultural factor with 4 items, policy-making-official factor (legal status) with 4 items, education-research and planning factor with 4 items, cost-investment factors (financial resources) and the human resources are prioritized into 4 items, and finally the technology factor, with 4 items are prioritized.

The categories are developed and each category will include subcategories and the relationship of each of them will be specified in axial coding. The axial coding step requires constant data comparison. The researcher compares the encoded data with each other and breaks it down into categories that fit together and puts the same codes into a single category.

Table 1. Results of axial coding (Dehkordi, 2018)

Categories	Sub – categories
policy-making-official factor (legal status)	There are interest groups like oil companies or coal companies that leverage renewable energy.
	Legal frameworks and energy policies are a major obstacle to renewable energy.
	The position of renewable energy in national energy policies is often ambiguous.
	Policies prevent the private sector from investing in renewable projects.
	The long process and bureaucratic procedures for obtaining electricity generation licenses can be an obstacle for investors to set up renewable energy projects.
	The renewable energy industry must be influenced by the macroeconomic policies of the government, which is very weak.
	Renewable energy systems and their components are subject to import duties or other heavy taxes, which is an important deterrent.
	The government still does not have a strong belief in the use of renewable energy as a substitute for conventional energy.
education-research and planning	Agencies or NGOs are weak on renewable energy.
	Such plans include high levels of ambiguity.
	The lack of reliable scientific data on renewable energies is common in developing countries.
	The scarcity of renewable energy research in the region is one of the barriers to the use of this technology.
	Lack of planning for renewable energy use
	Lack of supervision to the rural areas regarding the potential assessment of the areas

continues on following page

Table 1. Continued

Categories	Sub – categories
cost-investment factors (financial resources)	Many renewable energy technologies regarding cost are not competitive compared to conventional forms of energy.
	On the one hand, the economic growth rate is low, on the other hand, the unemployment rate was very high, and the development of the renewable energy industry, especially wind energy, has a major impact on both of these problems that require investment.
	Market players in renewable energy are scarce and suffering from a lack of capital.
	The high cost of new technology equipment and the low income of rural residents
cost-investment factors (financial resources)	The most important reason for failing to make the optimal use of these natural resources is that they have lost their place in the general culture of society.
	In some parts of the province, coal and wood are still used for heating and cooking, due to the lack of awareness of renewable resources.
	There is a lack of information in the field of maintenance.
	The market for renewable systems in the developing world is not very wide.
	There are few organizations in the developing world that promote renewable energies by disseminating information or leveraging non-governmental and governmental organizations.
	People do not have adequate and proper acceptance of renewable energy use in rural areas.
	Broadcasting organization does not have appropriate plans for renewable energy use in rural areas.
	Lack of training is seen as a deterrent.
	Audience preference over conventional energy use
	Lack of information in potential areas
Human resources	Lack of skilled manpower in the field of renewable technology
	Hard access to customer and skilled manpower in the village
	Such plans involve high risk elements.
	People are not welcomed and involved enough to use new energy.
Technology	Poor quality of some of the renewable energy technologies that are produced and sold in developing countries are an important obstacle.
	The cost of maintaining renewable energy equipment is high.
	The initial cost of purchasing renewable energy systems is seen as an important deterrent.

SOCIAL DYNAMICS OF ENERGY TRANSITION

An inductive research approach was applied by Kent (2018) to study how community energy initiatives can support social innovation in local energy transitions. For this purpose, a combination of GT and case-study methods is used by way of an examination of the community energy sector in Bristol, United Kingdom. An iterative and emergent analysis grounded in the experiences of various community energy initiatives in the city was conducted which resulted in a conceptual framework including dynamics of social change surrounding and realized by these initiatives. Using an inductive method like GT, it is possible to consider situational factors that may have otherwise been overlooked to emerge from data collected from participants and then incorporated with other methods as part of a wider contextual analysis.

Field studies on 7 rural renewable energy projects were conducted by Kunze and Busch (2011) in Brandenburg, Germany, in which the social dimensions of renewable energy technology were identified by organizational complexity, technology acceptance, participation by local people and funding models. The research on renewable energy in rural areas has mainly focused on technical or economic aspects. However, little attention has been paid to social dynamic of the transition from non-renewable to renewable energy in a micro-sociological context. The following research questions were developed based on the first findings of this GT approach: How can different technical solutions be categorized based on the social complexity of the respective projects? What are the typical social barriers in the development towards local energy autarky? According to the findings of this research, social complexity that accompanies renewable energy projects can be equally challenging as economic or technical aspects.

In order to provide empirically structured data which could serve as a structured and empirical foundation for a conceptual framework, a mainly qualitative method was applied based on GT aimed to answer the following question: How do people understand and assess community-based renewables and the connected issues of an induced community transition? In order to gain an in-depth and grounded understanding of people's perspectives on climate change and related issues, a qualitative research was used. The results of a quantitative household survey based on comparing the interviews undertaken, are less profound in scope and content but provide statistical data and a larger sample. However, interviews helped to develop the model conceptual grounding, statistical data informed parameters and values for the computational model.

Energy systems are known to be important contributors to community structure and complexity. Research results show that growth, stability or decline in energy depends on the bilateral relationship between energy and social structure. Therefore, the transition from a fossil fuel-based energy system to a new system also requires a social transition. Successful implementation of new energy technology needs social and institutional change, a skill-based technical infrastructure, appropriate financial networks, and appropriate social adoption models (Iskin et al., 2013).

Figure 6. Social dimensions of renewable energy technology (Kunze and Busch, 2011)

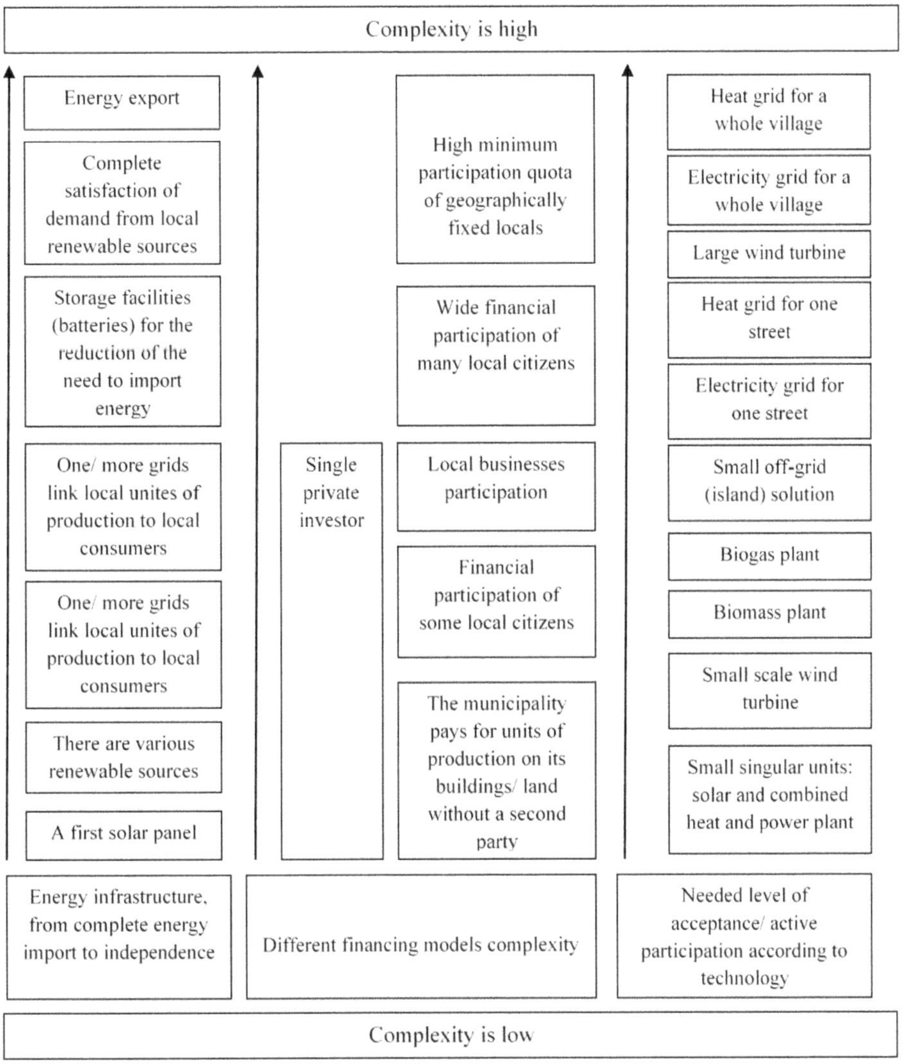

As a societal challenge demanding transformation in our social and economic systems, it is needed to face climate change in order to adapt to expected changes and to reduce a temperature increase above 2 degrees Celsius. The question of how to enable low-carbon energy transitions based on renewable-energy technologies such as wind turbines, solar panels, biogas plants or geothermal plants should be answered in this regard. Such a transition initiates a physical (re)shaping of places and social change in communities.

Today, it is found that individual households and communities are increasingly making important contributions in energy transition, driven by the emergence of community wind farms, energy cooperatives and initiatives etc. This trend has led to the fact that citizen's energy and community renewable energy are high on the political agenda. Despite the emergence of 'community renewable energy' as a grassroots-based innovation concept, the local places of energy transition and their underlying social processes and structures are not sufficiently studied and often remain underestimated. What place-based social and geographic aspects needed to enable communities to become the places of local energy transition?

By applying a place-based perspective on mitigating climate change with renewable-energy technologies, Süsser (2016) seek an in-depth understanding of the multifaceted and complex nature of the social phenomenon of community-based renewable energy. This research is focused on place, local agents and their relationships and interactions in order to analyze and deal with the complexity of the system. The climate change and renewables in people's localities, places as sources of experiences, memories, knowledge and innovation; and represents local benefits and challenges of mitigating climate change with community renewables are considered in a place-based approach. Firstly, analytical categories for the meanings of climate change were determined, compared and further explained along the course of the interview analysis by GT. Secondly, the analytical concepts of psychological distances and place attachments are addressed in the study which permeate these meanings of climate change (Charmaz, 2014; Corbin and Strauss, 2015).

The current situation of community energy planning in northern Europe is evaluated by Petersen (2016) via a review of literature, practice and the performance of a barrier analysis for successful community energy planning. According to the research finding, there is lack of systematic approach in current community energy planning; it also suffers from insufficient information, tools and resources. Municipalities are also generally unable to play a leading role in the planning of community energy. Hence, a decision-support methodology, based on community energy profiles (CEP), is presented to overcome these barriers and guide municipalities in the pre-project phase. This research is conducted in two parts: GT-based theoretical research and application of the acceleration method in a case study, after the concept of action research. The methodology was applied in a case study in Germany. The possibility to merge qualitative data from local settings into generic energy modeling is shown with CEPs, which could help improve community energy strategies.

CONCLUSION

Studies in the field of energy transition using the Grounded Theory (GT) approach were examined in this study. As the first component of the energy transition, the goal of reducing energy efficiency is to reduce energy demand in order to lower production levels and thus carbon dioxide emissions. The most important element of green building is energy efficiency. Hoffer's (2015) study, which discusses energy-building policy and capital investment decision-making, was also reviewed here; in this study, GT's approach have been applied to study the change experience by real estate developers in improving construction through demand changes to greener buildings.

As one of the major research topics in energy consumption reduction, behavioral changes are deeply rooted in behavioral and social sciences. Studies have been conducted to investigate the perceptions and behaviors of energy saving using the GT approach, which we reviewed here. GT seems to be suitable for such research because of its special features. Among these is the suitability for new topics or the presentation of new points of view that have now been undertaken in numerous studies. Several investigations have also been conducted on the diffusion of renewable energy technologies to create a diffusion model. Also, GT-based and social-science analyses have been conducted to help inform ideas that help better understand the customer's perspective and develop policy interventions to reduce climate change with renewable energy technologies.

REFERENCES

Ann, C. M., & Abualrejal, H. M. (2015). Energy efficiency in green building to achieve company sustainability. In *Proceedings of Symposium on Technology Management and Logistics (STMLGoGreen)*. Universiti Utara Malaysia.

Berkhout, F., Marcotullio, P., & Hanaoka, T. (2012). Understanding energy transitions. *Sustainability Science*, *7*(2), 109–111. doi:10.100711625-012-0173-5

Chien, M. K., Chang, T. M., & Kuo, W. C. (2012). *Applying Grounded Theory to study green supply chain management practices in Taiwan's industry. International Technology Management Conference*, Dallas, TX. 10.1109/ITMC.2012.6306381

Corbin, J., & Strauss, A. (2008). *Basics of qualitative research: Techniques and procedures for developing grounded theory* (3rd ed.). Thousand Oak, CA: Sage Publications. doi:10.4135/9781452230153

Dehkordi, M. K., Einodin, H. K., Yadavar, H., & Roshandel, R. (2018). Qualitative analysis of inhibitors of the use of renewable energy using grounded theory (Case Study: Kahkash Village of Chaharmahal va Bakhtiari Province). *Journal of Geography and Planning*, *22*(66), 207–229.

Elahi, S., Gharibi, J., Majidpour, M., and Anvari Rostami, A. A. (2005). The path to diffusion of renewable energy technologies: A grounded theory approach. *Journal of Innovation Management*, *4*(2), 33-56.

European University Association (EUA). (2017). *Energy transition and the future of energy research, innovation and education: An action agenda for European universities*. European University Association. Retrieved September 13, 2019, from https://energy.eua.eu/downloads/publications/energy-transition.pdf

Foster, D., Lawson, S., Winn, J., Noble, H., & White, D. (2011) Using grounded theory to inform the design of energy interventions for the workplace. In Digital Engagement 2011, Newcastle, UK.

García, O., Prieto, J., Alonso, R. S., & Corchado, J. M. (2017). A framework to improve energy efficient behaviour at home through activity and context monitoring. *Sensors (Basel)*, *17*(8), 1749. doi:10.339017081749 PMID:28758987

Hoffer, E. R. (2015). *Green building policy and capital investment decision-making: A grounded theory study*. Northeastern University. Retrieved September 14, 2019, from https://repository.library.northeastern.edu/files/neu:349730/fulltext.pdf

Iskin, I., Abu Taha, R., & Daim, T. U. (2013). Exploring the adoption of alternative energy technologies: A literature review. *International Journal of Sustainable Society*, *5*(1), 43–61. doi:10.1504/IJSSOC.2013.050534

Joo, J., & Kim, L. (2013). Diffusion ofs Smart Grid for Low-Carbon Green Growth: Grounded Theory Approach. *Pacific Asia Conference on Information Systems (PACIS)*.

Kent, S. (2018). *Powering social innovation through community energy initiatives? Towards a conceptual framework*. Erasmus Mundus Master Course in Urban Studies (4Cities).

Kunze and Busch. (2011). The social complexity of renewable energy production in the countryside. *Electronic Green Journal, 1*(31), 1–18. https://portal.research.lu.se/ws/files/4291309/2203760.pdf

Luthra, S., Kumar, S., Garg, D., & Haleem, A. (2015). Barriers to renewable/sustainable energy technologies adoption Indian perspective. *Renewable & Sustainable Energy Reviews, 41*, 762–776. doi:10.1016/j.rser.2014.08.077

Mosly, I., & Makki, A. A. (2018). Current Status and Willingness to Adopt Renewable Energy Technologies in Saudi Arabia. *Sustainability, 10*(4269), 1–20. doi:10.3390u10114269

Osarumwense Asemota, G. N. (2013). Electricity use in Namibia: Developing algorithms to encourage more efficient consumer behavior and motivate more environmentally friendly utility practices. iUniverse.

Petersen, J.-P. (2016). *Optimization of energy planning strategies in municipalities Are community energy profiles the key to a higher implementation rate of renewable energies?* Paper presented at International Conference on Sustainable Built Environment 2016, Hamburg, Germany. Retrieved September 15, 2019, from https://orbit.dtu.dk/files/120656652/SBE16Hamburg_Community_Energy_Planning_Jens_Phillip_shortend_final2_1.pdf

Pulla, V. (2014). Grounded Theory Approach in Social Research. Special Methodology Edition plus Miscellaneous. *Space and Culture, 2*(3), 1–23.

Singh, M. K., Mahapatra, S., & Atreya, S. K. (2010). Green building design: A step towards sustainable habitat. In *National Conference on Renewable Energy 2010 (NCRE2010)*. Tezpur University.

Sony, M., & Mekoth, N. (2018). A qualitative study on electricity energy-saving behavior. *Management of Environmental Quality, 29*(5), 961–977. doi:10.1108/MEQ-02-2018-0031

Süsser, D. (2016). *People-powered local energy transition: Mitigating climate change with community-based renewable energy in North Frisia* (PhD Dissertation). Faculty of Mathematics, Informatic, and Environmental sciences, Hamburg University. Retrieved September 14, 2019, from https://ediss.sub.uni-hamburg.de/volltexte/2016/8034/pdf/Dissertation.pdf

Sweeney, J. C., Kresling, J., Webb, D., Soutar, G. N., & Mazzarol, T. (2013). Energy saving behaviors: Development of a practice-based model. *Energy Policy*, *61*, 371–381. doi:10.1016/j.enpol.2013.06.121

Trevarthen. (2011). Stakeholder perceived barriers to the use of solar energy in Thailand's buildings (Master's dissertation). Massey University, Palmerston North, New Zealand.

Unuigbe, M., Zulu, S., & Johnston, D. (2020). Renewable energy sources and technologies in commercial buildings: Understanding the Nigerian experience. *Built Environment Project and Asset Management*, (ahead-of-print). doi:10.1108/BEPAM-11-2018-0151

Zhao, J. (2014). Applying grounded theory methodology with mixed methods in occupant energy behavior research. *The European Conference on Social Sciences 2014 Official Conference Proceedings.*

Chapter 6
Grounded Theory Approach in Knowledge Management

ABSTRACT

Knowledge management (KM), as a new field having many concepts and strong conceptualization, is a vital business process in organizations that, because of the nature of knowledge, is closely linked to individuals. Because sociological research is mainly qualitative and KM contains sociological components, KM can take advantage of methods such as grounded theory (GT) approach that are specific to qualitative research. Accordingly, the chapter provides an understanding of the use of GT in KM. For this purpose, the chapter focuses on understanding process of transforming knowledge into wisdom, presenting KM model, determining factors of knowledge sharing, and consequently, developing a framework of knowledge sharing and determining the critical success factors (CSFs) of KM and their relationships within a model.

INTRODUCTION

According to Wang and Noe (2010), knowledge as a critical organizational resource, in a dynamic and competitive economy, provides a competitive advantage to its holder. Jelenic (2011) believes that knowledge is a strategic resource for the organization as well as a factor of competitive advantage and business success, so the knowledge management (KM) process is the most important process in a modern company. In order to empower people, improve learning efficiency and increase competitive advantage, KM provides

DOI: 10.4018/978-1-7998-4252-1.ch006

people with the tools and techniques to manage large volumes of information that they receive (Gao et al. 2018). KM has been used in many settings since the 1990s, especially in non-profit companies of all sizes, as well as in the non-profit sector (Agrawal & Marouf, 2016). Because of its important role in knowledge transfer for decision making at all levels of corporate governance and structure, the KM process is a routine business process in the organization. KM is also related to the management of business processes that deal with resources, in addition to manage knowledge as a resource (Jelenic, 2011).

The dissemination and sharing of knowledge and its application within and between specific organizations is an essential part of a KM system that seeks to guide and support the flow of ideas and experiences of the organization's people. Knowledge, in its exact sense, cannot be shared and therefore, unlike commodities, relies on cognitive matter and cannot be freely distributed. Re-shaping behavior is an integral part of acquiring knowledge that uses knowledge to obtain and thus, sharing knowledge. In knowledge sharing, there is at least a relationship between the two parties, one having knowledge and the other acquiring knowledge (Zheng, 2017). Knowledge sharing as a knowledge-focused activity is an essential tool whereby employees can participate in the application of knowledge, innovation and, ultimately, the organization's competitive advantage. Exploiting and investing in knowledge-based resources is possible through knowledge sharing within and between teams in the organization. According to research in this regard, knowledge sharing and combination is positively associated with lower production costs, faster completion of new product development projects, team performance, firm innovation capabilities, and firm performance including growth of sales and revenue from new products and services (Wang and Noe, 2010).

When we want to study in depth an issue or problem in the organization, a qualitative research approach should be used. Integrating theories, extracting some undiscovered relationships, clarifying some concepts, and offering connections are among the benefits of using a qualitative approach in the field of KM that was not achievable with the quantitative approach (Luciana, 2013). Direct observation, interviews, documents, and texts as well as researcher's feelings and reactions are generally used in qualitative approaches such as action research, case studies, and Grounded Theory (GT). When we aim to understand contextual information about people's way of living, the use of qualitative methods is preferred (Grossman and McCarthy, 2005).

Because of the importance of knowledge and its widespread application in the organization, KM is inextricably linked to individuals (Onions, 2006). Because sociological research is mainly qualitative, and KM contains sociological components, KM can take advantage of methods such as GT approach that are specific to qualitative research. However, before claiming the relevance of the GT methodology to KM research, examples of the application of this approach to the field must be examined, as obtained from the research of Smith (2004) by using the original GT method and study of Wastell (2001) with the use of the Straussian approach.

In Smith's (2004) research, the KM practices of the three organizations are examined and the GT approach is used to discuss about their commonalities. The purpose of this study was to provide some tools and methods for KM in successful organizations. According to Martin and Turner (1986), GT is appropriate for studies dealing with qualitative data obtained using semi-structured or unstructured interviews, and since the field of KM is at its early stage of development, using such approaches can be beneficial.

In similar fields, such as information systems and organizational research, some research has been conducted using the GT methodology that suggests that GT is more applicable to sociological contexts and KM has a strong sociological basis. KM is generally defined as any planned, formalized, or recognized activity and management of the knowledge application in organizations, which represents a social process that is appropriate field to apply the GT methodology. Since KM is related to a social construct, the application of qualitative methods is preferred to quantitative methods, which is consistent with previous research findings that quantitative methods are not appropriate in management research; because management research is generally deductive, quantitative, and positivist, involved with the complexity, ambiguity, and dynamics of the environment and subject. In the field of KM, there are various definitions, theories and hence, it needs GT methodology because of its qualitative nature. On the basis of these claims, Onions (2006) believes that the GT approach can be a good way to study KM.

The applicability and constraints of GT strategy in performing KM research is studied in Omona et al. (2010). In their study, aimed at developing a framework for KM using ICT in higher education in Uganda, inductive-hypothetical research strategy based on GT methodology is used along with soft systems methodology based on action research. Adopting a Knowledge-Based View (KBV) considering the competitive character of KBV consultants, is investigated by Akhavan et al. (2007) that used the GT approach. In sum, since 1) KBV and related fields provide little theoretical guidance, 2) the research manager's views and experience should shape the development and appropriateness of the theory, and 3) management and knowledge concepts are ambiguous, the GT approach is appropriate for conducting research in this field.

Attempts to achieve an early theory of the role of leaders in KM through the application of the GT approach are evident in Lakshman (2007). According to the findings of this study, leaders are fully aware of the role of information and knowledge sharing and the design of knowledge networks to maximize organizational effectiveness. Also, leaders utilize information technology and KM to better focus on internal and external customers. Therefore, GT's focus is on both the leadership behavior dimension of information and knowledge sharing. A case study of outsourced software maintenance operations in e-commerce unit of a large UK retailer using the GT approach is performed by Brome (2012) aimed at providing a framework for evaluating and improving KM capability in software maintenance teams that evaluates the operation in five areas of leadership, communication, tools, processes and cultures.

The process of knowledge creation in nursing education is investigated by Hassanian et al. (2015) using GT approach. Striving for growth and reduction of ambiguity, use of knowledge resources, dynamism of mind and social factors, converting knowledge, and creating knowledge are the main categories obtained in this study. Knowledge was transformed by mind processes, individual and group reflection, praxis and research, and resulted in the creation of nursing knowledge.

This chapter reviews the application of GT in KM focusing on:

1) Understanding the process of transforming knowledge into wisdom,
2) Presenting KM model,
3) Determining the factors of knowledge sharing, and developing a framework of knowledge sharing,
4) Defining CSFs of KM and their relationships in a form of a model.

KNOWLEDGE INTO WISDOM

According to the interviews, Atarodi et al. (2019) defined the concept of knowledge and the way it was formed. Extracted categories were recorded in the axial coding of how to transform knowledge into wisdom from the experts' perspective (Figure 1) as follows.

Based on the findings of the interviews and data analysis, the process of converting knowledge to wisdom can be the result of a main category (central issue) that is at the heart of the theory of knowledge to wisdom transformation.

Figure 1. Axial coding of how to transform knowledge into wisdom (Atarodi et al., 2019)

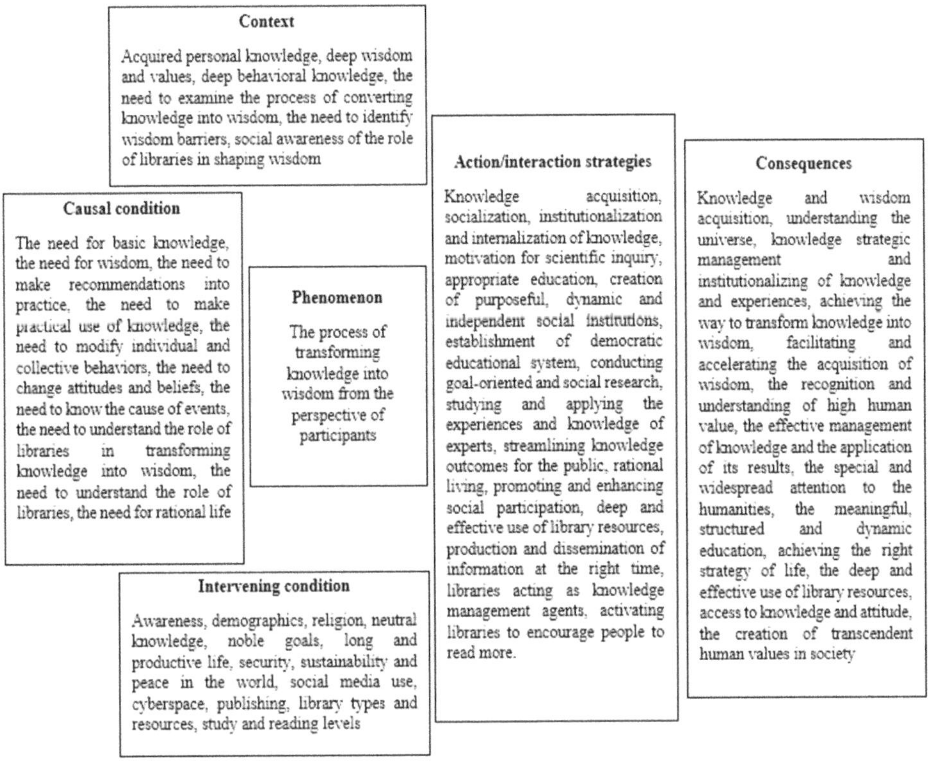

Achieving this goal, of course, requires removing obstacles from the path and process of knowledge to wisdom through the discovery and application of wise and rational strategies and solutions based on rational wisdom as well as through process modifications.

KNOWLEDGE MANAGEMENT MODEL

In a qualitative GT-based study by Tajedini et al. (2018), the feasibility of identification, extraction, organization and sharing of personal knowledge is evaluated in Kerman public librarians. The knowledge and information science experts in public libraries of Kerman were determined as the research population among them, a sample was selected using snowball sampling. The research data was gathered using in-depth interviews. The Lincoln and Guba's evaluative criteria (credibility, confidence in the 'truth' of the findings, transferability to show the findings applicability in other contexts, dependability to show findings consistent and repeatability, and conformability as the degree of neutrality or the extent to which the findings are shaped by the respondents and not affected by the researcher bias, motivation, or interest) was used to ensure the research validity and reliability and data collected from the interview, were coded and analyzed.

In open coding, as a first step in analyzing findings, interview texts are categorized and analyzed for breaking information analysis into information categories. The data are divided into different sections, scrutinized and compared according to their differences and similarities. Finally, 74 conceptual statements were extracted according to the data collected from interviews with knowledge and information science experts in public libraries in Kerman. During axial coding, as the second stage, the data broken during the coding process were again combined and more relevant categories were selected from the relevant codes and notes. In this stage, 19 conceptual statements from the interviews with knowledge and information science experts in public libraries of Kerman were detected from among conceptual statements of the first stage. Then, the core category was determined in selective coding and linked to other categories. In addition, the extracted information categories are divided into four groups, which will be explained in theoretical framework. Identification of personal knowledge, organization of personal knowledge, extraction of personal knowledge and sharing of personal knowledge are four categories obtained from interview analysis.

The statements derived from the analysis of interviews with knowledge and information science experts in public libraries of Kerman according to 4 categories obtained from data analysis are explained in detail in Figure 2.

As essential factors for the personal KM, causal conditions affect personal KM in public libraries. Consequences, as the results of strategies, are influenced by causal conditions. Also, conditions and backgrounds affect causal conditions. In addition to the specialized knowledge in their work, specialists may have personal knowledge in a variety of areas and can implement the process of personal knowledge management in these areas. Strategies show that the phenomenon of personal KM is affected by several factors in the public libraries of Kerman.

In all organizations, including in the energy sector, KM is seen as an important competitive advantage. Much of the knowledge is generated, shared and reused as a result of the implementation of research and development (R&D) projects of energy industry (RDEI) that few organizations know the

Table 1. The flow of data management concerning knowledge and information science experts in three coding stages (Tajedini et al., 2018)

Open coding stage: 74 conceptual statements	Axial coding stage: 19 conceptual statements	Selective coding stage: 4 categories
Acquisition of knowledge, knowledge discovery, facing problem, memories, need, knowledge use, daily teachings, information access, need fulfilment, opinion statement, efficient use of time, personal creativity, job development, income acquisition, job creation, access to information resource, useful reading, in-service training, nurturing known information, personal interests, interactive communication, note taking, timing, providing secondary memory, recording personal skills, information personal equipment, setting priorities, information integration, proper analysis, relationship discovery, knowledge division, systematic information, notebook, knowledge classification, checklist, organized signs, using personal abilities, information utilization, purposeful knowledge representation, information analysis, use of previous experience, responding needs, quick access, random retrieval, information search, information evaluation, finding information, reviewing known information, acquisition of information, remembering known information, personal information, social knowledge, discussion and idea exchange, meet the others' needs, social networks, facilitating communication, consulting with others, information enhancement, current awareness, interaction promotion, conversation, improving cooperation, idea exchange, research objective fulfilment, known information sharing, satisfaction, exploiting, cyber-space, transferring experience, practical training, cheerfulness, self-confidence increase, unique experiences, personal communication.	Applying knowledge (3 categories), discovery of knowledge (3 categories), understanding information resources and their application (5 categories), using educational facilities (4 categories), information preservation (4 categories), knowledge coherence (6 categories), information ranking (4 categories), knowledge coding (4 categories), indexing (5 categories), information access (4 categories), provision of information (5 categories), information assessment (6 categories), knowledge retrieval (2 categories), known information extraction (3 categories), specialized information sharing (4 categories), communication media (4 categories), personal interactions (3 categories), information communication (2 categories), emotional engagement (3 categories)	Identifying personal knowledge, Organization of personal knowledge, Extraction of personal knowledge, Sharing personal knowledge Core category: personal knowledge management

Figure 2. Personal Knowledge management model for knowledge and information science experts in public libraries in Kerman derived from codes (Tajedini et al., 2018)

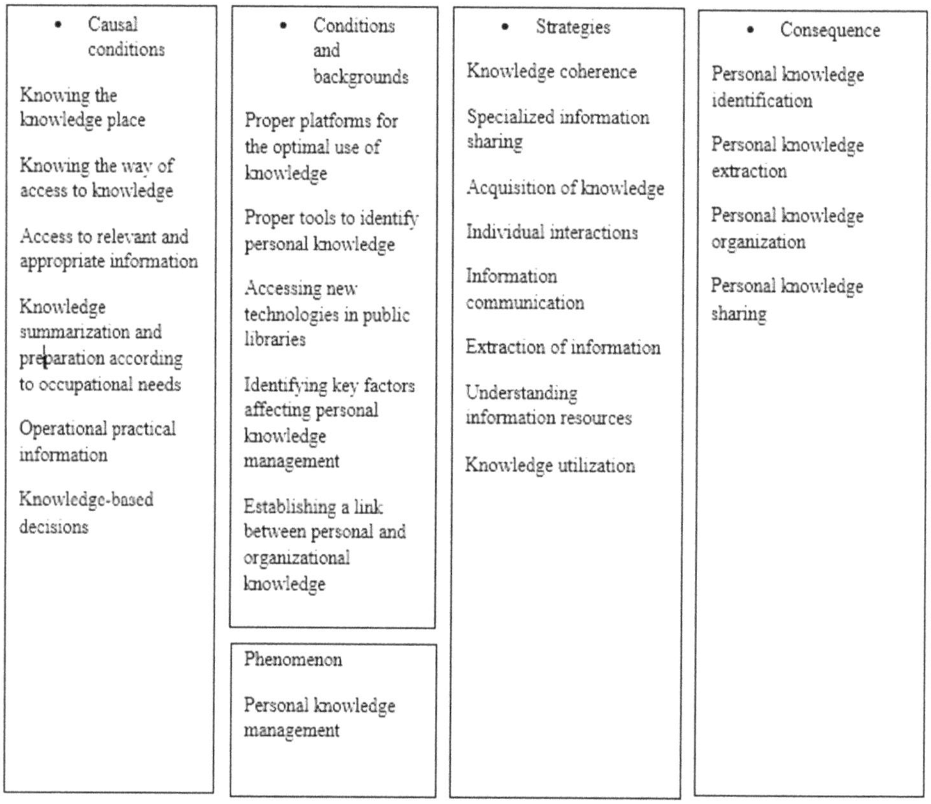

way of managing it, effectively. Hence, a major concern for managers is to find a custom KM model compatible with specific RDEI factors. A customized KM pattern for the R&D projects of the studied sector considering project-based organization characteristics is provided by Amidi et al. (2019) using GT. The required information is collected by semi-structured interviews with experts and the components of the final model and their relations are found using open, axial, and selective coding. according to the results, 48 open codes, 15 main concept, and 5 secondary concepts were extracted which are all categorized in "causal situations", "intervention situations", "strategies", "core phenomena" and "effects".

The categories found based on the opinions of the selected experts group in the survey include "organization context," "causal conditions," "strategies," "intervening factors," and "effects and results of KM." The factors of organization context shape, the situation nature, conditions, or

Figure 3. KM Pattern of the R&D projects for the studied energy industry (Amidi et al., 2019)

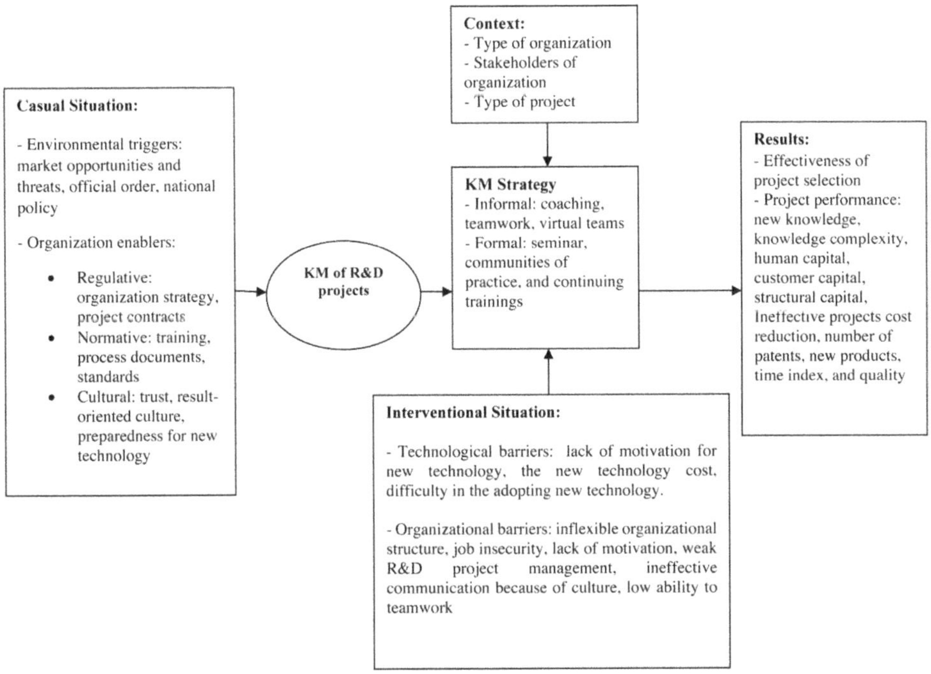

the problem in which individuals interact in the micro to macro levels. The causal conditions include factors forming or influencing the primary category. Strategies show the interactions or actions by activists. Interventional factors include organizational and technological barriers.

The validation by respondents is one of the pattern validation methods in which, the results of coding are presented to the research team to verify the findings validity. Next, the final pattern is presented to the respondents, and their opinions were asked about the conceptual pattern. Kappa coefficient index is used to find the reliability among the group which is described below:

$$K = \frac{(P_0 - P_e)}{(P_1 - P_e)} \tag{1}$$

Equation 1: Kappa coefficient in which P_0 is the relative observed agreement among raters, and P_e is the hypothetical probability of chance agreement that uses the observed data to calculate the probabilities of each observer by randomly seeing each category. The Kappa coefficient shows the agreement between the two encoders. The obtained index is equal to 0.83, which indicates that the agreement intensity is almost complete and the pattern is understandable for the interviewees and hence, the proposed pattern accuracy is confirmed.

CRITICAL SUCCESS FACTORS OF KM

Critical Success Factors (CSFs) that represent managerial areas that require constant and sustained attention to achieve high performance, are among the few things that should be at the desired level to ensure success for managers and/or organizations. Certain CSFs are required to effectively develop and implement a KM (Yang et al., 2010). Because it provides researchers and practitioners with the basic requirements for implementing a successful KM initiative and building a successful KM system, knowing the CSFs is useful.

CSFs for KM within project-based organizations are studied in Akhavan and Zahedi (2014) using a multi-case approach. For this purpose, they used GT approach to segment and analyze the data accordingly. Also, CSFs of KM and their relationships is investigated by Sousa and Hendriks (2006) using a GT research approach. In this study, the stages of GT were used to categorize and analyze the collected data. A semantic network has been developed in which the categorized data indicate the relationships between the extracted CSFs and finally, a theory has been obtained. The KM success roadmap for the organizations is obtained using the semantic network and the emerged theory.

In this study, after reviewing the data of each case study, some data were selected based on the research needs to answer the following questions:

- Why do these companies should apply a KM system?
- What are the main problems of KM programs in these companies?
- What are the CSFs of KM adoption in these companies?

Chronological descriptions of project activities due to the KM deployment in companies is constructed in the first stage of data analysis which shows the formation, start-up time, people involved (based on the authority in the company), level of participation, and the main outputs. An in-depth case history of the project was completed in this study. The second stage of analysis includes coding the in-depth case history regarding its characteristics, origin, and effects. This highly repetitive procedure includes moving between the in-depth case history, existing theory, and the raw data. The next stage is to find relationships through identifying concepts that may somehow explain the phenomenon under consideration. This process is usually related to axial coding, which is achieved by identifying the main relationships or structures within which the concepts are formed. Axial coding is the understanding of concepts in terms of their dynamic interactions and forming the basis for the theory construction.

The construction of core categories, which include concepts to explain the phenomenon, is the next step in the process of developing the theory. In order to build the theoretical framework, there should be theoretical significance which is traceable back through the data and then integrate categories through selective coding. The main mechanism of emerging and appearing new ideas and concepts is the literature comparison with the results of each stage which will be continued until saturation stage. Also, no new cases will add any new concept to the findings in this stage.

According to the semantic network shown in Fig. 4 based on the final analysis of input data, the above factors directly and indirectly influence the success of KM as well as each other whose relationships are clearly shown in this figure. The overall findings of the research are visualized in a semantic network that to gain a better understanding.

By examining the deterrent and debilitating factors of KM initiatives, and using the GT approach to present a model of KM success, Wastell (2001) contributes to the literature in this area. Although the field of KM has been the subject of much research, the theory presented in this work and its generalizability can be discussed. Many aspects of the proposed model are derived from existing KM research.

Although the evidence suggests that KM has failed to perform successfully in many cases, little research has been done into the causes of these failures. An action research (AR) project is described in this study, focusing on one of their key knowledge processes (Design for Manufacturability, DFM) in a major motor manufacturer (WWM). Extensive field work with the GT method has led to the development of a model relating to the effectiveness of knowledge creation and the use of a set of success factors. Many of the factors like the need for a shared knowledge repository, a formal KM process, and a culture disposed towards knowledge sharing and re-use resonate with key issues described in previous KM research. The model provides a rigorous platform to design interventions to improve the DFM process in WWM. Bringing about cultural change is less tractable and process improvements in WWM

Figure 4. Roadmap of success in KM area for the organizations (Sousa and Hendriks, 2006)

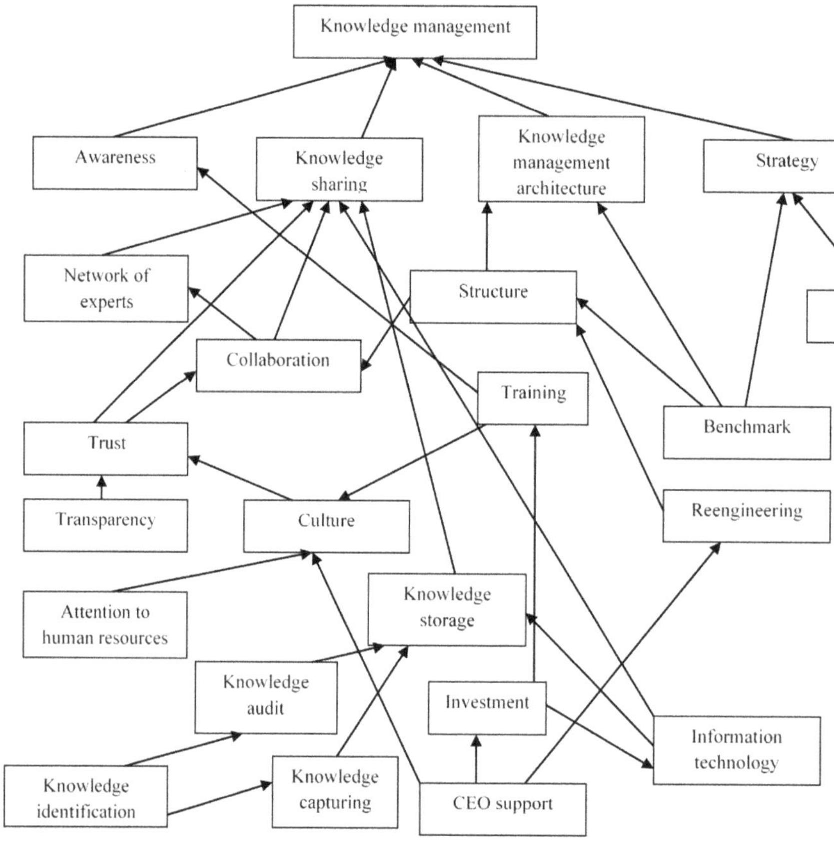

have tended to focus on the former rather than the latter although technical changes (creating infrastructure, defining processes) are readily feasible. GT can help to inform the design of organizational interventions and the evaluation of their impact in relation to the problem-solving aspect of AR; also, GT adds rigor and method to the theory building process in relation to research, thereby raising the status of AR as a research tool.

The final form of the GT derived from the data and the concepts above is showed in Figure 5 that deliberately shows the simplified model. Two basic ontological constructs, namely knowledge processes and perceived success factors, are connected by arrows that represent dependencies. Two key processes of KM that indicated in this figure are knowledge creation and application. The consistent distinction both in interviews and in the DFM documentation, between the creative process of generating design knowledge and the implementation activity entailed in carrying this through into the actual manufacturing process are the result of the distinction between knowledge creation and its application. As defined in the KM literature, these categories (and their implicit subcategories) crudely map well into models of the KM process. Various success factors that influence these two processes have also been indicated. Although it is possible to clearly divide these factors into different sub-categories (e.g. cultural, organizational, technological), a single notation is used given for simplicity so that they all belong to a common high level ontological class (i.e. success factor) and that individual provenance can be readily inferred from the construct label. Also, the diagram shows thc links (arrowed lines) between categories that were induced from the statements made by interviewees. These links, at an abstract conceptual level, simply reflect the existence of a dependency of some sort amongst the success factors, and between the factors and the knowledge processes. For instance, it has been shown that knowledge generation depends on the commitment of the Design Release Engineer's (DREs), who has the charge of the design work for that component/sub-system from inception to fruition, to the DFM process, and in turn, this commitment is critically affected by the degree of active support for DFM from their senior line managers.

There are several ways to validate the theory. The first way is to track back the main constructs to documentary evidence through the open-coding process (i.e. conceptual labeling of field notes, comprising paraphrased and quoted comments, scenario descriptions etc.). The second way is to present the model formally to company members and receive their endorsement (e.g. the DFM user group). The third way is to informally triangulate it in the course of individual interviews. The fourth way is to provide further endorsement by the fact that it has provided a basis for practical recommendations, some of which have been implemented (see below).

The model is applicable only to the WWM domain and there is no claim to generalize it beyond its scope. However, more fieldwork is needed to develop the model, for example through comparative analysis and theoretical sampling of organizations to create more generalizable theories. This is partly realized today. First, most of the data was collected in only one division of WWM (Truck); as the work continues, theoretical sampling has been carried out in other sectors, resulting in a rich set of categories applied throughout the company. Of course, despite the theoretical saturation in a particular organization, other empirical work is needed in other automotive companies

Figure 5. A model of KM success (Wastell, 2001)

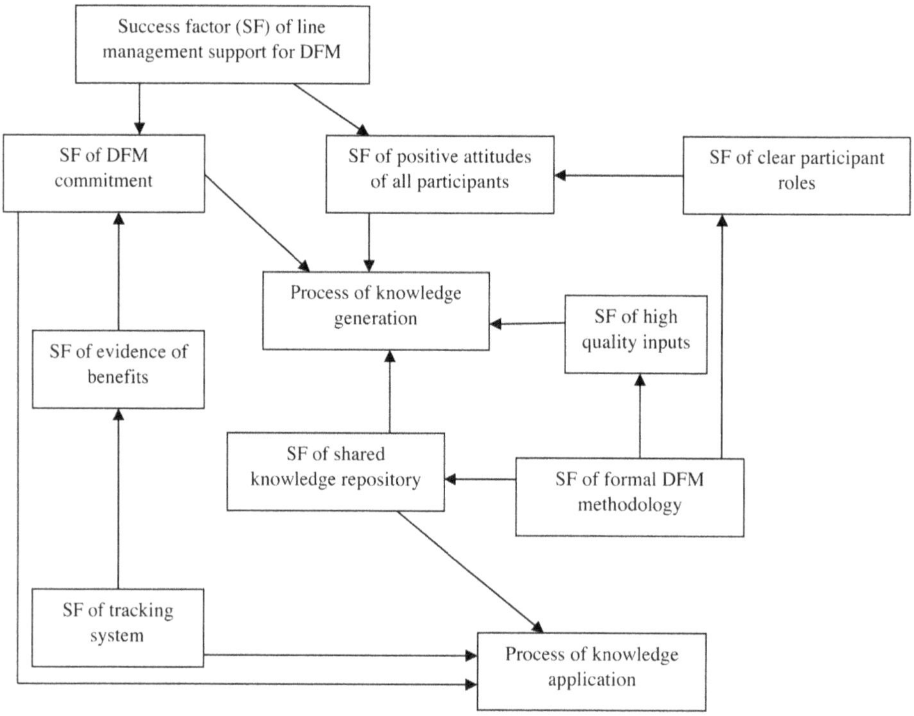

(as well as other manufacturing and non-manufacturing environments) to fully generalize the theory to the substantive domain of KM.

The keys to KM success influencing both knowledge generation and application are repositories, commitment and formal process. The first one emphasizes the need for a shared knowledge repository. The absence of such an infrastructure seriously inhibited the efficacy of the DFM process in WWM because much of the KM literature focuses on technologies for knowledge management. This shows the critical role of technology as an enabler of KM. Hence, it is expected that the introduction of a shared DFM site can make a major effect. But as many others have pointed out, technology is not a sufficient condition for effective KM whilst it is arguably a necessary one. In order to encourage knowledge sharing and re-use of knowledge assets, it is critical to make changes in attitudes and working practices; also, a knowledge environment "conducive to more effective knowledge creation, transfer and use" is necessary which is much more difficult than changing infrastructure. To this end, the coordination of cultural practices is needed, and the main reason for many KM failures is the lack of attention to this issue. There are strong cultural barriers. The company design culture is that of heroic individuals not team players; the traditions of WWM emphasize design ingenuity often at the expense of manufacturing efficiency. Of course, the company can take steps to fix these problems that can focus on demonstrating DFM performance and making knowledge accessible (e.g. through changing incentive and accountability structures to enforce the DFM approach).

The need to strengthen the existing DFM methodology and encourage greater compliance is the third key element of the model. According to the author, as a KM tool in multidisciplinary design teams, methodology has considerable potential which is arguably more important than its traditional role as a control and co-ordination mechanism which is rarely emphasized. Methodology proposed a robust structure for creating and binding together a community of practice through providing a shared linguistic and ontological framework. Therefore, strengthening adoption and use of a formal DFM process has a key role in creating a vigorous DFM community within WWM. In addition, access to a defined collaborative process enables the system to define metrics without which the KM processes are unmanageable.

Finally, as the contribution of the present research methodology, GT's important role in AR and consulting practice should be mentioned. As we have seen, GT can reinforce the theory formation mechanisms in AR and thus add to its status and effectiveness as a research tool, which is one of the criticisms that come to it. Of course, the potential is one subject and its realization is another that needs changing in attitude and understanding of the AR community. Specifically, more focus should be on research rather than problem solving, and of course reinforcing research on the AR side, GT can also lead to strengthening the problem-solving side.

The benefits of a well-defined theoretical model are two-fold. First, it allows for systematic interventions to address maximum leverage points. Second, it allows to evaluate these interventions and understand their outputs. A set of interventions in WWM based on the recommended model and some of them have been applied. Although it is too early to assess the impact of these changes, they have been under continuous evaluation. However, the important point is that this model provides a framework for measuring the impact of changes and understanding their effectiveness (or lack of it). In a pessimistic state, the model predicts that whilst some gains will be yielded, but the benefits might be expected to be marginal since the pivotal problem (of DRE commitment) is not yet being directly addressed. The value of this model is in providing a framework to guide future improvement measures.

The concepts or tentative theories of employees' perceptions and experiences about electronic knowledge sharing is investigated in Matayong et al. (2010) research aimed at explaining the employees' behavior in electronic knowledge sharing. A GT approach is proposed in their research to conceptualize the electronic knowledge sharing phenomenon in the Malaysian oil and gas sector. First, electronic knowledge sharing is one of the employees' concerns. Thus, there is a link between access to information and resources and the sharing of electronic knowledge in the oil and gas sector. Second, the role of management and leadership is very important in encouraging employees to share their knowledge in the environment. Third, employees are eager to have guidance on e-knowledge sharing practices and processes, because they are skeptical about what should and should not be shared, as well as how to share knowledge electronically. Finally, the lack of system-friendly tools and support may prevent employees from sharing their knowledge to the environment.

KNOWLEDGE SHARING

Because people think that their knowledge is valuable and important, knowledge sharing is usually unusual and people having it are reluctant to share it. Research in this area (Liang et al., 2008) also shows that changing the people behavior, especially in relation to knowledge sharing, is the most important challenge facing organizations. A GT research project is performed by Jones and Alony (2014) to study the collaboration and knowledge sharing phenomena in the Australian Film Industry. The use of GT's powerful, systematic and detailed approach results in flexibility and freedom in the study of complex multidimensional phenomena because GT is capable of addressing social issues.

The determinants of knowledge sharing at the individual level are identified in a study by Jabbary and Madhoshi (2014) using GT methodology. For this purpose, the purposive sampling and snowball method were used to select 23 faculty members of Iranian universities as the research sample. The in-depth, semi-structured interview using Strauss and Corbin's constant comparative method were used to collect data. According to the obtained results, social-emotional relations, market value, personal growth and development, and requirements (internal and external) were obtained as the most significant factors influencing knowledge sharing among faculty members.

As a gap in the tacit knowledge (TK) sharing literature, a framework for promoting TK sharing in multinational corporations (MNCs) from the ICT perspective has been developed by Al-Qdah et al. (2018). ICT channels have a vital role to play in connecting people in headquarters (HQs) and subsidiaries that, in the absence of such channels, this communication would not be possible as a major advantage for the organization. According to this study, classifying TK into distinct levels and matching these levels to the most appropriate ICT channel can lead to the realization of TK transfer. It has also been argued that the issues facing specialists and practitioners in MNCs when transferring TK among employees can be largely resolved through the effective utilization of ICT tools. Using GT, three coding procedures are applied in scquential data analysis, which is a duplicate procedure for identifying relationships. Table 2 shows the selected coding procedure in GT in the field under study.

In this study, the nature and complexity of TK, the barriers affecting transfer, and its transferability mechanisms are explored to reach key themes

Table 2. Selective coding procedures used in GT (Al-Qdah et al., 2018)

OPEN CODING	AXIAL CODING	SELECTIVE CODING
Managerial procedures, attitudes and beliefs, culture, technical capacity; complexity of tacit knowledge, low motivations, process and political factor	The nature of tacit knowledge and problems affect the transfer of tacit knowledge.	Conceptualization of tacit knowledge include nature and complexity of tacit knowledge, managerial and technical problems that affect tacit knowledge management
Identifying the tacit knowledge needed by the organization to transfer and understand the knowledge and skills at risk of loss as important factors in knowledge sharing improvement	Identifying who has the experience and skills and who needs these skills	Recognizing the tacit knowledge
Grouping tacit knowledge into levels in terms of complexity, makes the tacit knowledge transfer from HQ to subsidiaries easier.	Tacit knowledge classification into high, medium and low degree of being tacit	Tacit knowledge categorizing based on degree of tacitness
Tacit knowledge meetings, trainings and workshops, documentation of tacit knowledge, planning; infrastructure development, evaluation, create tacit knowledge department, management, increasing resources, Research and Development	Promoting tacit knowledge transfer in companies	Applying mechanisms for improving the transfer of tacit knowledge
Video-conferencing, groupware, document sharing, networking, SCADA communication channels, Skype and telephone, HyTechPro software, chat rooms, e-mail, voice mail, e-forum, social networks	Diverse ICT tools with different capacities to enhance tacit knowledge transfer	Selecting the right types of ICT tools to transfer tacit knowledge

that contribute to a deeper understanding of the TK transfer phenomenon. The conceptualization of TK includes the nature of TK and the managerial and technical issues affecting TK transmission, TK identification, TK classification, exploitation of TK transmission improvement mechanisms, and the selection of appropriate types of ICT tools for TK transmission are the five main categories identified. These categories are then linked together with other important categories to develop a theoretical plan scheme of TK transfer among team members working in MNC subsidiaries. In order to overcome the complexity of the ambiguous nature of TK that affects its transferability, a GT approach has been used which has led to the development of understanding of the nature of TK.

In their research, Akhavan and Iman (2016), have investigated the factors affecting knowledge sharing in order to find the most important factors in this regard. For this purpose, the GT methodology has been used along with gathering and analyzing the researchers' opinions. Factors were first collected from library sources, reviewing the literature and the reporters' views, and after coding by open, axial, and selective methods, 9 categories of factors including social, competitive, organizational, motivational, cultural, leadership and management, occupational, technology and individual were extracted.

- Social factors include awareness of other's needs, eliminating employee stress and discomfort, developing the willingness to talk about self and awareness of the importance of communication, informal social interactions among employees, increasing the time for positive interaction, membership in social networks and access to social media and socializing employees through training programs.
- Competitive factors include attention to type and level of competition (visible and invisible), confidentiality of personal knowledge, promotion and preserve the competitive advantage, and unique position.
- Organizational factors include the organizational perspective and having strategy on knowledge sharing, the need for creativity, innovation and learning, paying attention to the role of coaches and organizational training to increase the ability to share knowledge, knowledge sharing processes as a part of job duties, presenting guideline for practical action, understanding the organizational structure, and attracting capacity for the organization;
- Motivational factors include creating interest among knowledge collaboration partners and satisfaction with ability recognition, commitment in a dynamic work environment, trust, learning

opportunities, motivation for work behavior and reduction of employees' resistance, empathy (unexpected kindness, voluntary help, personal satisfaction), helping (feeling happy and satisfied, no matter what he or she has received), recognizing people's contributions and increasing credit in sharing knowledge, paying attention to appraisal method and rewarding (tangible, intangible) practices, motivation for organizational competition, job security, organizational performance, lowering production costs, increasing innovation capability, enhancing interpersonal relationships, and fostering altruism for the benefit of the organization.

- Cultural factors include creating a sense of usefulness for the individual, appreciating personal knowledge for the organization, enhancing the sense of responsibility, linking the culture of knowledge sharing, national culture, organizational culture and knowledge-based culture, supporting ethical and mental norms, and promoting citizenship behavior.
- Leadership and management factors include the senior manager's support and commitment to sense employee safety, shared leadership, and coordination among employees.
- Occupational factors include increased job stability, job diversification and job rotation, job identity, job feedback, job importance, work with quality, job design, financial turnover, job satisfaction, job security, and team working.
- Technology factors include the creation of a knowledge-based bank for recording and searching of knowledge, the adoption of educational technology, information and communication technology, the installation of monitoring systems, and media services.
- Individual factors include collaboration among employees, sharing goals and priorities, individual plans and gain benefits from the others, understanding the perception level of learner, low individualism, unified community, group loyalty and commitment to organization, support and empowerment of staff knowledge levels, individual authority in the job planning and determining the method used, satisfying the primary needs, and the type of controlling or independence personality.

CONCLUSION

In this study, the application of the grounded theory (GT) methodology in knowledge management (KM) is reviewed. It is assumed in the GT that since theory is a process, complexities and organizational context must be involved when discovering it to better understand the phenomenon rather than simplifying and ignoring some aspects. As an inductive, theory discovery methodology, The GT facilitates the creation of theories of process, sequence and change related to organizations, positions, and social interactions.

This chapter focused on knowledge sharing and critical success factors (CSFs) of KM. Since GT is suitable for studying the complex multifaceted phenomena and is also well-equipped to explore socially related subjects, it helps identify the determinants of knowledge sharing, and therefore develop a framework for tacit knowledge sharing improvement. CSFs of KM and their relationships were presented in the form of a model.

Since KM is an important competitive advantage for all kinds of organizations, every company might attempt to have its own KM model. In this chapter, two knowledge management frameworks, one about the personal KM model in public libraries and the other related to the KM model in R&D projects for the energy industry, were examined. Furthermore, a study on the process of transforming knowledge into wisdom using GT has been reviewed.

REFERENCES

Agarwal, N. K., & Marouf, L. (2016). Quantitative and qualitative instruments for knowledge management readiness assessment in universities. *Qualitative and Quantitative Methods in Libraries*, *5*, 149–164.

Akhavan, P., Fathian, M., & Jafari, M. (2007). Exploring the basic elements of successful knowledge management system with presenting a theory through a semantic network. *International Journal of Engineering Science*, *18*(3-4), 31–38.

Akhavan, P., & Imani, S. (2016). Review and determination of the factors influencing knowledge sharing using grounded theory and techniques using DematelISM fuzzy. *Journal of Information Processing and Management*, *32*(1), 93–122.

Akhavan, P., & Zahedi, M. R. (2014). Critical success factors in knowledge management among project-based organizations: A multi-case analysis. *The IUP Journal of Knowledge Management*, *12*(1), 20–38.

Al-Qdah, M. S., AbuAli, A. N. F., Salim, J., & Khalil, T. (2018). A grounded theory for ICT-mediated tacit knowledge transferability in MNCs. *Interdisciplinary Journal of Information, Knowledge, and Management*, *13*, 311–335. doi:10.28945/4107

Amidi, M., Hashemzadeh, G., & Alizadeh, A. (2019). Knowledge management pattern for project-based organizations in energy industry: A Grounded Theory Study. *Journal of Petroleum Business Review*, *2*(2), 52 59.

Atarodi, A., Hariri, N., & Babalhavaeji, F. (2019). Transforming knowledge into wisdom: a grounded theory approach. *Library Philosophy and Practice,* 2955. Retrieved September 13, 2019, from https://digitalcommons.unl.edu/libphilprac/2955

Brome, K. (2012). Team knowledge management within an outsourced business systems software maintenance environment: a case study using grounded theory methods. *VISTAS: Education, Economy and Community*, *2*(1), 90–111.

Gao, T., Chai, Y., & Liu, Y. (2018). A review of knowledge management about theoretical conception and designing approaches. *International Journal of Crowd Science*, *2*(1), 42–51. doi:10.1108/IJCS-08-2017-0023

Grossman, M., & McCarthy, R. V. (2005). Qualitative approaches to knowledge management assessment. *Issues in Information Systems*, *VI*(2), 90–95.

Guta, L., & the Quantitative Versus Qualitative Research in Knowledge Management. (2013). Available at SSRN: https://ssrn.com/abstract=2218594

Hassanian, Z. M., Ahanchian, M. R., Ahmadi, S., Gholizadeh, R. H., & Karimi-Moonaghi, H. (2015). Knowledge creation in nursing education. *Global Journal of Health Science*, *7*(2), 44–55. PMID:25716383

Jabbary, N., & Madhoshi, M. (2014). Factors affecting knowledge sharing behavior in academic communities: Grounded theory. *International Journal of Education and Practice*, *Conscientia Beam*, *2*(6), 126–136.

Jelenic, D. (2011). The importance of knowledge management in organizations – with emphasis on the balanced scorecard learning and growth perspective. *Management, Knowledge and Learning International Conference*, 33-43.

Jones, M., & Alony, I. (2014). The use of grounded theory in research: knowledge sharing in thc Australian Film Industry. In H. Hasan (Eds.), Being Practical with Theory: A Window into Business Research (pp. 113-122). Academic Press.

Lakshman, C. (2007). Organizational knowledge leadership: A grounded theory approach. *Leadership and Organization Development Journal*, *28*(1), 51–75. doi:10.1108/01437730710718245

Liang, T.-P., Liu, C.-C., & Wu, C.-H. (2008). Can Social Exchange Theory Explain Individual Knowledge-Sharing Behavior? A Meta-Analysis. *ICIS 2008 Proceedings*. https://aisel.aisnet.org/icis2008/171

Martin, P. Y., & Turner, B. A. (1986). Grounded theory and organizational research. *The Journal of Applied Behavioral Science*, *22*(2), 141–157. doi:10.1177/002188638602200207

Matayong, S., Mahmood, A. K., & Ariffin, M. M. (2010). *Electronic knowledge sharing in Oil and Gas Sector: A grounded theory approach*. Retrieved September 15, 2019, from https://pdfs.semanticscholar.org/ebb0/965b0f78 5a378ca538a1251253e612bbf9b5.pdf

Omona, W., Weide, T. V. D., & Lubega, J. T. (2010). Knowledge management research using grounded theory strategy: applicability, limitations and ways forward. In *Special Topics in Computing and ICT Research, ICCIR 10: Proceedings of the 6th Annual International Conference on Computing and ICT Research*, (pp. 163-185). Academic Press.

Onions, P. E. W. (2006). *Grounded theory applications in reviewing knowledge management literature. Leeds Metropolitan University Innovation North Research Conference*, Leeds, UK.

Smith, A. D. (2004). Knowledge management strategies: A multi-case study. *Journal of Knowledge Management*, *8*(3), 6–16. doi:10.1108/13673270410541006

Sousa, C. A. A., & Hendriks, P. H. J. (2006). The diving bell and the butterfly: The need for grounded theory in developing a knowledge-based view of organizations. *Organizational Research Methods*, *9*(3), 315–338. doi:10.1177/1094428106287399

Tajedini, O., Sadatmoosavi, A., & Esfandiarpour, Y. (2018). Identification, extraction, organization and sharing of personal knowledge: Using grounded theory. *International Journal of Information Science and Management*, *16*(2), 143–160.

Wang, S., & Noe, R. A. (2010). Knowledge sharing: A review and directions for future research. *Human Resource Management Review*, *20*(2), 115–131. doi:10.1016/j.hrmr.2009.10.001

Wastell, D. G. (2001). *Barriers to effective knowledge management: Action Research Meets Grounded Theory*. Global Co-Operation in the New Millennium The 9th European Conference on Information Systems, Bled, Slovenia. 10.1108/13287260180000764

Yang, Y.-C. O., Yeh, J.-Y., & Lee, T. C. (2010). The critical success factors for knowledge management adoption a review study. *The 3rd International Symposium on Knowledge Acquisition and Modeling*.

Zheng, T. (2017). A literature review on knowledge sharing. *Open Journal of Social Sciences*, *5*(3), 51–58. doi:10.4236/jss.2017.53006

Chapter 7
Explaining Empowering Employees by Grounded Theory Methodology:
In Particular for Health Services

ABSTRACT

This chapter initially studies the concept of empowerment. Then, it moves on to a review of empowerment approaches, strategies, and processes. It also provides an overview of the application of the grounded theory in employee empowerment, and empowerment in nursing and the health services in particular. It is concluded that empowerment as a dynamic process results from the interrelationship between personal, culture, and organizational factors. To put it in other words, it is required in the process of empowerment that both the structure of the organization and the employees' perception of themselves and their roles undergo changes. This chapter provides discussion on factors influencing employee empowerment, such as supportive manager, employee resistance to challenge managers, communication without dialogue to recognize employees' viewpoints, manager's lack of visibility and employees' inability to interact with the manager, as well as organizational contexts such as budget, education, increasing authority and self-confidence, and participative decision-making.

DOI: 10.4018/978-1-7998-4252-1.ch007

INTRODUCTION

Most developing countries, regarding the problems of investing in the human resources, have now realized that their backwardness is not only due to a lack of physical capital, but also lack of human capital such as technical and professional skills, and lack of sufficient attention to sustainable growth. It is associated with the way of industrialization and development of these countries. Since the shortage or weakness of human resources leads to a reduction in the productive capacity of the economy and as a result, the economy will not be able to make full and proper use of the available physical capital. For this reason, many economists believe that concentrating and enhancing the vigor of human capital is a more important factor than concentrating on the physical capital during the economic development of developing countries. In fact, economic and social progress is impossible without reforming and improving the quality of human resources. Studies show that investing in this area is one of the most important factors that guarantees the growth of developed countries.

According to economists, investment in education or human capital is an important source of economic growth. Output, over the past 40 years, has been increased about 3.5 percent a year. The labor productivity growth, which is considered to be the major driver of increases in wages and standards of living, has measured about 2.4 percent per year. Education contributed to this growth, as estimated in different countries, between 13 and 30 percent of the total increase. Regardless of the extent of the contribution of education to growth in the past, the investment in other forms of capital may result in increased investment in human capital, due to the emergence of a post-industrial, knowledge-based economy (Sawhill et al., 2006). As economists asserted, physical capital in each country is regarded as the most important constituent of productive wealth. However, in the mid 1990's, the World Bank's assessment indicated that physical capital on average accounts only for 16% of total wealth, natural wealth for 20% and more importantly human capital for 64% and the potential investment on human capital is duly recognized. Based on this large scale recognition of the significance of human capital, the Governments are naturally forced to pay more attention and give due importance for education as an essential component of human development (Sethunath, 2009).

Human resources play a key role in enhancing the empowerment of the organization, and in fact, it is human resources that have the power of creativity by utilizing the ability to exercise their physical and spiritual power and knowledge. Certainly without these efficient human resources, the tool would be nothing more than solid and lifeless, and human resources would be able to produce and present their potentials with the synergy of groups, using past experience and skills. Empowerment has now become one of the managers' concerns since they have found that empowering employees increases the power base and dignity in the workplace. Staff who have self-awareness work more and have a stronger sense of participation in work. In general, empowerment occurs when well-trained employees are satisfied with their work, motivated, well-led, and rewarded for their decision-making in proportion to their performance.

Regarding the necessity of staff empowerment, it should be noted that factors such as rising public expectations, globalization growth and advanced technology, among others, are considered as distinguishing features that have made the 21st century organizations different from traditional ones. Traditional organizations only managed the employees' physical strength and energy. However, the modern organizations need to manage the employees' brainpower and creativity besides their energy. Under these circumstances, the hierarchical methods of command are not appropriate and, in addition, the employees must also show initiative and act fully autonomously, and quickly on the basis of problems. Therefore, the need to train employees who have self-management abilities has led to the empowerment of human resources as a new paradigm, attracting the attention of many management experts. These experts believe that both employees and managers will benefit from the advantages of empowerment. On the other hand, empowering by nurturing motivated and empowered employees will allow managers to respond faster and more appropriately to the dynamics of the competitive environment. In addition, empowerment is now recognized as a tool by which managers will be able to manage efficiently modern organizations with features such as the variety of channels of influence, the growth of reliance on horizontal and collaborative networks, the slight difference between managers and employees, and reduction of organizational belonging.

Today, organizations need to be managed in a highly competitive environment with fast-moving developments. In this context, managers do not have much time to control the staff and should devote most of their time and energy to scan the external and internal environment of the organization and delegate other daily-based tasks to the employees. Employees can perform assigned tasks well when they have the required skills, knowledge, ability and motivation, and understand organizational goals well. The empowerment process is the useful and helpful tool in this regard. Thus, empowerment is the process of giving power to individuals, through which people can overcome their feelings of helplessness. Empowerment in this sense results in the mobilization of individuals' intrinsic motivations.

This chapter initially studies the concept of empowerment. Then, it moves on to a review of empowerment approaches, strategies and processes. It also provides an overview of the application of the grounded theory (GT) in employee empowerment, and empowerment in nursing and the health services in particular.

EMPOWERMENT

Empowerment is defined, in Oxford Advanced Learner's Dictionary, as "the act of giving somebody more control over their own life or the situation they are in". Literally, it is providing somebody with the power or authority to do something. This term has been liberally applied since the late 1970s by academics and aid workers in the English-speaking world, including in social services and psychology, public health, adult literacy and community development (Simon 1994). Many sources of inspiration of the notion of empowerment can be traced back to various domains such as feminism, Freudian psychology, theology, the Black Power movement, and Gandhism (Simon, 1994). Empowerment encompasses the principles such as individuals and groups' ability to act in order to guarantee their own well-being or their right to participate in the process of making decisions; the decisions that concern them and have guided conducting research and social intervention among poor and marginalized populations for several decades in the United States (Simon, 1994).

Since employee empowerment has the potential to increase the opportunities of participation and involvement in decision making, it is regarded as a motivational practice aiming at increasing the performance. The core issues of employee empowerment include developing trust, motivation, participating in decision-making process, as well as removing any boundaries between an employee and top management (Meyerson and Dewettinck, 2012). It essentially contributes to organizational success and, for many authors, it is a factor with direct effect on employee performance, job satisfaction and organizational commitment (Meyerson and Dewettinck, 2012).

Empowerment also encourages people to participate more in decision-making process that affects their activities. In this way, we can provide opportunities for individuals to demonstrate that they can create and implement good ideas. Empowerment means simply encouraging people to play a more active role in their work and moving forward to take responsibility for improving their own activities and eventually achieving the level of competence they need without resorting to responsibility. Above all, they can make key decisions. Empowerment is to provide individuals with the tools they need to use to achieve their goals.

According to Conger and Kanungo (1988), power is considered to be the central point of empowerment, which contributes to strengthening this belief or weakening the belief in personal powerlessness. Transferring control results in redistribution of power and hence, it gives the authority to the employees to make and implement their own decisions. The relational and motivational meanings of empowerment are distinguished by the authors. The relational aspect concerns with studying the relationship between managers and workers both before and after empowerment. The motivational dimension is concerned with the suggestion of a process through which the employees can feel motivated by the initiative provided in this process. As Conger and Kanungo (1988) assert, empowerment is not simply empowering subordinates with power and resources but an intrinsic construct meaning "enabling".

Empowerment means to provide someone with power to do something. Power has a variety of meanings. Power in legal sense refers to authority, and in this case empowerment has the same meaning. On the other hand, power can also be interpreted as energy. In this case, empowerment means to energize. Energy transfer is the most plausible statement for the motivational sense of empowerment (Thomas and Velthouse, 1990).

Furthermore, the studies on the management revealed two complementary perspectives on empowerment at work; that is, the social-structural and the psychological perspectives. Table 1 shows that the differences between these two perspectives.

The social-structural empowerment perspective is aimed at limiting the conditions that prevent employees from gaining access to the organization's opportunity, information, support and resources required to make relevant decisions on their job or role (Spreitzer 2007). On the other hand, psychological empowerment deals with the psychological state of a subordinate perceiving

Table 1. Differences between the social-structural empowerment approach and the psychological empowerment approach (Spreitzer 2007)

Approach of social-structural empowerment	• Macro orientation. • Supervisor's behaviour as he/she empowers his/her subordinates. • Focusing on the social-structural or contextual conditions including empowering structures, policies, and practices that give employees the empowerment in the workplace.
Approach of psychological empowerment	• Micro orientation. • Subordinate's psychological state caused by his/her supervisor's empowering. • Focusing on the psychological experience related to empowerment in the workplace (meaningfulness, competence, self-determination and impact).

four dimensions of meaningfulness, competence, self-determination and impact, which is affected by empowering behaviors of the supervisor.

EMPOWERMENT STRATEGIES

The management of the organization is expected to provide facilities to implement the empowerment strategy. These strategies directly or indirectly change the attitudes and behaviors of employees and pave the way for specialized and empowered staff. Depending on the purpose and philosophy of the organization, its characteristics and employees and their roles, it is possible to implement a variety of strategies. Chadiha et al. (2004) point out three important strategies in employee empowerment.

Strategy 1- Increasing collective awareness through storytelling: when employees take responsibility for solving their problems, they are prone to striving to improve their individual and organizational lives. The storytelling approach as an essential factor of empowerment reinforces collaborative efforts. When people discover, create, or reflect their stories of collaboration, they actually tell the story of their own life in the organization in a positive way. Accepting staff's descriptions of problems and identifying their abilities are important elements of the empowerment approach in practice. Employees collaborate in small groups to tell their personal story of their tasks or experiences that occurred to them each month, and to think and talk about their own problems.

Strategy 2- Training problem-solving skills: employees need to increase their capacity for problem-solving skills. Problem-solving skills can lead to the empowerment of staff at the individual, interpersonal, and group levels, which is considered as a necessary step in changing an unfavorable situation. This strategy should allow employees to identify and solve their problems based on the content of stories that are formed in a collaborative environment. In this case, the group first summarizes the problem-solving goals. These goals include: problem identification, choosing one of the most important problems, choosing the goal to solve the problem, creative thinking to solve the problem and realizing the goals, and identifying resources to help achieving the goal.

Strategy 3- Supporting skills training: through support, employees are assured of building a large social structure within empowered groups. There are three types of support:

- self-support,
- manager's support of the individual,
- law protection of the individual.

The organization can extend collective support by writing, speaking, or presenting lectures by a legislator or political individual. Empowerment can be quickly achieved if the employees know that resources are available for

Table 2. Strategic employee empowerment (Sahoo and Das, 2011)

Authority delegation	Organizations have found that delegation of authority to the executives will promote the hidden talents or competencies to meet the business requirements in the areas like construction of new projects, operation and methods, effective employee engagement, etc.
Formation of several joint forums	Several joint forums comprising of equal representation from both workers and management side at all the levels of organization are formed to foster healthy employee relations climate and better organizational performance.
Sense of trusteeship	The employees trust their employers since they can rightly identify and implement several welfare measures for them. Moreover, the employers can motivate them for organizational achievements and fulfil their individual desires and needs.
Employees suggestion scheme	This provides opportunity to all employees to influence the managerial decision- making and involve themselves in organization building activities. The abilities of employees are fully utilized through encouraging them to make suggestions, and rewarding them.
Interaction with top executives	All employees are addressed at least once or twice a year in the meetings by the chief executive officer (CEO) along with the board of directors to discuss about the business issues of the company. It is, in fact, a platform for the employees to raise several issues, offer their views, and provide suggestions for survival and sustainability of the organization. The management can make the employees more emotionally attached with the organization by hosting a meal, lunch or dinner, after the meeting with the employees.

Keerthika et al. (2018) provided strategies to enhance employee empowerment.

Table 3. Strategies to enhance employee empowerment (Keerthika et al., 2018)

Training	These strategies include motivation and new hires throughout career, more education, and less supervision and guides. It also includes problem-solving and stimulating thinking.
Motivation	Taking advantage of opportunities is achieved if the employees are motivated. Motivation should be found in the nature of a person; it can't be taught or given. Autocratic leadership can de-motivate the employees.
Involvement	Making the employees involved in problem-solving process and quality circles can lead to their empowerment.
Job enlargement	The management can offer additional opportunities and tasks. Learning new skills provides individuals with new perspectives, resulting in identify new ways for quality improvement and innovations.
Job enrichment	Employees should make suggestions to improve vertical opportunities for promotion.

their personal development in the organization and there is support available along the way.

Sahoo and Das (2011) presented several strategies utilized to empower the existing employees.

Based on the managers' interpretation of the meaning of empowerment, their perceptions of organizational needs and the benefits of employee involvement, they employ different forms or applications of empowerment (Lashley and McGoldrick, 1994).

EMPOWERMENT PROCESS

Nowadays, no organization can survive without empowered staff and an annual calendar of training needs. Empowerment is neither a task nor an end in itself but a process, and should be seen as a part of organizational culture. Empowering employees is a process through which the culture of empowerment is developed. This culture allows sharing the visions, goals, decision boundaries and outcomes of their influences and efforts throughout the organization. In such a culture resources are also shared. Empowerment is provided and supported in order to obtain the resources needed for the effectiveness of the employees' activities. Some empowerment processes are as follows:

- **Information Sharing**: This means that information is easily accessible to employees. Access to information builds self-confidence and awareness of the current state of affairs and fosters the culture of trust and empathy. Lack of enough information prevents the employees to make

Table 4. Different forms of empowerment used by managers (Lashley and McGoldrick, 1994)

Employee empowerment	Empowerment by participation	Autonomous groupwork	As a group or team, the employees can enhance work life and productivity through exercising some form of responsible autonomy.
		Job enrichment	Job enrichment can be achieved when an employee is given greater responsibility and scope to make decisions and is expected to use the new skills.
		Empowerment via ownership	Employees can be provided with an opportunity to comment on, and maybe influence the policies applied at the most senior levels.
	Empowerment by involvement	Suggestion scheme	As a formalised mechanism, it can be applied to encourage employees to think creatively about their jobs and their job environment and to create ideas contributing to the development of the organization; thus, they can be rewarded on a specific basis as well.
		Quality circles	The interested employees can voluntarily join quality circles to meet regularly to identify, analyse and recommend solutions to common job-related problem usually under the guidance of a supervisor or a facilitator. Such employees tend to be more committed to the organization and have higher self-esteem.
		Team briefing	They provide a mechanism for managers and employees to meet on a regular base to consider operational problems. Thus, the consultation and suggestions from employees can be collected.
	Empowerment by delayering	Empowered manager	The removal of layers of managers often results in unit or junior managers, which provides the manager with a wider span of control. The manager will have to operate with more responsible autonomy and without direct supervision.

the right decisions. Employee access to information leads to a sense of belonging, performance improvement and a sense of responsibility. Information is the lifeblood of empowerment. Information shows the way to the employees and guides them what to do. Unfortunately, it is a misconception that if information is made available to employees, the role of managers will be diminished. Identification of the boundaries of decision-making and information enables the employees to adjust their activities within the permissible boundaries.

- **Work Autonomy**: It must be within the boundaries of the organization to prevent wasting energy. One of the main factors of determining the boundary of activities is the mission of the organization.

- **Restructuring Traditional Organizational Hierarchy Structure to Autonomous Groups**: A self-governing group includes employees who are fully responsible for executing a task or producing a product from the beginning to the end. Through the training courses, these groups are able to acquire the necessary skills, and at the same time, feel less dependent on managers and supervisors. The autonomous groups do not interfere with each other unless it is a step towards empowerment. The top management of the organization must have a strong belief in the support of the autonomous groups. The performance of the self-governing groups is so collaborative that it is not clear who is the leader of the group. These groups are empowered for doing things that wcrc previously only possible for managers, so these groups can be replaced by traditional hierarchies of the organization.

Empowered employees need less supervision and are more self-reliant. The organizations that have implemented the empowerment process have different roles for managers and supervisors rather than other organizations, in that they have changed roles and delegated part of their authority and power to employees. The manager has more of a coaching and goal setting role and spends most of his/her time in modifying the behaviors and perspectives, guidance of staff, removing obstacles and setting ideal goals, and believes that his/her power depends on having empowered employees. Thus, s/he takes actions to empower the staff and himself. Managers need to consider this fact that sometimes empowered employees are only willing to accept responsibility and decision in a specific job, and thus, there may be felt lack of required skills in other areas of task.

GROUNDED THEORY

The main focus of an exploratory approach is gaining an insight into a situation, phenomenon, thing, community or person that is little known. A different range of causes and alternative options for a solution of a specific problem are presented in the result section of the exploratory research; such a research leaves rooms for further researches. Moreover, as Saunders et al (2009) argued, reviewing the literature of the subject under investigation, interviewing with experts in the subject and/or conducting focus group interviews are used in the exploratory research. In exploratory research, it can be said that finding of the new data or insight determines the process of the research. Also, the

Table 5. Structural, cognitive and behavioral empowerment (Vali Nazari Ali Abadi and Goudarzvand Chegini, 2013)

Structural empowerment	
Information availability	More information leads people to experience self-regulating, self-control and more confidence. Authority and accuracy of decision-making can be achieved through accurate, timely, and relevant information. Participation in information is the initial step in empowering people and organizations. It provides opportunities for: • providing a deep understanding of the current situation; • making confidence throughout the organization; • eliminating the traditional hierarchy mentality; • helping people to be most responsible; • raising people to act like owners of the organization.
Reward system	Effects of a reward system include the followings: • increasing the frequency of optimal behaviour; • identifying and enhancing individual competence; • increasing participation in decision-making process in the workplace.; • improving initiative and creativity; • increasing job satisfaction; • improving the quality of work life; • increasing the quality of goods and services;, • increasing the organizational productivity, and making the organization ready for competition.
Psychological empowerment (behavioral)	
Meaning	It provides a match between the requirements of work role and the person's beliefs, values, and behaviours. It makes people in meaningful job, who have a higher sense of commitment, more involved.
Competence	It refers to: • self-efficacy; • the belief of the capacity to work; • the belief to have the capacity to apply the necessary effort; • the belief that any external barrier will be prevented.
Self-determination	It is a sense of choice in initiating and regulating actions. Self-determination refers to the efforts of individuals and group to increase their control over the way of working. It is concerned with job satisfaction

outcomes of the research that is referred to as interpretative research or GT approach provide answers to questions like what, how and why.

In qualitative method, the data collection techniques (such as interview) or data analysis procedures (such as categorizing data) are used that generate or use non-numerical data including pictures and video clips (Saunders et al. 2009). Moreover, qualitative methodologists described three major purposes for qualitative research: exploring, explaining or describing a phenomenon. These terms can be replaced by understanding, developing or discovering.

The human world can never be understood scientifically. What can best contribute to understanding this world is to arrive at a truth that makes a difference that opens up new possibilities for understanding. The methodological framework is qualitative approach that is mainly focused on GT approach. This approach is concerned with thinking about the concepts and building theories rather than testing the theory or hypothesis. Qualitative research is considered as an interpretive and naturalistic approach (Khan, 2014).

The GT approach has been used since 1970 in the studies on nursing that have focused on nursing practice and education. Since empowerment is regarded as a process rather than a static factor, a GT approach is preferred to conduct the studies on this concept. Furthermore, this approach has been selected due to the setting of nurses' practice, that is, a multidisciplinary team. Besides, GT focuses on identification, description, and explanation of interactional processes between and among individuals or groups within a given social context (Adib Hajbaghery and Salsali, 2005).

GROUNDED THEORY IN EMPOWERMENT

Using a GT approach, Mohammadnezhad et al. (2017) identified factors affecting employee empowerment presented in Islamic Azad University. The data collection tools were in-depth interviews and semi-structured interview. They recorded interviews and coded data using the coding stages, that is, open coding, axial coding, and selective coding. The following Table shows the participants' quotes, basic codes, axial codes, and core codes.

Regarding the mission of nursing, i.e. providing safe and high quality nursing care, the concept of empowerment is frequently used in nursing and the health services, particularly in relation to the quality of care. Patients, through safe nursing care can achieve their maximum level of wellness. Considering the importance of nursing services in any health system, the focus of the 54th World Health Assembly was on designing programs to strengthen and promote the nursing profession. In this regard, Adib Hajbaghery and Salsali (2005) designed a model for empowering nurses in Iran. The research questions were what processes influence the empowerment of nurses and what a suitable model is for empowerment of nurses in Iran.

They analyzed the nurses' experiences, their perceptions and the strategies affecting empowerment by using GT. Three main categories emerged from the data: personal empowerment, collective empowerment, and the culture and structure of the organization. The participants believed that empowerment is a dynamic process and is the result of mutual interaction between personal and collective traits of nurses as well as the culture and the structure of the organization. Power dynamics within the health care system is one of the

Table 6. Factors affecting employee empowerment (Mohammad Nezhad et al., 2017)

<table>
<tr><th>Core codes (as a process of selective coding)</th><th>Axial codes (as a process of axial coding)</th><th>Basic codes (the result of a coding process)</th><th>Quotes of the participants (coding process)</th><th>Row</th></tr>
<tr><td rowspan="17">Factors affecting employee empowerment based on the opinions of experts</td><td rowspan="3">Objectives</td><td>Intention</td><td>Essential objectives for employee empowerment.</td><td rowspan="3">1</td></tr>
<tr><td>Mission</td><td>Organization's mission and philosophy of existence of activities. Each organization is created for the purpose to meet a need.</td></tr>
<tr><td>Vision</td><td>Vision is the projection of a future status of an organization and answer to the question of where the organization intends to go.</td></tr>
<tr><td rowspan="3">Planning</td><td>Program</td><td>Determination of the way of doing a job for employee in order to achieve a predetermined objective.</td><td rowspan="3">2</td></tr>
<tr><td>Strategic planning</td><td>Planning process to achieve long-term objectives. Planning for staff empowerment must be performed at the top level of organization.</td></tr>
<tr><td>Operational planning</td><td>It is done to achieve short-term objectives of the employee empowerment aligned with strategic planning for growth and decision making.</td></tr>
<tr><td rowspan="2">Compliance</td><td>Acceptance of responsibility by executives</td><td>Having highly responsible executives towards employees encourages employees to comply with orders.</td><td rowspan="2">3</td></tr>
<tr><td>The presence of executive</td><td>The importance of executive presence as a factor that leads people to obey.</td></tr>
<tr><td rowspan="2">Accountability</td><td>Task</td><td>Employee empowerment for being responsible to do duties and tasks.</td><td rowspan="2">4</td></tr>
<tr><td>Commitment</td><td>Empowerment of employees to be committed to do what they are responsible for.</td></tr>
<tr><td rowspan="2">Environmental conditions</td><td>Appropriate work environment</td><td>The workplace must have necessary resources and facilities.</td><td rowspan="2">5</td></tr>
<tr><td>Psychological and social environment</td><td>The most important factor of the workplace is psychological and social conditions of the workplace.</td></tr>
<tr><td rowspan="5">Job nature</td><td>The value of work</td><td>One of the factors with a great value is coordination among people in the organization. People tend to work in such an organization.</td><td rowspan="5">6</td></tr>
<tr><td>Self-independence</td><td>Independence is one of the human needs. This means that one can make decisions to have experience, do mistakes, and learn skills.</td></tr>
<tr><td>Job opportunities</td><td>Employees follow job opportunities.</td></tr>
<tr><td>Job facilities</td><td>Facilities in organization helps employee to achieve personal goals and organizational objectives.</td></tr>
<tr><td>Job challenge</td><td>More empowered employees pursue a career that has more challenges.</td></tr>
</table>

impediments that hinders nurses from presenting their capabilities that can be required as essential ingredients of empowerment.

- **Personal Empowerment**: personal empowerment, according to the participants, depends on three variables: having authority, professional self-confidence for the application of professional knowledge, and skills.
- **Collective Empowerment**: the participants stated that collective power of nurses or the power of the profession of nursing is the result of the interaction between supportive management and unity. They believed that unity of nurses and assembling in nursing organizations act as an efficient way to increase their professional power. The participants were aware they can obtain better working condition as well as professional self-regulation by collective power through which their voices are also stronger and more influential. Thus, they will be able to develop standards for their profession as well as a clear definition of the scope of authority and responsibility of each nurse in his/her specific setting, giving them the possibility to apply their professional power in their practice settings to provide high-quality patient care.

Nurses frequently emphasized on the role of supportive management on empowering them. Three subheadings were categorized based on the participants' views and experiences on supportive management; they include provision of job-related supports, financial support, and emotional support. However, most nurses felt unsupported. Factors such as shortage in the nursing workforce and lack of supplies such as sheets, dressing equipment and so on, prevented nurses from using their professional knowledge and skills. As a result, the clients' needs were not met, causing the feeling of inadequacy and dis-empowerment in nurses.

- **The Culture and Structure of the Organization**: this is a two-dimensional factors; it can either motivate or inhibit nurses to feel empowered. As the participants noted, these factors prevented the nurses to show their competence and power in the patient care settings. Two sub-headings were determined for the data related to the cultural and organizational variables: the public culture and organizational culture and structure.
- **The Public Culture**: according to the most of the nurses participating in this study, the Iranian people have a poor image of nursing. They

believed that the general public did not recognize nursing as a specialized profession. In fact, the public status physicians have in the society has affected the culture of health care organization and the inter-professional relationships have been affected by this culture, resulting in an uneven power relation in which the doctors have the last word.

- **Organizational Culture and Structure:** as the majority of the participants stated, public and organizational culture has caused development of a structure in which the physicians are in a higher position in the health care system. Such physician-centered structure affected the design of the nursing system. Three parts of this system, according to the participants, included nursing services, nursing education, and nursing research.
- **The Structure of Nursing Services:** one of the barriers and limitations to the true potential and capability of the nursing profession is classifying nursing services as in-patient settings. According to the participants, this problem is a result of the ambiguity of scope and standard of practice for nurses in the national healthcare system.
- **The Structure of Nursing Education**: despite of the integral role of education in the process of empowerment, there was great concern regarding the education system, which originates from entry into nursing school. Another factor with a significant role in the weakness of nurses is role models. Lack of confidence, competency, and autonomy of the nurse educators led to ineffectiveness of these models for students. Continuing education was considered to be critical for nurses to maintain competency in the clinical setting. In this context, they can contribute, with high confidence, to improving nursing practice and building a community of empowered professionals. However, the cycle of empowerment is blocked by the Ministry of Health and Medical Education due to low staffing and lack of staff development resources.
- **The Structure of Nursing Research:** there are reasons affecting research utilization or the implementation of evidence-based practice by nurses. The traditional structure of hospitals, poor quality of education, lack of continuing education, heavy workloads, no time, no mentoring and/or training in designing and conducting research, lack of financial resources, poorly defined nursing roles, lack of team work, and no opportunities for interdisciplinary relationships can be mentioned as the influential factors on the structure of nursing research.

Figure 1.GT approach for empowering nurses (Adib Hajbaghery and Salsali, 2005)

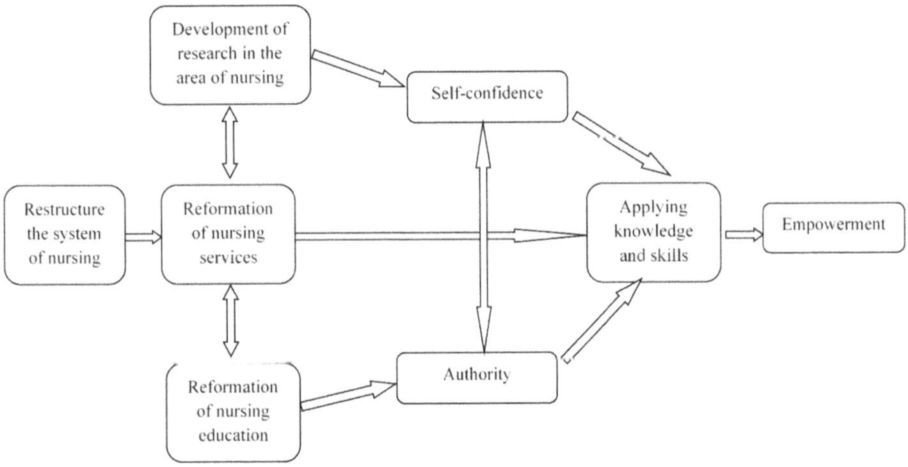

According to the model, empowerment as a dynamic process results from interrelationship of personal and organizational factors. In other words, some changes are required in the process of empowerment in both the structure of the organization and in the nurses' perception of themselves and their role. The results of these changes are transformation and the development of new perspective by the nurses, both about themselves and their organization. This transformation will lead the individuals to seek new knowledge, and develop new problem-solving skills. Moreover, they can acquire a variety of solutions that can be observed in their thinking and actions. As a result, nurses will apply evidence-based practice to support their nursing care actions rather than subservient behavior and routine-based nursing care. Thus, it is a need to make nurses to function at this level.

The cornerstone for restructuring the nursing system is reforming and the close inter-relationship of the three sub-systems. In this sense, competent and confident nurses are the result of nursing education; supporting high quality patient care and other subsystems is the outcome of nursing services; and the interaction of nursing research and other sub-systems will lead to form an interdisciplinary team which will provide the knowledge and skills for conducting research through which the issues will be identified and creative solutions will be provided.

Both micro and macro levels of empowerment of nurses/nursing has been of consideration in studies (Fig. 2). The macro level concerns the domain of nursing in the health system. Findings of this study indicated that nursing, its mission and its position have not been clearly defined in Iran. So, initially and most importantly, nursing, and its mission should be defined and its position in the national healthcare system should be established. Thus, a committee as "the Scientific Committee for Defining Nursing and its Mission" (SCDNM) is recommended to be established. The members of the Iranian

Figure 2. Micro and macro levels of empowerment of nurses (Adib Hajbaghery and Salsali, 2005)

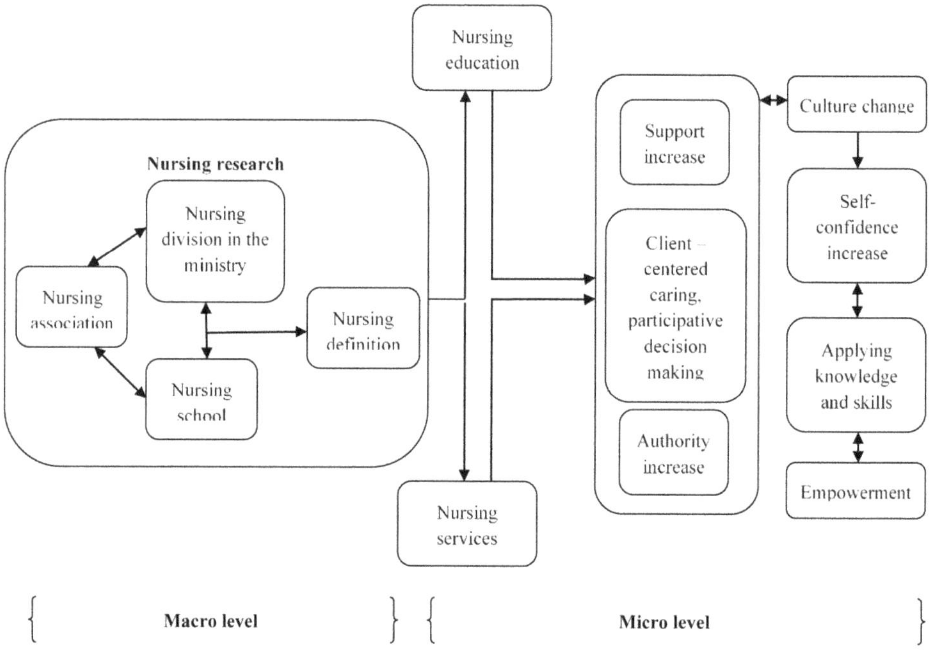

Nursing Organization (INO), nursing schools and the division of nursing in the Ministry of Health are considered to be the members of this committee. These three parts are now separate but they will be connected through their research subsystems for the execution of important mission (see Fig. 2).

To provide a better understanding of what fosters or constrains staff nurses' empowerment and to extend the theory of nurse empowerment, Udod (2014) investigated the way of exercising power in a hospital setting by staff nurses and their managers. Power is an integral part to empowerment, and there is a need to advance a theoretical understanding of power in the nurse–manager relationship, based on the challenges in nurses' work environment and nurse outcomes that have been considered by administrators, researchers, and policy-makers. The methodology used in this study is GT. The basic social process was seeking connectivity. It indicated the critical role of the manager in the work environment and the need to managers in order to share power with nurses in the provision of a safe, quality patient care.

While responding to organizational demands, the nurse empowerment theory was extended to the theory of seeking connectivity formed by conditions, actions, and consequences. First, the relationship between nurses and their managers was affected by the conditions caused by five contextual factors. Second, five themes showed how nurses and their managers exercised power in their relationships: (a) working without an anchor, (b) silencing forms of communication, (c) stepping up of power, (d) positioning to resist, and (c) experiencing the potentiality of enabling. The two latter factors are concerned with nurses' responses to the relationship of power. The nurses responded to and shaped the situations in which they found themselves in order to provide patient care in satisfying ways through with the contextual factors (conditions), and as a result of nurse–manager actions and interactions.

- **Organizational Context:** The relationship between nurses and their manager in the hospital setting was affected by five key contextual factors. First, the budget was the common-used term by the nurses; their function and practice was influenced by economic efficiency and resource constraints. Second, working short, according to the nurses, was the result of a lack of nursing personnel; the budgetary reasons preventing filling the sick days and hence, it affected the way nurses managed their workloads. Shortage of professional nursing staff influenced the nurses' work activities become less controllable. Third, all nurses expressed concern about being interfered with the organizational priorities; they had to respond immediately to overcapacity alerts, provide documentation, and dispense medications at the designated time, while also responding to myriad non-nursing duties rather than paying attention to direct patient activities. Fourth, the nature of policies dominantly influenced the nurses' work since the institutional policy decisions made the nurses' judgment and actions in line with managerial priorities. Such policies occasionally affected nurses' ability to provide good care as they had to meet the organizational demands instead of caring for the patients. Finally, organizational priorities caused an increase in the scope of nurses' workloads, guiding them to perceive the importance and significance of their actions for patient safety and their professional licenses.

- **Working Without an Anchor**: In this category, nurses expressed concerns about lack of consistent support of their manager. However, the extent of this experience for each nurse was different. The manager was defined by nurses as nursing and patient care practices subordinate to organizational priorities. Invisible manager and lack of interaction between nurses and the manager led the nurses to think they were working in isolation. It also adversely affected nurses' access to knowledge and engagement in decision-making, as well as manager's understanding of patient needs and time constraints. From nurses' perspective, managers had limited clinical knowledge and experience, hindering them from understanding the complexities of nurses' work and advocating the interests of nurses and patients. In general, working without an anchor indicated the nurses' tension in meeting organizational demands while providing patient care, without the consistent and active engagement of the manager in facilitating and guiding professional responsibilities.
- **Silencing Forms of Communication**: Silencing forms of communication indicates how communication patterns were restricted between managers and nurses, and hence, they reinforce the isolation that nurses experienced. According to nurses, they have to follow the policy changes posed by the manager and have no chance to express their viewpoints. Regarding staffing levels, the patient delivery model, and documentation as either restricted or non-existent, nurses described input into policy changes. The policies communicated to the subordinates in a way that it seemed they are mandatory rules. The management usually uses an educator to push the policies instead of communicating them with the staff by preparing and meeting with them. In general, one-way communication with minimal ability to exchange ideas could be a way for managers to minimize conflict and retain power. They could also respond to organizational mandates over which they had little control.
- **Stepping Up of Power:** This factor was categorized by the nurses as the manager's supportive attitudes, guidance, and behaviors; nurses can control their work despite of the contextual demands of the workplace. The manager played a mediating role to support nurses and/or resolve conflict between nurses and patients, families, or other health professionals, especially in case of a power differential. According to one of the nurses, the manager is someone who could support nurses in ways that they can perform their patient care activities more easily. Nurses expressed that they could respond favorably if the manager

engaged with nurses, asked for feedback, and exchanged ideas with them. Moreover, nurses characterized stepping up of power as the manager's accessibility on the unit, seeking the demands of nurses' work and redirecting her/his activities to actively support nurses in their provision of patient care, which resulted in raising nurses' comfort level in interacting with the manager and nurses' trust in their manager.

- **Nurse Responses Positioning to Resist:** Nurses used different resistance strategies in an intermittent manner to challenge the power imbalances between themselves and their managers. They deployed these strategies in different forms and through different approached rather than applying all or no approach Data analysis showed that there were deep-rooted resistances with significant but unapparent roles. Yet, there were also overt resistances at other times. Positioning to resist was also identified as the means used by nurses to give their manager an opportunity to ascertain her/his fitness for the role of manager. The subtle and not so subtle strategies used by nurses were convincing to the manager to function in a way they perceived acceptable. Nurses had many suggestions for a manager in an informal meeting to persuade her to change her behavior. The forms of resistance were more overt when nurses' workload was unmanageable; these forms of resistance were particularly evident in the actions related to policies. For example, they did not adhere to the new patient care delivery model and not documenting immediately. One way adopted by nurses to cope with workload was performing the required minimum. Occasionally, some acts of resistance remained unproductive, yet the most successful acts of resistance resulted from their collective decision to act as patient advocates. A more detailed analysis of resistance related to the exercise of power between nurses and their manager will be outlined in a future publication.
- **Experiencing the Potentiality of Enabling:** Nurses experienced the potentiality of enabling, in case that the manager showed supportive behaviors, as advocating for good-quality patient care. Nurses could believe in the manager's reliability and dependability and could gain their sense of control over their work when the manager minimized the demands of the organization, which, in turn, made the nurses able to provide the quality of care they believed necessary to promote and enhance patients' health and well-being. Nurses had experiences of the paralyzing fears that patients felt about advanced medical therapies or life-threatening surgeries. Nurses saw patients as being attentive

> and as feeling confident that the nurse was making a difference to their recovery and well-being. Nurses believed that the intervention of the manager in organizational processes and practices made them able to focus on direct patient care. In this sense, the nurses had the opportunities to use their knowledge and expertise to promote good health behaviors and health outcomes.

A substantive theory developed by Slatyer et al. (2015) explained the hospital nurse's perspective of caring for patients in severe pain using GT. The significant pain can delay healing and increase the risk of developing chronic pain. Nurses are affected by patients' ongoing pain and distancing from such patients may be their strategy to cope with consequent anxiety and helplessness. The strategies to support nurses' coping, their patients and, ultimately, their retention in the nursing workforce will be demonstrated through understanding nurses' responses to patients in severe pain. Data collection tools, based on theoretical sampling, were semi-structured interviews with nurses and participant observation, including structured observations of nurses who cared for patients in pain. Persisting severe pain of patients caused a basic psychosocial problem of feelings of disempowerment in the nurse participants. In response, they used a basic psychosocial process of seeking empowerment through which they could feel comfort in order to resolve distress and exhaustion associated with disempowerment. This coping process included three stages: building connections; finding alternative ways to comfort; and suppressing emotional distress. The substantive theory suggested a link between the nurses' disempowerment and a coping response that contributes to supporting nurses' practice. Strategies indicated include enhanced communication protocols, access to advanced practice nurses, use of nonpharmacological comfort measures, utilization of ward-based pain resource nurses, and unit-specific pain management education.

Various organizational practices can cause agile workforce empowerment. Khodabandeh et al. (2018) using GT pointed out that the agility of human resources is due to a set of individual-organizational, individual-personal, organizational and occupational attributes. Yazdkhasti et al. (2019) designed a model for the empowerment of Iranian women in managing menopause using the GT on 40-60-year-old women to understand the actual needs and provide a divergent view for health policy-makers.

CONCLUSION

Employee empowerment exists in the framework of the purpose of the organization. Empowerment enables the employee to take the right decision, keep the right priority, and do the right action without extra supervision. This happens in conditions provided by the organizational culture. Employee empowerment provides the opportunities for the management to gain competitive advantage. This chapter initially studies the concept of empowerment. Then, it moves on to a review of empowerment approaches, strategies and processes. It also provides an overview of the application of the grounded theory in employee empowerment, and empowerment in nursing and the health services in particular.

Each of the staff working in the hospital as a part of the service industry has the potential to interact with all types of patients. In health services, employee empowerment makes the employees extremely patient-centric. Each interaction is considered as a unique experience and provides an opportunity to build the image of the hospital in the patients' eyes. Nurses need to be empowered to make their optimum contribution.

As a conclusion, empowerment is viewed as a dynamic process resulted from interrelationship of personal, culture, and organizational factors. In other words, some changes, in the process of empowerment, are required in the structure of the organization and the employees' perception of themselves and their role. This study discussed about the factors influencing employee empowerment, including supportive manager, employee resistance to challenge managers, communication without dialogue to elicit employees' viewpoints, manager's lack of visibility and employees' inability to interact with the manager, as well as organizational contexts such as budget, education, increasing authority and self-confidence, and participation in decision-making process.

REFERENCES

Adib Hajbaghery, M., & Salsali, M. (2005). A model for empowerment of nursing in Iran. *BMC Health Services Research*, *5*(1), 24. doi:10.1186/1472-6963-5-24 PMID:15769297

Chadiha, L. A., Adams, P., Biegel, D. E., Auslander, W., & Gutierrez, L. (2004). Empowering African American women informal caregivers: A literature synthesis and practice strategies. *Social Work*, *49*(1), 97–108. doi:10.1093w/49.1.97 PMID:14964522

Conger, J. A., & Kanungo, R. N. (1988). The empowerment process: Integrating theory and practice. *Academy of Management Review*, *13*(3), 471–482. doi:10.5465/amr.1988.4306983

Keerthika, R., Henry Edward Roy, S., Karthikeyan, G., & Chennai, R.E.C. (2018). Employee empowerment- challenges and strategies. *IOSR Journal of Business and Management*, *20*(6), 54-57.

Khan, S. N. (2014). Qualitative research method: Grounded theory. *International Journal of Business and Management*, *9*(11), 224–233. doi:10.5539/ijbm.v9n11p224

Khodabandeh, N., Mohammdi, N., Doroudi, H., & Mansouri, A. (2018). Designing a human resource agility model based on grounded theory approach (Study Case: Social Security Organization), Iranian journal of educational. *Sociology*, *1*(7), 163–179.

Lashley, C., & McGoldrick, J. (1994). The limits of empowerment: Critical assessment of human resource strategy for hospitality operations. *Empowerment in Organizations*, *2*(3), 25–38. doi:10.1108/09684899410071671

Meyerson, G., & Dewettinck, B. (2012). Effect of empowerment on employees performance. *Advanced Research in Economic and Management Sciences*, *2*, 40–46.

Mohammad Nezhad, M., Nazem, F., & Abolmaali, K. (2017). Identification empowerment predisposing factors in Islamic Azad University – A grounded theory approach. *Iranian Journal of Educational Sociology*, *1*(4), 64–72.

Sahoo, C. K., & Das, S. (2011). Employee empowerment: A strategy towards workplace commitment. *European Journal of Business and Management*, *3*(11), 46–54.

Saunders, M., Lewis, P., & Thornhill, A. (2009). *Research methods for business students* (5th ed.). Harlow: Prentice Hall.

Sethunath, R. (2009). Universal Education: where we stand? (a review of the role of India's Sarva Siksha Abhiyan in Achieving Universal Primary Education. In J. Godwin Prem Singh (Ed.), *Millennium Development Goals edited*. Allied Publishers Pvt. Ltd.

Simon, B. L. (1994). *The empowerment tradition in American social work: A history*. New York: Columbia University Press.

Slatyer, S., Williams, A. M., & Michael, R. (2015). Seeking empowerment to comfort patients in severe pain: A grounded theory study of the nurse's perspective. *International Journal of Nursing Studies*, *52*(1), 229–239. doi:10.1016/j.ijnurstu.2014.06.010 PMID:25035166

Spreitzer, G. (2007). Taking stock: A review of more than twenty years of research on empowerment at work. In C. Cooper & J. Barling (Eds.), *The Handbook of Organizational Behavior* (pp. 54–72). Sage Publications.

Thomas, K. W., & Velthouse, B. A. (1990). Cognitive Elements of Empowerment: An "Interpretive" Model of Intrinsic Task Motivation. *Academy of Management Review*, *15*(4), 666–681. doi:10.5465/AMR.1990.4310926

Udod, S. (2014). Seeking connectivity in nurses' work environments: Advancing nurse empowerment theory. *CJNR*, *46*(3), 110–127. doi:10.1177/084456211404600307 PMID:29509488

Vali Nazari Ali Abadi, M., & Goudarzvand Chegini, M. (2013). Process of employee empowerment (Concepts and dimensions). *Kuwait Chapter of Arabian Journal of Business and Management Review*, *2*(11), 76–83. doi:10.12816/0001261

Yazdkhasti, M., Negarandeh, R., & Behboodi Moghadam, Z. (2019). An empowerment model of Iranian women for the management of menopause: A grounded theory study. *International Journal of Qualitative Studies on Health and Well-being*, *14*(1), 1665958. doi:10.1080/17482631.2019.1665958 PMID:31589094

Chapter 8
A Grounded Theory Approach for the Study of Organizational Burnout:
Particularly for Caregivers in the Workplace

ABSTRACT

Burnout is a kind of psychological withdrawal as a particular response to stress. As a costly coping mechanism, it can have adverse impacts on the motivation, performance, and personal wellbeing of special service providers. Ineffectiveness of direct and active problem-solving efforts gives rise to the burnout response. The professions dealing with high levels of stress, including healthcare, social work, police work, teaching, and customer services are regarded as the occupations most at risk of burnout. There is limited qualitative research and in particular grounded theory (GT) on a subjective definition of job burnout by employees. The present study is organized to contribute more qualitative studies to concentrate more on the application of GT approach in the field of occupational burnout. Since it examines current studies of occupational burnout that focused on GT, it is of particular value.

DOI: 10.4018/978-1-7998-4252-1.ch008

INTRODUCTION

Organizational burnout is a state of fatigue or frustration caused by one's self-sacrifice as well as one's lifestyle or relationships that do not lead to the desired outcome (Vahdani et al., 2013). Organizational burnout is defined as the psychological response to chronic job stress (Zarei et al., 2012). The inconsistency between the nature of the job and the nature of the job holder results in negative consequences; For example, teacher burnout leads to depression, fatigue, and a severe decline in performance that causes illness and early retirement (Zarei et al., 2012). Occupational burnout is an occupational hazard that reduces the employees' physical and mental energy (Tabarsa et al., 2011).

An exploratory-qualitative research started the initial basis of studying burnouts. The social and clinical psychology-based ideas composed the topics of studies conducted mostly by the researchers involved in these fields. The concepts involving interpersonal relations, i.e. how people perceive and respond to others, were utilized in studies based on a social perspective. These concepts included detached concern, dehumanization in self-defense, and attribution processes. Moreover, concepts such as motivation and emotion (and especially coping with emotional arousal) were investigated. These two concepts were the topics of studies with a clinical perspective as well, but the difference is that these concepts, in clinical perspective, were examined more in terms of psychological disorders, such as depression. The subsequent studies with a perspective of industrial-organizational psychology emphasized on work attitudes and behaviors. Burnout, at this point, was conceptualized as a form of job stress, primarily focused on the organizational context rather than on the physical characteristics of the experienced stress (Maslach and Leiter, 2016).

Though all jobs dealing with human health can be stressful, it is of great importance and sensitivity how the caregivers cope with occupational burnout. In addition, generating theory in behavioral and social sciences can be resulted from using grounded theory (GT) in these fields. This chapter is aimed at examining application of GT in the field of job burnout and in particular for caregivers in the workplace.

ORGANIZATIONAL BURNOUT

Psychological burnout syndrome is a response to chronic social stressors at work, which encompass the strongest emotional stressors such as exhaustion, pessimism and indifference to work, feelings of inadequacy and failure (Bianchi et al., 2018). In fact, burnout occurs when people feel overwhelmed by emotional stress in their workplace and their activities are not as productive as they might expect and are blamed by clients for lack of productivity (Azarbarzin, 2009). A satisfactory and compatible job may lead to dissatisfaction and incapacity and makes the individual having inconveniency. Undoubtedly, many jobs are stressful. Many employees in organizations know how to manage these pressures while some others may feel tense due to unbearable pressure or poor awareness and ability to cope. Constant worrying causes traumas, which is called job burnout (Rahimi, 2009).

Job burnout is the result of a particular type of coding and mental interpretation of individuals' work stressors and pressures (Swider and Zimmerman, 2010). Occupational burnout is considered to be a global phenomenon, which is associated with the quality of the working environment, workload, relationships, and conflict (Squires et al., 2014). Maslach and Jackson (1981) found that burnout can reduce the person's ability to cope with stressors and syndromes such as physical and emotional exhaustion, which can lead to a negative self-concept, a negative attitude toward work, and a lack of communication with colleagues and clients while on duty. Generally speaking, stress and burnout are the two professional risks everyone is exposed to.

Thus, there is a great deal of similarities between the definitions of burnout, and it can be concluded that there is an agreement on them.

1. Burnout consists of multiple dimensions: emotional exhaustion, depersonalization, and reduced personal accomplishment.
2. Burnout occurs in the workplace.
3. Burnout is somehow linked to job stress.
4. Burnout has many symptoms; that is why referred to as burnout syndrome.

Emotional exhaustion, depersonalization, and reduced personal accomplishment can be mentioned as the symptoms of burnout. Burnout is often illustrated as a process caused by work variables, individual variables, and loss of interest or detachment from one's services (Maslach, et al., 2001). The

Maslach Burnout Inventory (MBI) is used to measure three levels of burnout: emotional exhaustion, depersonalization, and personal accomplishment.

A. Emotional exhaustion: it implies excessive physical and mental fatigue and develops when one feels s/he no longer has enough energy to work (Shojafard et al., 2014). In fact, emotional exhaustion as a negative emotion is overwhelmed in the individual and makes him/ her helpless (Spooner, 2004). It makes the individual feel drained and left with no adequate resources to cope (Hosseinzadeh, 2012). As the central quality of burnout, it is associated with the emotional demands of work that may limit the capacity of a clinician to be engaged and receptive to clients (Maslach et al., 2001).

Some symptoms of emotional exhaustion are as follows:

1. Continuous and distressing complaints of feeling tired after a brief mental or physical effort,
2. Feeling confused,
3. Feeling pain and muscle discomfort,
4. Tension headaches (not migraine headaches),
5. Sleep disorder,
6. Irritability.

B. Depersonalization: as a severe negative response, it happens to people who are usually recipients of service (Hosseinzadeh, 2012). Detachment within the self and distancing oneself from work via depersonalization often causes ignorance of personal strengths and qualities and thereupon makes unfavorable relationship with others (Shojafard et al., 2014). The feeling of detachment oneself from work is, in fact, a response to the emotional strains of work. In addition, depersonalization has been illustrated as a form of cognitive distancing and cynicism resulted from emotional exhaustion (Maslach, et al., 2001).
C. Reduced personal accomplishment: it refers to the individual's sense of success and ability to perform on the job (Hosseinzadeh, 2012). It occurs when the sense of competition and the sense of pleasure to work with others are reduced (Shahnaz Doost et al. 2011). On the other hand, it reveals the sense of dissatisfaction with work activities as well as low motivation and low self-esteem, which leads to low professional performance and less productive job turnover (Shojafard et al., 2014).

Emotional exhaustion and depersonalization prevent one to realize his/her abilities to be effective and competent (Maslach et al., 2001).

BURNOUT AND QUALITATIVE RESEARCH

The qualitative research is functioned to find the meaning constructed by people; that is, how people make sense of their world and the experiences they have in the world (Merriam, 2009). Unlike the quantitative approach that seeks to enumerate the nature of the phenomenon via surveys, statistics, or other quantitative methods, a qualitative design lets the investigator find the meaning and experience of a phenomenon for the population under study rather than regarding straightforward descriptions of the occurrences (Tracy, 2013). Further, qualitative research is not concerned with identifying cause and effect relationships but emphasizes more on understanding human nature and investigation of their lived experiences (Willig, 2012).

The approach used in qualitative research methodology is inductive; it explores the experiences, perceptions, and meaning for the phenomena (Morgan, 2014). Data collection and analysis take place at the same time (Morgan, 2014). Qualitative research contains intensive interviews of open-ended questions that contribute to eliciting each participant's interpretation of his or her experience (Charmaz, 2006). Listening, observing with sensitivity, and encouraging the person to respond are regarded as the roles of an interviewer (Charmaz, 2006). Dual subjectivity is considered in open-ended interviewing, through which the research participant's beliefs and interpretations as well as the researchers' subjective processes are emphasized (Morgan, 2014). As a major strength of qualitative research methodology, it gives the researcher the opportunity to learn more about other's beliefs and meanings; that is, the subjective preferences and expectations that can be observed in their behaviors (Morgan, 2014). Open-ended questions make the chance to discuss about the topics that emerge during the course of the conversation (Morgan, 2014). Moreover, an exceptionally wide range of factors, perhaps relevant, and the connections among those factors can be checked through open-ended interviewing (Morgan, 2014).

For exploring the phenomenon of burnout, the qualitative methods can be best suited. Since it takes into account the dynamic nature of human beings and understands that humans largely construct reality themselves, the statistical description cannot be used. In fact, reality is not something to be determined and then quantified (Creswell, 2013). The use of qualitative methods to study the phenomenon of work burnout allows the researcher to dig deeper into this occurrence than has been done in available studies. Furthermore, the vague characterizations of burnout in the research literature can be unpacked through a qualitative approach to this phenomenon.

The qualitative methodology has not been widely used in studying burnout. Using a mixed approach with a semi-structured interview and the Occupational Fatigue Exhaustion Recovery Scale, Steege et al. (2017) explored nurse leader fatigue. According to the results of this study, nurse leaders experience fatigue, and in comparison to other nurse roles, nurse managers in particular experience relatively high levels of chronic fatigue. In a study conducted with the aim of measuring compassion fatigue and burnout in a trauma team, Berg et al. (2016) used a focus group methodology. The findings of this qualitative approach study confirmed the presence of compassion fatigue and burnout syndrome in the minds of the trauma team. Keyvanara et al. (2019) investigated factors affecting job burnout among operating room staff of teaching hospitals affiliated to Isfahan University of Medical Sciences using qualitative content analysis. They concluded that internal factors of the organization (e.g. lack of recruitment, ignorance of employees' mental health, etc.), external factors (e.g. economic problems, cultural issues, etc.), and individual and personal factors (e.g. personal problems, lack of motivation, etc.) are the main causes of job burnout.

Observation is the initial step in GT and then, it seeks to find patterns, themes, or common categories. GT is built as an inductive-deductive feedback loop in which hypotheses or hunches are tested as the conceptual model. Then, meanings in the patterns can be developed to concepts and hypotheses. According to Charmaz's (2006) description of GT, it refers to systematic, yet flexible, guidelines for collection and analysis of qualitative data in order to construct theories grounded in the data themselves. Constant comparisons must be utilized, while conducting more interviews, by comparing new information to the concepts and hypotheses made in previous interviews as well as the examination of contrasts across respondents, situations, and settings. New questions may be raised based on topics and themes made by participants in previous interviews; these ideas can be challenged, refined, and extended by the researcher (Morgan, 2014) in future interviews. New questions can be added in the list of the interview guide as the study proceeds. What is of great concern in qualitative research design is the quality, not quantity of the data, and hence, sampling is not aimed at maximizing breadth or reach, but achieving saturation of information about a specific topic. According to Charmaz (2006), identifying a phrase, a code, to identify the content of these phrases is the first step in qualitative coding. In the second step, these codes are compared to other phrases, codes, in the data. Then, the codes develop into categories. As the process of interpretation data continues, the categories turn to theoretical framework describing the experiences of the subjects studied.

BURNOUT AND GROUNDED THEORY

Rafii et al. (2004) used GT to study nurses' responses to burnout. Due to intense and long-standing problems in burn centers in Tehran, nurses are suffering from burnout that has provoked serious responses and made the nurses, patients and the organization feel they are under pressure. The managers and nurse executives are challenging with understanding the factors affecting the nurses' responses to burnout as well as developing delivery systems that promote positive adaptation and facilitate quality care.

The data collection tools in the present study were tape recorded and unstructured interviews. The data was collected after obtaining the ethical approval. The data, initially, was collected in one center and analyzed. Then, the second center was studied and data was collected. Based on the initial review of the literature on the concepts of the subject of the study, researchers used a topic guide to conduct unstructured interviews, which included the structure, process and outcome of care. The main question was: "please tell me about the nursing care in your unit". The subsequent questions were raised based on the participants' responses and demands of the emerging theory. Data redundancy was the sign to terminate interviews Terminating the interviews, participant observations were performed in all wards of each center in the morning, evening and at night. During focused and selective observations, theoretical sampling happened. To obtain the theoretical sampling, some questions were asked: what are the differences, if any, between the nursing cares received by different patients? Is there any difference in nursing care in a large or small ward? During the observations, the researcher conducted some informal interview. Systematic completion of the field notes was the next step immediately after each session of observation. The contextual conditions were determined through the analysis of the field notes; also, the variations in the nurses' responses in each context were explained, contributing to the proposition of several hypotheses.

Using GT, the data collection, analysis and interpretation happened at the same time. The transcript of each interview was manually transcribed by the main researcher onto a personal computer, through which the themes were identified. Then, a print- out was obtained and the tape replayed to make notes onto the transcripts. Comments about tone of voice, recurrent themes and the researcher's own initial thought and feelings concerning the nature and importance of the data included the items of these notes. Typing and analysis of the field notes of each session of observations were performed. Rereading the transcripts, recurrent themes were coded. In fact, the data are examined word by word and line by line in the process of open coding and codes are freely generated, often reflecting the words of the respondents themselves. For example, the responses describing a heartfelt, positive, and supportive relationship between the patient and the nurse can be coded under *head nurse support*. The codes with similar meaning were grouped in the same categories. The analytical tools, including asking questions and making comparisons, were contributing to finding the properties of each concept. In axial coding, the relations of categories and their subcategories were determined; the coding process was around the axis of a category, and hence, categories were associated at the level of properties and dimensions. In this stage, the association between structures of care and the processes was realized. For example it attributed a group of factors to the nurses' distancing from patients.

In selective coding, the theory was integrated and refined. The core category, i.e. the emergence of negative trends: nurses' responses to burnout were identified in this stage. A very helpful action was selective sampling of literature related to job stress and burnout. Other main categories (emotional, attitudinal, psychosomatic, behavioral, and organizational responses) and their subcategories were linked by the core category. Table 1 displays the main categories and their subcategories.

Table 1. Emergence of negative trends: nurses' responses to burnout (Rafii et al., 2004)

Main categories	Subcategories
Emotional responses	Personal despair Professional despair
Attitudinal responses	Depersonalization Negativity
Psychosomatic responses	Physical attrition Psychological attrition
Behavioral responses	Intolerance Justification
Organizational responses	Inattentive care Performance decline

Guba and Lincoln provided a perspective that was accepted by the researchers. They replaced credibility for validity, transferability for external validity, dependability for reliability, and confirmability for objectivity.

Credibility was achieved through prolonged engagement and persistent observation, which was confirmed by data triangulation and method triangulation. The ways to meet this criterion included maximum variation sampling, participant observation and using published literature. Furthermore, after completing the description of the phenomenon, 4 participants of each center verified and validated the descriptions. The original context was adequately described, helping the readers to make a judgment of transferability. To meet dependability, the process of the study was audited.

Confirmability needs one to show the way in which interpretations have been arrived at via the inquiry. In this study, since credibility, transferability and dependability were achieved, confirmability was also established.

The findings obtained from the factors involved in the nurses' responses to burnout are presented. The two factors, according to the analysis and interpretation of data, were personal characteristics and social support. Table 2 presents these two factors.

Table 2. Factors involve in nurses' responses to burnout (Rafii et al., 2004)

Personal characteristics	Characteristics of nurses Characteristics of patients
Social support	Support of the head nurse Support of the nursing administrator Support of peers

The nurses' responses to burnout and altered caring behaviors were modified by the characteristics of nurses and patients. As further analysis and interpretation of data indicated, a more powerful combination of these two variables was the result of the interaction between them, which alters responses to burnout and identifies the kind of caring behavior.

Camargo M.R. (2008) used GT and studied the relationship between e-mail and burnout. This qualitative study investigated the role of e-mail in burnout at work among high technology employees working full time and on-site for Internet, hardware, and software companies. GT was the selected methodology to study the relationship between email and burnout since a researcher, through this method, can explore a phenomenon and build theory or theoretical models for contexts that are subject to change processes and transitions such as the high technology work environment.

According to this methodology, high technology workers were interviewed based on the prepared interview protocol. The open-ended questions of the interviews were designed to collect information in respect of the interviewees' views on the advantages and disadvantages of e-mail at work, their habits with regard to their use of e-mail both inside and outside their organization and the volume and type of messages they received and sent on a given day.

The initial ideas were drawn from the literature were useful to study the common issues related to the phenomenon under investigation. However, as required by the GT approach used in this study, the researcher is expected, in accordance with the requirements of GT, not to be contaminated and excessively influenced by previous studies. To do comparison and have a source of ideas, technical and non-technical literature was also used.

The interview transcripts formed the core issue of the study and then, the researcher started the GT process with a line-by-line analysis to elicit the concepts behind what people were saying. The first analysis of data is called open coding. The researcher tried to find any association between the concepts generated in the open coding in order to group similar items with common properties or characteristics. This analysis called as axial coding allowed the researcher to create initial categories, i.e. the concepts that stand for the phenomena. The open and axial coding is illustrated in Table 3 as below.

Table 3. Open and Axial Coding (Camargo M.R., 2008)

Question	Extracted transcript	Open coding	Axial coding
What do you think are the advantages of using e-mail in your workplace?	The written communication can be tracked and used as an evidence to keep someone to his/her word. This is especially needed in large projects with huge amounts of data.	Information tracking, documentation history, project management, data management.	Different applications and uses of email
	a. Recording things can help you easily find anything when searching for project history. b. Communicating with multiple users at the same time is fast and easy. c. It, as an archive, helps me to find information about happenings, solutions, and researchers of the old projects. d. It functions as a to-do list.	record keeping, message distribution tool, archiving, list of tasks	

Memos that are the researcher's notes can support each coding phase. These memos play an important role in documenting ideas and connections as they occurred in the analysis process. An example of a memo is below: as this interviewee expressed the shared view, e-mail is essential for documenting and tracking everything that occurs at work.

Axial coding developed categories and then the association between these categories, based on the study paradigm, were identified. This process is called selective coding through which the main categories of the theoretical model are created: 'Different perceptions on e-mail role in the workplace' was emerged from the axial coding 'different applications and uses of e-mail' shown in Table 3.

In GT, when no new information can be found in the data obtained from the participants, the category saturation is achieved. As the final requirement of the GT approach, it is needed to define a process to explain the actions and interactions among the elements of a theoretical model.

It should be noted that one of the basic assumptions of the GT methodology is that it does not cause reaching findings, but creates a theory or theoretical model to provide a tentative explanation of the phenomenon under investigation. According to the theoretical model resulted from this study, alongside the evolvement and change of the context with its subjects, the evolution of a social phenomenon needs constant verification and updating.

The central category that emerged, after careful consideration, and became the title of the theoretical model was: misuse and overuse of e-mail as key element to job burnout, as shown in Figure 1.

Figure 1. Misuse and overuse of e-mail as precursors to job burnout (Camargo M.R., 2008)

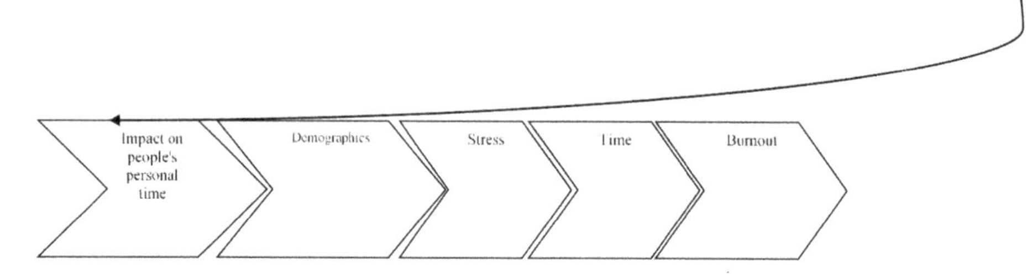

The description of the relationship between e-mail and burnout is the first step of theoretical model. It is done by showing how e-mail is perceived in the high technology industry. According to the data obtained from the interviewees, people have various interpretations on the representation of e-mail in their environments and the best way to apply it for communication and productivity purposes. It was emerged during the open coding processes that people use e-mail to meet their goals including documentation, tracking, record keeping, information sharing, distribution lists, broadcasting, project management, data management, task management, archiving, data transferring, file swapping, troubleshooting and reminders.

As Jackson et al. (2018) stated, many critical care nurses experience burnout; however, promise is shown as a potential solution to burnout in resilience. This study was aimed at providing a better understanding of nurse burnout and resilience in response to workplace adversity in critical care. A GT is applied according to the Corbin and Strauss methodology. The research tool was qualitative, open-ended interviews about burnout and resilience. Findings showed that the indicators in a process of responding to workplace adversity are burnout and resilience. The adversity in workplace can be reflected in many forms, leading to a negative impact on nurses. Nurses must have knowledge or perception of this impact to take action. The process of managing exposure is what nurses make sense of workplace adversity and how they address using variety of techniques, such as protecting, processing, decontaminating, and distancing. The nurses can identify this process through these indicators: thriving, resilience, survival and burnout. Organizational policies can affect this process. It is shown that resilience and burnout are connected, as indicators of the same process for critical care nurses show. This process can be intervened by nurse leaders, resulting in reduced workplace adversity, and supporting resilience among nurses.

Billeter-Koponen and Fredén (2005) tried to find a deeper understanding of the solutions applied by nurses to deal with long-lasting stress and burnout. The central concerns in the study were professionalism and especially patient–nurse relations. GT methodology was used to analyze the open interviews. Participants included 10 nurses (at age range of 30–61) from different care institutions. They had experienced long-lasting stress and burnout, which made them distance from work for two or more months. The main core emerging from the data was that no one can neglect or influence the valuation of the work of nurses. It reflects the process of decision making, particularly in the context of reorganizations in which the knowledge and experience of nurses are often disregarded, despite of significant influence of these decisions on their daily work. The participants believed that the patient–nurse relationship was an important part of care. The nurses always concerned about their relationship with patients and tiredness could not affect it, but they did not have the power to meet patients and secure quality of care, and hence, they had to go off sick leave the work place.

According to Oser et al. (2013), the counselors believe that the following factors affect the emergence of burnout; challenging and difficult clients, large caseloads, excessive paperwork, office politics, and low prestige. They used GT methodology in this study. Furthermore, they found that co-worker support, clinical supervision, and self-care can affect preventing burnout. Burnout may result in poor client care, reversing roles, clients changing counselors, and job turnover.

The vulnerability of substance abuse counselors to burnout can cause negative repercussions for the counselor, employing organization, and clients. However, there is not much information about what are differences between counselor burnout and the counselors' perspective in rural versus urban treatment centers. In 2008, 28 rural and urban counselors in a southern state were investigated and the analysis of focus group data revealed three burnout themes across all counselors: causes, consequences, and prevention. However, various differences were found between rural and urban counselors in sub-themes; only rural counselors cited office politics and low occupational prestige as causes of burnout. Only urban counselors reported responses that emphasized on the sub-themes of role reversal, clients trying to choose their counselors, and changing jobs as consequences of burnout. According to all counselors, co-worker support, clinical supervision, and self-care were important strategies for managing burnout. In brief, since rural counselors mentioned more causes of burnout, context obviously matters; yet, poor quality clinical care is the universally accepted implication of burnout. It is needed to understand addiction as a disease, which would reduce stigma, especially in rural areas, as well as increase the prestige and earning potential of the substance abuse counseling occupation.

The focus groups identified three main burnout themes: causes, consequences, and prevention of burnout. It should be noted that both rural and urban counselors identified these three themes; however, the difference was in the sub-themes, based on rural versus urban locale. Table 4 depicts the themes and sub-themes emerging from the analyses as well as those that were rural only, urban only, or discussed among both rural and urban counselors.

Table 4. Burnout themes and sub-themes among rural and urban counselors: causes, consequences, and prevention (Oser et al, 2013)

Themes:	Causes	Consequences	Prevention
Sub-themes:	Challenging–clients B	Poor client caring-B	Supporting of co-worker –B
	Large caseload–B	Reversing roles–U	Clinical supervising–B
	Paperwork–B	Attempting to choose counsellor by clients–U	Self-caring–B
	Office politics–R	Changing jobs-U	
	Low prestige–R		

NOTE: R=rural counselors only, U=urban counselors only, B=both rural and urban counselors

First, multiple sub-themes regarding the causes of burnout emerged from the counselor focus group data included clients who are difficult to treat, high caseloads, massive amounts of paperwork, office politics, and the low level of prestige associated with the counseling occupation. One sub-theme that was similar in both rural and urban counselors as a cause of burnout was providing services to clients who are difficult to treat. Oftentimes substance abusers suffer from co-occurring mental health problems and issues with their physical health. The social problems these clients are faced with include employment difficulties, lack of housing, minimal social support, and/or no childcare, challenging them in treatment. Thus, it's not surprising that this theme emerged from all the focus group transcripts since those refer to counselors all have substance use disorders, regardless of treatment services are performed in rural or urban areas. High caseloads resulting in volumes of paperwork has also led to burnout. This sub-theme was identified by both rural and urban counselors.

The other two sub-themes were identified by rural counselors only. Frustration with colleagues and management was a form of office politics that was discussed in both rural groups. Oftentimes, fewer full-time equivalent employees and more part-time staff work in rural facilities. Thus, in case of occurrence of any conflict in the workplace, counselors will have to keep on working with co-workers who are the cause of frustration on a daily basis. The rural counselors also discussed about the lack of prestige or value in being a substance abuse counselor as a cause of burnout. The counselor's effort to bring prestige to the field and his idea about this issue was really critical to being an effective substance abuse treatment counselor.

Rural and urban counselors also discussed the consequences of burnout, among which poor quality client-care was a sub-theme among all participants; however, the result of the urban focus group only indicated that the effects of burnout included reversing roles (i.e., taking on the counseling role by the client to address the counselor's personal problems), clients trying to choose their counselor, and changing jobs. Counselor burnout obviously affects the client's recovery process to be slowed down or failed. That is why the sub-theme of poor quality clinical care was identified by all counselor participants regardless of geographic locale. Specifically, as each of the four focus groups mentioned, clients can realize and tell when their counselor is not engaged, affecting counselor-client rapport.

Other sub-themes of the effects of burnout were cited by urban counselors only. When clients sense that their counselor is burned out, reversing roles can occur. In this case, the client takes on the psychotherapist role and the counseling session can become a therapy session for the counselor rather than the client. In this context, the client's therapeutic process is disrupted. Clients may seek to be engaged in role reversal for a variety of reasons including it can provide the client with a sense of self-worth, or it can be used as a strategy to avoid dealing with their substance use disorder(s). Regardless of the reason, it is considered as a problem since it is wasting the time that should be devoted to addressing the client's issues.

Another sub-theme emerged from the urban focus group data was that burnout can lead to clients try to select their counselor. Requesting specific counselors can be resulted from a range of different reasons; for example, difficulties in establishing rapport with certain counselors (e.g., because they are burned out) or selecting a counselor who will force the client to focus on the difficult personal issues s/he has been avoiding. Discerning the difference between a client who is not engaged in the recovery process versus a counselor who is really burned out and is not therapeutically effective can be mentioned as the difficulties raised by requesting counselors. Thus, allowing clients to select who they work with while in substance abuse treatment is a problematic issue.

The final sub-theme of the consequences of burnout mentioned by the urban counselors only was changing jobs. According to the counselors in urban areas, just a little change up with your job would help. Since disorders mostly occur together, counselors could change their positions to focus on (and bill for) mental health treatment. Such changes in positions within the same organization may occur more frequently in urban community mental health centers; these centers are larger and may offer more employment opportunities. Leaving the field was suggested by other counselors, which is costly to the treatment organization.

Kavalieratos et al. (2017) documented sources of burnout on four interrelated levels: individual (lack of boundaries, feeling like one cannot make a difference, and self-judgment), interpersonal (interspecialty conflict), organizational (role monotony and system stress), and policy (regulatory issues) levels. A variety of potential solutions were also suggested to burnout by the participants, corresponding to the aforementioned four-level hierarchy: individual (self-regulation strategies, reaffirming one's positive impact), interpersonal (relying on colleagues to avoid to be harmed by being part of a group), organizational (culture change to reduce burnout), and policy (appeals for American Academy of Hospice and Palliative Medicine (AAHPM)'s involvement to promote resilience and regulatory changes such as repayment policies).

Although, based on the prior surveys, the rates of self-reported burnout among palliative care clinicians was reported as high as 62%, there is limited data to clarify the causes, ameliorators, and effects of this phenomenon. They explored burnout among palliative care clinicians. The issues of the main concern in this study included the palliative care clinicians' experiences with burnout, their perceived sources of burnout, as well as potential individual, interpersonal, organizational, and policy-level solutions to address burnout. During the 2014 AAHPM/Hospice and Palliative Nurses Association Annual Assembly, three focus groups were conducted to examine personal narratives of burnout, the differences of burnout within hospice and palliative care, and strategies to reduce burnout. Template analysis was used to analyze data; it is an inductive/deductive qualitative analytic technique. 20 palliative care clinicians (14 physicians, four advanced practice providers, and two social workers) were interviewed. Common sources of burnout were identified as increasing workload, tensions between non-specialists and palliative care specialists, and regulatory issues. There also found some essential concerns about the stability of the palliative care workforce and providing high-quality palliative care in light of a distressed and overburdened discipline. Some anti-burnout solutions were proposed by the participants, such as promoting the provision of generalist palliative care, frequent rotations on-and-off service, and organizational support for self-care.

As Grafstrom (2017) stated, the qualitative research study will explore the role of adult day social workers in identifying and mitigating caregivers burnout. Data collection tool used in this study was semi-structured interviews (eight interviews) conducted with adult day social workers to analyze their

Table 5. Questions asked in the focus groups (Kavalieratos et al., 2017)

1	How about we go around and state your names, where you live, what your roles are in hospice and palliative care (HPC), and for how long you have been working in HPC.
2	What do you sense of the term burnout? What is your definition of this term? What does being burnt out feel like? How can you successfully deal with burnout? Is burnout an acute, discrete event for you, or is it more of a chronic feeling?
3	Think back over all the years that you have been in HPC. Please tell us an instance of a stressful event when you felt burnt out. What about that experience caused you perceive burnt out? What happened to help you pass the burnout?
4	From what or where do you find support to help you pass feelings of burnout? How open are you about your feelings when you are feeling burnt out? Who do you talk to when you feel burnt out? What do they tell you?
5	Let us suppose that you are mentoring a medical student who is keen on a career in HPC. What would you tell him and/or her to preserve him or herself from burnout?
6	How do you think that burnout in HPC relates to burnout in various medical specialties? How is burnout in HPC different than or similar to burnout in other specialties? How prevailing do you feel that burnout is among your HPC colleagues?
7	We have spent a lot of time this (morning/afternoon) for the discussion about burnout, what it is, and how it influences on you and your colleagues.

experience with caregivers, their role in recognizing burnout and their response to caregivers experiencing burnout. A GT approach was used to analyze data. According to the findings, adult day social workers play an important role in identifying burnout among caregivers by providing support that is supported by practices in the adult day setting.

Definition of burnout, causes of burnout, burnout reduction as multi-pronged approach and formal supports as interventions included the four themes. Six sub-themes were identified within the theme of definition of burnout: overwhelmed, crying, exhaustion, appearance, guilt and anger. Four identified sub-themes within the theme of causes of burnout were: dementia behaviors, role overload, lack of sleep, and lack of support. Within the theme of burnout reduction as multi-pronged approach, eight sub-themes were identified: sitting in the moment, encouragement, and informal check in and normalizing, dementia process, self-care, future planning, and how to ask for help. Four sub-themes emerged within the theme of formal supports as interventions: community resources, support group, caregiver coaching, and respite. Table 6 presents a visual representation of themes and corresponding subthemes.

- **Overwhelmed:** In response to the question what burnout looks and sounds like, the participants answered they feel being overwhelmed

Table 6. Themes and sub-themes (Grafstrom, 2017)

Themes	Burnout definition	Burnout causes	Decrease of burnout as multi-pronged strategies	Supporting formally as interventions
Sub-themes	Overwhelmed	Dementia behaviors	Sitting in the moment	Community resources
	Crying	Role overload	Encouragement	Support group
	Exhaustion	Shortage of sleep	Check in's informally	Caregiver coaching
	Appearance	Shortage of support	Normalizing	Respite
	Guilt		Dementia process	
	Infuriation		Self-caring	
			How to plan for the future	
			How to apply for help	

as the main sub-theme that emerged. The task of caregiving makes caregivers feel overwhelmed and are often confused what to do to move forward or strike a balance in their role as caregiver.

- **Guilt:** According to the answers of four of the participants, the caregivers feel guilty because they wish to be the sole supporter of their care recipient, internal pride and beginning to realize they need help.
- **Crying:** Many emotions may lead to crying; in this case, five participants believed that crying is the physical and emotional sign of burnout among caregivers.
- **Exhaustion**: Exhaustion is common among those who are extremely burnt out from the demands of caregiving while caring for an older adult and the complex set of needs that can occur.
- **Appearance**: Things related to physical appearance such as lack of grooming and body language can be an indication of caregiver's burnout.
- **Anger:** Four participants believed that anger is as an indication of caregiver's burnout and discussed various ways anger is expressed.

Causes of burnout was the second theme consisting of four sub-themes. The sub-themes were identified based on what the participants stated regarding the challenges of caregiving they hear most often from caregivers. Dementia behaviors, lack of sleep, lack of support and role overload were identified from challenges stated by the burnt out caregivers in conversations or during interactions.

- **Dementia Behaviors:** As the level of disease approaches higher percentages, normal behaviors in the people living with dementia can be changes as well as their responses to the world around them; which can be challenging for those providing daily care.
- **Lack of Sleep:** Three of the participants had difficulties in sleeping as a result of dementia. These people cannot sleep at night, or need help from caregivers to use the bathroom.
- **Lack of Support:** Multiple participants illustrated struggles they have heard from caregivers; they were not supported by other family members or adult children in helping with duties and tasks of caregiving.
- **Role Overload:** The signs of the role overload included lack of freedom, wanting to do it all, taking on tasks the care receiver used to complete, and learning to accept assistance or request for help from others to reduce overload.

Burnout reduction as multi-pronged approach: eight participants, in response to the question how they define their role as a social worker in the adult day setting, expressed that being a source of support and providing education were important items. The participants were asked to describe the types of informal support and education they provide to caregivers. The answers led to the identification of four sub-themes: sitting in the moment, encouragement, informal checks-ins, and normalizing. Sub-themes of education included various aspects of the dementia process, the importance of self-care, teaching caregivers how and when to ask for help, and planning for the future.

- **Sitting in the Moment:** According to three of eight participants, being present in the moment with caregivers and allowing them to express their feelings are ways to support their needs at the moment.
- **Encouragement**: Considering validation, acknowledgment, recognizing expertise and strengths, six participants described providing encouragement and emphasized that they do this repetitively over time.

Normalizing the experience of caregiving for a person with dementia can feel isolating before being involved with supportive service or support groups.

- **Informal Check-ins**: The participants defined informal check-ins as typically brief encounters, either at the center during drop off/pick up, check in phone calls or a meeting outside the quarterly meeting requirement.
- **Dementia Process**: The process of dementia is complex, ever-changing and different from person to person. Participants described they do education with caregivers on the dementia process and the reasons why it's of importance to make problem be solved.
- **Future Planning**: The challenge that caregivers face on knowing how to plan for the future when caregiving becomes too much to handle were discussed by 5 participants they also discussed about the ways they can support and provide education on future planning.
- **Self-care**: Taking care of themselves and learning how to find balance while taking care of an older adult are vital in reducing stress. According to seven participants, the burnt out caregivers require guidance to explore simple ways they can add self-care to their daily routine.
- **How to Ask for Help:** The participants reported that a main challenge they hear from or observe in caregivers is that their concern is to know when and how to request for help. Topics of education on this subject were concerned about asking for help from doctors and asking for help from family, friends and neighbors.

All participants believed that infusing formal supports in interventions is crucial and was a main function of their role as an adult day social worker. Formal supports, as defined by participants, are the resources and referrals they most often provide to caregivers; sources and referrals such as a number of community resources, caregiver coaching, referring to their or another support group, and additional respite.

- **Community Resources:** All eight participants indicated a variety of community resources they most often refer to caregivers. Four participants pointed out that they often refer caregivers to home care agencies for extra services.
- **Caregiver Coaching:** Three participants described caregiver coaching as a resource through the Alzheimer's Association that performs as

a focused support coach to caregivers and one they often refer for struggling families.

- **Support Group**: Seven adult day programs participants referred to offering support groups for caregivers through their program.
- **Respite**: Four participants described respite as one of the items by which caregivers can take care of their loved one or family member for as long as possible in the community. It was discussed broadly regarding the different work forms of caregiving task and specific examples were also given such as respite in assisted living, adult day programs, companion care, or from other family members.

Kung et al. (2019) studied the relationship between burnout and the clinic's capacity to meet social needs. They used GT and phenomenology approaches in urban clinics serving low-income patients. According to the results, increasing the social needs resources alongside other burnout-prevention initiatives may decrease burnout symptoms.

CONCLUSION

Feeling constant pressure while having few opportunities to take real breaks from work can lead to higher levels of stress, resulting in feeling overwhelmed and burnt out. The professions dealing with high levels of stress, including healthcare, social work, police work, teaching, and customer services are regarded as the occupations most at risk of burnout. Thus, providing backgrounds and necessary knowledge to adopt strategies to reduce or control occupational burnout and stressors and to strengthen strategies and risk factors that threaten physical and psychological health of employees requires the process of identifying employees' coping with job burnout which is linked with their deep and authentic experiences in relation to job stress, the hidden and visible factors, strategies and methods of staffs' coping, and also the factors and conditions affecting the coping process of employees..

The present study provided the basics for more qualitative studies to consider the application of grounded theory (GT) approach in the field of occupational burnout in more details. GT as a general research approach that applies a set of systematic procedures for the collection and analysis of qualitative data is designed to support the inductive development of theory about a phenomenon. There is limited qualitative research and in particular GT on providing a subjective description of job burnout provided by employees.

Since the present study examined current studies of occupational burnout that focused on GT, it can be considered as a valuable study in this regard.

REFERENCES

Azerbarzin, M. (2009). *The effect of exercise on job burnout reduction of managers and staff of Ministry of Agriculture Jihad* (M.Sc. Thesis). Faculty of Management, University of Tehran.

Berg, G. M., Harsbarger, J. L., Ahlers-Schmidt, C. R., & Lippold, D. (2016). Exposing compassion fatigue and burnout syndrome in a trauma team: A qualitative study. *Journal of Trauma Nursing*, *23*(1), 3–10. doi:10.1097/JTN.0000000000000172 PMID:26745533

Bianchi, R., Laurent, E., & Schonfeld, I. S. (2018). Burnout syndrome and depression. In Y.-K. Kim (Ed.), Understanding Depression. Singapore: Springer Nature Singapore Pte Ltd.

Billeter-Koponen, S., & Fredén, L. (2005). Long-term stress, burnout and patient–nurse relations: Qualitative interview study about nurses' experiences. *Scandinavian Journal of Caring Sciences*, *19*(1), 20–27. doi:10.1111/j.1471-6712.2005.00318.x PMID:15737161

Camargo, M. R. (2008). A grounded theory study of the relationship between e-mail and burnout. *Information Research*, *13*(4), 1–15.

Charmaz, K. (2006). *Constructing grounded theory: A practice guide through qualitative analysis*. London: Sage.

Creswell, J. W. (2013). *Qualitative inquiry and research design: choosing among five approaches* (3rd ed.). Sage Publications.

Grafstrom, A. (2017). Identifying and mitigating caregiver burnout: The role of adult day social workers. *The St. Catherine University*. Retrieved September 5, 2019, from https://sophia.stkate.edu/msw_papers/747

Hosseinzadeh, D. (2012). The relationship between management styles with job burnout and organizational health in Taleghani Hospital. *Journal of Cognitive Psychotherapy*, *2*, 108–127.

Jackson, J., Vandall-Walker, V., Vanderspank-Wright, B., Wishart, P., & Moore, S. (2018). Burnout and resilience in critical care nurses: A grounded theory of managing exposure. *Intensive & Critical Care Nursing*, *48*, 28–35. doi:10.1016/j.iccn.2018.07.002 PMID:30033214

Kavalieratos, D., Siconolfi, D. E., Steinhauser, K. E., Bull, J., Arnold, R. M., Swetz, K. M., & Kamal, A. H. (2017). It is like heart failure. It is chronic and it will kill you: A qualitative analysis of burnout among Hospice and Palliative Care clinicians. *Journal of Pain and Symptom Management*, *53*(5), 1–10. doi:10.1016/j.jpainsymman.2016.12.337 PMID:28063867

Keyvanara, M., ShaarbafchiZadeh, N., & Alimoradnori, M. (2019). Effective factors on occupational burnout among the operation room staff in teaching hospitals affiliated with Isfahan Medical Universty: A qualitative content analysis. *Evidence Based Health Policy, Management and Economics*, *3*(3), 202–211.

Kung, A., Cheung, T., Knox, M., Willard-Grace, R., Halpern, J., Olayiwola, J. N., & Gottlieb, L. (2019). Capacity to address social needs affects primary care clinician burnout. *Analysis of Family Medicine*, *17*(6), 487–494. doi:10.1370/afm.2470 PMID:31712286

Maslach, C., & Jackson, S. E. (1981). Measurement of experience burnout. *Journal of Occupational Behaviour*, *2*(2), 99–113. doi:10.1002/job.4030020205

Maslach, C., & Leiter, M. P. (2016). Understanding the burnout experience: Recent research and its implications for psychiatry. *World Psychiatry; Official Journal of the World Psychiatric Association (WPA)*, *15*(2), 103–111. doi:10.1002/wps.20311 PMID:27265691

Maslach, C., Leiter, M. P., & Shaufeli, W. B. (2001). Job burnout. *Annual Review of Psychology*, *52*(1), 422–479. doi:10.1146/annurev.psych.52.1.397 PMID:11148311

Merriam, S. B. (2009). *Qualitative research: a guide to design and implementation*. San Francisco, CA: Jossey-Bass.

Morgan, D. L. (2014). *Integrating qualitative & quantitative methods*. Thousand Oaks, CA: Sage.

Oser, C. B., Biebel, E. P., Pullen, E., & Harp, K. L. H. (2013). Causes, consequences, and prevention of burnout among substance abuse treatment counselors: A rural verses urban comparison. *Journal of Psychoactive Drugs*, *45*(1), 17–27. doi:10.1080/02791072.2013.763558 PMID:23662328

Rafii, F., Oskouie, F., & Nikravesh, M. (2004). Factors involved in nurses' responses to burnout: A grounded theory study. *BMC Nursing*, *3*(1), 1–10. doi:10.1186/1472-6955-3-6 PMID:15541180

Rahimi, F. (2009). A look at Burnout or Burnout Syndrome and its presence in the library profession. *Book Quarterly*, *77*, 289–302.

Shahnaz Doost, M., Maghsoudi, S., & Tabari, R., & Kazemnejad, L. (2011). Relationship between burnout and job support of nurses. *Majallah-i Danishgah-i Ulum-i Pizishki-i Gilan*, *20*(80), 49–59.

Shojaeifard, J., Poursadegh, N., Shahr-Ashub, G., & Zangisheh, S. (2014). The relationship between burnout and resiliency in Medical Emergency Personnel of Tehran. *Journal of Rescue Research*, *2*, 58–67.

Spooner, L. R. (2004). *The influence of work stress and work support on burnout in public hospital nurses* (Unpublished PhD thesis). Queensland, Australia.

Squires, A., Finlayson, C., Gerchow, L., Cimiotti, J. P., Matthews, A., Schwendimann, R., ... Sermeus, W. (2014). Methodological considerations when translating "burnout". *Burnout Research*, *1*(2), 59–68. doi:10.1016/j.burn.2014.07.001 PMID:25343131

Steege, L. M., Pinekensten, B. J., Knudsen, E. A., & Rainbow, J. G. (2017). Exploring nurse leader fatigue: A mixed method study. *Journal of Nursing Management*, *25*(4), 276–286. doi:10.1111/jonm.12464 PMID:28244184

Swider, B. W., & Zimmerman, R. D. (2010). Burn to burnout: Ameta- analtic path model of personlity, job burnout, and work outcome. *Journal of Vocational Behavior*, *73*(3), 487–506. doi:10.1016/j.jvb.2010.01.003

Tabarsa, G. A., Yazdani, Z., Yazdani, M., Raisi, H., & Taheri, A. (2011). The relationship between organizational structure and job burnout among staff of Shahid Beheshti University. *Journal of Career and Organizational Counseling*, *3*(9), 88–93.

Tracy, S. J. (2013). *Qualitative research methods: collecting evidence, crafting analysis, communicating impact*. West Sussex, UK: John Wiley & Sons, Ltd.

Vahdani, M., Moharramzadeh, M., & Seyed Ameri, M. H. (2013). Factors influencing job burnout and coping strategies in Personnel of Youth and Sports Departments of Iran. *Journal of Sport Management and Development*, *5*(2), 1–6.

Willig, C. (2012). *Qualitative interpretation and analysis in psychology*. Maidenhead: McGraw-Hill Education.

Zarei Matin, H., Seyed Kalali, N., & Akhavan Anvari, M. (2012). The effect of burnout on job outcomes of employees. *Quarterly Review of Public Administration*, *9*(3), 73–90.

Chapter 9
Using Grounded Theory Methodology to Explore Women's Sense of Insecurity

ABSTRACT

The focus of this chapter is reviewing the studies on sexual harassment and sexual violence, focusing on definitions, statistics, forms, consequences, and prevention strategies. Moreover, it concerns the grounded theory (GT) as a qualitative research methodology and provides a comparison between this methodology and constructivist GT that is considered to be more compatible with feminist inquiry. To study the theories with inappropriate or inadequate features and to study the subject under investigation, such as the analysis of women's sense of insecurity, GT methodology seems most appropriate. This chapter provides a detailed discussion of the impact of sexual violence on mental and physical health as well as social well-being, all of which may be equally long-lasting. Preventive strategies, as mentioned in this chapter, are concerned with changing people's attitudes and behaviors by formulating and implementing appropriate policies and empowerment programs.

INTRODUCTION

Since 1970s, women's sense of insecurity and violence against women have been widely discussed. There is some hidden form of bullying behind all forms of abuse, discrimination, prejudice, rape, assault and violence. Gender is the only aspect of identity which can affect the likelihood of experiencing sexual

DOI: 10.4018/978-1-7998-4252-1.ch009

assault. As the World Bank (2018) reported, protection against violence can also guarantee women's economic empowerment. Since violence against women prevents employment and blocks access to financial resources, it undermines economic empowerment. Violence hinders women's free function in societies and the business world. The scope of existing legislations, in any, on violence against women is examined by the indicator of protecting women from violence such as domestic violence and sexual harassment. Domestic violence is gender-specific violence perpetrated by family members or intimate partners, which includes different types of abuse. Around the world, nearly 1 in 3 women have experienced physical or sexual violence from an intimate partner. As many as 38% of all murders of women were committed by their intimate partners. Domestic violence legislation as an important first step can take significant steps towards ensuring women's protection.

The focus of a qualitative research can be one or more characteristics of a sole individual, social group or category of population of a region or even an entire country. New approaches and explanatory theories have been developed within the framework of qualitative research, among which the feminist theories can be also found. The feminist researchers prefer using qualitative method, as compared to the quantitative one, since it does not have standard models or situations to examine. In qualitative research studies, there is no restriction imposed to the researcher by assumptions and selecting predetermined forms, and thus, s/he is encouraged to continuously discover new issues and see reality from the examined subjects' eyes. The most basic characteristics of feminist research conducted by women, who are feminist, is that the main focus is on women. Secondly, "male" quantitative methods must be differentiated from feminist qualitative ones. Thirdly, feminist research is considered as a political research since women are promoted to engage actively in changing their lives (Stanley and Wise, 1990).

This chapter focuses on grounded theory (GT) as a qualitative research methodology to examine current studies of sexual harassment and sexual violence. In addition, it compares constructivist GT and classic GT, and sexual harassment and sexual violence are defined by presenting their types, consequences, and preventive strategies.

SEXUAL HARRASSMENT

Despite of greater risk of violence from an intimate partner, women are also exposed to other forms of violence. They may experience sexual harassment in the workplace and other arenas. Sexual harassment refers to the abuse of a position of hierarchy or a significant power disparity. Traditionally, it was linked to employment, but it may happen in other spheres including education.

More than four decades have passed since sexual harassment and insecurity have been of consideration but there is limited research on the issue of insecurity in the workplace. Even in some societies, such issues are considered as a kind of social taboos. Gender inequality is manifested, at the macro level, in forms of sexual harassment and feelings of insecurity in the workplace. Apart from various gender discrimination, women are even vulnerable to insecurity because of their bodies. Women in senior positions in an organization with both work and time management and ethical behavior are not also secure in the workplace.

Due to unreported harassments, Barker (2017) stated, there is no clear data about the statistics of sexual harassment. In addition, there were 6,862 sexual harassment claims were filed with the U.S. Equal Opportunity Employment Commission, of which 92.5% were filed by female employees. Sexual harassment in the workplace negatively affects the employees, and the performance and image of an organization. Psychological and physical effects on employees, illnesses, and several negative work-related behaviors can be mentioned, among others, as the negative impact of sexual harassment in the workplace. The employees can prevent these negative effects and be productive and efficient members of the organization if they feel secure in their workplace. Sexual harassment in organizations is common; about 68% of women in the UK experience sexual harassment in their lifetime (Ministry of Defense, 2015).

Insecurity in the workplace leads to women's psychological burnout, and causes disorders such as anxiety, fear, aggression, depression, confusion, disruption of work activities and family life, and also impedes women's ability to flourish. It results in disregarding the abilities of women to be used effectively. Consequently, half of the active population in the society are deprived from their natural right. In this regard, fear of dishonor and stigma make women be silenced in face of insecurity.

According to the definition by the U.S. Equal Employment Opportunity Commission (EEOC, 2011a), harassment is unwelcome manners based on race, color, religion, sex (including pregnancy), national origin, age (40 or older), disability or genetic information. Unlawful harassment is proved where 1) the offensive conduct endures and becomes a condition of continued employment, or 2) the offensive conduct in workplace is severe or pervasive enough that a reasonable person would consider intimidating, hostile, or abusive. A person's unwanted sex-related conduct occurs to violate the dignity of a person, and to create an intimidating, hostile, degrading, humiliating or offensive environment. Sexual harassment, on the other hand, refers to unwelcome promise of rewards in exchange for sexual favors, and other verbal or physical conduct of a sexual nature, which interferes with one's employment or work performance or causes a hostile or offensive work environment (EEOC, 2011b).

One of the manifestations of the wider issue of the oppression of women is sexual harassment of women in the workplace. Sexual harassment is not only concerned with a boss-employee interaction, but in many cases an interaction between co-workers. Co-workers do have power over women's jobs and economic security since the public always blame the victim. Women's silence in this regard has several implications. It can lead to severe forms of sexual harassment such as rape, which will remain unreported as well. Women feel guilt and fear rather than anger after such incidents. Sexual harassment mainly happens to preserve the dominance of patriarchy. Sexual harassment has become a new version of an old phenomenon to push women out of specific jobs (Bularzik, 1978).

Sexual harassment can be prevented by adopting a stand-alone sexual harassment and assault policy or revisiting the current policies in the organizations. All employees' awareness of sexual harassment and assault policies needs to be ensured. In addition, empowering Human resource (HR) staff by the management to implement, train and enforce sexual harassment

Table 1.Types of sexual harassment (Center for Victim Advocacy and Violence Prevention, 2010)

Gender harassment	General sexist assertion and manner that relate to abusing and humiliating attitude such as humor about sex.
Seductive behavior	Unwanted, improper sexual move that cause a victim to feel deeply hurt, upset, or angry such as iterative and unwanted sexual invitation.
Sexual bribery	Request of sexual activity or other sex-related behavior in case of reward.
Sexual coercion	Sexual activity or other sex-related behavior by force and threat of punishment such as negative performance evaluation.
Sexual imposition	Imposing obscene sexual activity such as forceful touching.

polices within their organization is considered necessary (HRPA, 2019).

SEXUAL VIOLENCE

Sexual violence as a critical problem in the society is frighteningly common. Approximately one in four women will be or have been experienced such offensive behaviors. Between 1995 and 1996, a national telephone poll was conducted as The Violence Against Women Survey. The results indicated that 14.8 percent of women and 2.1 percent of men reported completed rape at some time in their lives while 54 percent of all rapes occurred before the age of 18. The prevalence of forced sexual intercourse and health-risk behaviors among a national sample of 4,609 female college students was examined by the 1995 National College Health Risk Behavior Survey. Restricting the estimation of rape rates in women since the age of 15, the survey found a prevalence rate of 15 percent (Bachar and Koss, 2001).

Jewekes et al. (2001) who discussed about teenage pregnancy in South Africa found a pattern of sexual activity which puts teenagers at risk of HIV. Currently the virus infects one in five pregnant teenagers. The results found by Leserman et al (1998) determined the impact of sexual and physical abuse history on a selected set of medical symptoms. They also aimed at testing how such abuse, medical symptoms and functional disability may affect subsequent health care visits. Women who had abuse history, particularly those with severe abuse, were much more likely to report somatic symptoms related to panic (e.g. palpitations, numbness, shortness of breath), depression (e.g. difficulty sleeping, loss of appetite), musculoskeletal disorders (e.g. headaches, muscle aches), genito-urinary disorders (e.g. vaginal discharge, pelvic pain, painful intercourse), skin disturbance (e.g. rash) and respiratory illness (e.g. stuffy nose). Thus, sexual violence is associated with both immediate and long-term consequences besides physical injury.

According to Acierno et al. (1999), past victimization, young age, and a diagnosis of active post-rape posttraumatic stress disorder (PTSD) affect the increase in women's risk of being raped. By contrast, the factors affecting increased risk of being physically assaulted include past victimization, minority ethnic status, active depression, and drug use. A history of depression, alcohol abuse, or experienced injury during the rape are considered as the risk factors for PTSD following rape. While, risk factors for PTSD following physical assault included only a history of depression and lower education. Creamer et al. (2001) provided a report on the epidemiology of PTSD in the Australian community. It was shown that most adult population in Australia were at exposure to trauma and that PTSD was a highly prevalent sequela of such exposure. Despite of similar overall rates between males and females in this population, females were at greater risk than males among the subsample of those exposed to trauma. Thus, sexual violence can have impacts on mental health as serious as on physical health, and may be equally long-lasting.

According to Darves-Boronz (1997), rape leads to a high proportion of PTSD. It can be said that the psychopathology following rape is severe. Levitan et al. (1998) found the association between the history of physical or sexual abuse in childhood and major depression with reversed neurovegetative features. Manic subjects might or might not be included in the analysis. There was a strong relationship between mania and childhood physical abuse.

Mollica and Son (1989) indicated that the prevalence of sexual trauma was high among refugee women. The victims' social well-being is profoundly affected by sexual violence that is a persistent worldwide problem. Using a stratified random sample of the general population, Elliot et al. (2004) examined the prevalence and impact of adult sexual assault. 22% of women and 3.8% of men, among 941 participants, reported adult sexual assault. Younger age, being female, having been divorced, sexual abuse in childhood, and physical assault in adulthood were the multivariate risk factors for adult sexual assault. 61% of sexually assaulted men and 59% of women had an experience of childhood sexual abuse.

Kilpatrick et al. (1987) examined lifetime criminal victimization experiences, crime reporting, and psychological impact on a sample of 391 adult females. In total, 75% of the samples had an experience of being victimized by crime, of which 41.4% were reported to the police. Reporting rates were different in accordance with crime type; burglary had the highest reporting rate (82.4%); and sexual assault was the lowest (7.1%). 27.8% of all crime victims subsequently developed PTSD. The prevalence of PTSD indicates that crime is followed by both an immediate and long-term psychological impact.

One in eight adult women, or at least 12.1 million American women, based on the U.S. Census estimates of the number of adult women in America, have experienced forcible rape sometime in her lifetime. Many were raped more than once. While 56%, or an estimated 6.8 million women have been the victims of one rape, 39%, or an estimated 4.7 million women were raped more than once, and five percent were unsure about the number of times they were raped (Kilpatrick and Seymour, 1992). The result of the survey revealed rape in America as a tragedy of youth; majority of cases occurred during childhood and adolescence. Twenty-nine percent of all forcible rapes happened for the children less than 11 years old, while another 32% occurred between the ages of 11 and 17. 22 percent of rapes occurred for the women between the ages of 18 and 24 years old; that is, slightly more than one in five rapes. Seven percent occurred between the ages of 25 and 29, with only six percent occurring when the victim was older than 29 years old. Three percent of the respondents did not answer or were not sure (Kilpatrick and Seymour, 1992).

The following are the concerns that rape victims mentioned (Kilpatrick and Seymour, 1992):

- Fear of family finding out about the incident (71%);
- Fear of being blamed by people (69%);
- Fear of her name being public by the news media (50%);
- Fear of getting pregnant as the result of the assault (34%);
- Fear of getting a sexually transmitted disease, other than AIDS/HIV (19%);
- Fear of getting AIDS or HIV (10%).

Unreported rapes threaten the public safety in America. After all, unreported rapes cause rapists cannot be apprehended, indicted, prosecuted, and incarcerated. Since the criminal justice system cannot detect rapists, they will remain invisible, remaining them free to continue raping (Kilpatrick and Seymour, 1992).

The mental health impact of rape was confirmed by the Nationals Women's Study. PTSD that is an extremely debilitating mental health disorder occurring after a highly disturbing traumatic event, such as military combat or violent crime was the first mental health problem examined. Almost one third (31%) of all rape victims experienced PTSD sometime during their lifetimes, and more than one in ten rape victims (11%) still suffer from PTSD at the present time. Rape victims in comparison to women who had never been victims of crime (31% vs. 5%) were 6.2 times more likely to develop PTSD. They were also 5.5 times more likely to have current PTSD, as compared to their counterparts who had never been victims of crime (11% vs. 2%) (Kilpatrick and Seymour, 1992).

Many women, not just rape victims, suffer from major depression. However, at least one major depressive episode occurred to 30% of rape victims in their lifetimes, and 21% of all rape victims were experiencing a major depressive episode when assessed. Only 10% of women never victimized by violent crime, on the other hand, had ever had a major depressive episode and only six percent had a major depressive episode at the time of assessment. Thus, the likelihood of a major depressive episode for rape victims were three times more than non-victims of crime (30% vs. 10%). Rape victims were also 3.5 times more likely to be currently experiencing a major depressive episode (21% vs. 6%) (Kilpatrick and Seymour, 1992).

Some mental health problems are in nature threats to life. 33% of the rape victims and 8% of the non-victims of crime stated that they had seriously considered suicide. Thus, rape victims tried committing suicide 4.1 times more than non-crime victims (13% vs. 1%). Considering the fact that 13% of all rape victims had actually attempted suicide, it can be said that it confirms the devastating and potentially life threatening mental health impact of rape. Finally, it was revealed, through substantial evidence, that rape victims had higher rates of drug and alcohol consumption, and hence, they were exposed to have drug and alcohol-related problems more than non-victims of crime. The following statistics indicate facts about non-victims of crime vs. rape victims: rape victims were 5.3 times more likely to have used prescription drugs non-medically (14.7% vs 2.8%); they were also 3.4 times more likely to have used marijuana (52% vs 15.5%); six times more likely to have used cocaine (15.5% vs 2.6%); 10.1 times more likely to have used hard drugs other than cocaine (12.1% vs 1.2%); and 6.4 times more likely to have used hard drugs or cocaine (19.2% vs 3.0%) (Kilpatrick and Seymour, 1992).

Koss and Dinero (1989) studied a representative national sample of 2,723 college women to examine the accuracy with which rape and lesser sexual assaults were predicted. Three vulnerability hypotheses were operationalized by a total of 14 risk variables. The hypotheses were: (a) vulnerability-creating traumatic experiences, (b) social-psychological vulnerability, and (c) vulnerability-enhancing situations. Testing each hypothesis individually, a composite model was developed using discriminant analysis. Only the variables of traumatic experiences clearly improved over the base rates in identifying rape victims. According to Sorenson et al. (1987) in the Los Angeles Epidemiologic Catchment Area project as one of five field sites of the National Institute of Mental Health-initiated program, women, non-Hispanic whites, and young people (younger than 40 years old) reported higher rates of sexual assault than men, Hispanics, and older people. Young non-Hispanic white women with some college education reported the highest rate (26.3%).

As Tjaden and Thoennes (2000) stated, women as compared to men experience significantly more partner violence (by a current or former spouse, cohabiting partner, or date (25% vs. 8% of the surveyed subjects). 1.5 percent of the surveyed women and 0.9 percent of the surveyed men said they were a victim of rape and/or physical assault over the past 12 months by such a perpetrator. This survey estimated that approximately 1.5 million women and

834,700 men are raped and/or physically assaulted by an intimate partner in the United States every year. The survey indicated, by using a definition of stalking requiring the victim to feel a high level of fear, that stalking is more prevalent than it was previously thought: 8 percent of women and 2 percent of men in this survey stated that they were stalked at some time in their life. 1 percent of the surveyed women and 0.4 percent of the surveyed men said they were stalked in the previous 12 months. The estimates of this survey showed that approximately 1 million women and 371,000 men are stalked in the United States every year. Considering these findings, stalking should be of great consideration as a serious criminal justice and public health concern.

Forms and Contexts of Sexual Violence

There are a wide range of sexually violent acts taking place in different circumstances and settings, including rape within marriage or dating relationships, rape by strangers, systematic rape during armed conflict, requests for sexual favors or sexual harassment, denial of the right to use contraception methods or to adopt other measures to protect against sexually transmitted diseases, violent acts against the sexual integrity of women, including female genital mutilation and obligatory inspections for virginity, sexual abuse of mentally or physically disabled people, children, forced marriage or cohabitation, including the marriage of children, forced abortion, forced prostitution and trafficking of people for the purpose of sexual exploitation.

Actions combating sexual violence are not appropriate as fast and easy solutions to the problem and so, are popular among politicians and crime prevention specialists. There are various reasons in this regard, including the following factors among others. The first is the fact that much sexual violence still remains hidden, or unrecognized. Thus, it is outside the social infrastructure of normalization.

Three prevention categories classify the public health interventions, which are based on when the intervention occurs.

It is necessary to understand what circumstances and factors influence the occurrence of sexual violence in order to prevent it. The root causes of such violent acts are described by many different theoretical models that contribute to a better understanding of sexual violence and help experts build programs that sustain protective factors and reduce modifiable risk factors. These models are biological models, psychological models, cultural models, and grassroots, feminist, and power-based models.

Table 2. Factors increasing men's risk of committing rape (WHO, 2019)

Individual factors	Alcohol and drug consumption, forcible sexual fantasies and other attitudes and beliefs urge someone to do sexually violent acts, impulsive and antisocial tendencies, preference for impersonal sex, hostile attitudes towards women, having an experience of sexual abuse in childhood, exposure to family violence as a child.
Relationship factors	Association with sexually aggressive and delinquent peers; witnessing physical violence in family and access to few resources; dominant patriarchy in relationship or family environment; growing up in a family that is emotionally unsupportive; the honour and dignity of family honour is considered more important than the victim's health and safety.
Community factors	Poverty, feeling pressured to preserve their masculinity, lack of employment opportunities; feeling unsupported from police and judicial system; general tolerance of sexual violence within the community; weak community and legal sanctions against sexual violence.
Societal factors	Social norms that support and reinforce sexual violence; supporting the dominance and superiority of men through social norms; laws and policies that are not strong enough to protect people against sexual violence and gender inequality; high levels of crime and other forms of violence.

Table 3. Sexual violence interventions (Brome et al., 2004)

Primary prevention	Pre-incident approaches that can prevent initial perpetration or victimization.
Secondary prevention	Immediate responses after sexual violence, dealing with the short-term consequences of violence.
Tertiary prevention	Long-term responses after sexual violence, dealing with the lasting consequences of violence and treating sex offender.

Changing behaviors that facilitate sexual violence caused achieving the overall goal of primary prevention; that is, a reduction in the incidence of such violent acts) (Fig. 1). The interventions are mainly focused on the interpersonal, community, and social level factors that promote and support behavior change. Finding the methods of achieving and implementing this in a best way is the next step.

The main focus of the prevention strategies is on women to take actions to avoid victimization. For example, the Project Sister USA runs a variety of programs with the purpose of preventing sexual assault. A list of tips to assist women in avoiding sexual assault has been suggested. Using the acronym PREVENT, they suggest women (Carmody and Carrington, 2000):

- Put change in your wallet for a ride home,
- Recognize the early signs of potential assault,
- Examine your surroundings and the environment constantly and carefully,

Figure 1. Steps to collective behaviour change for the reduction of sexual assault incidence (Quadara and Wall, 2012)

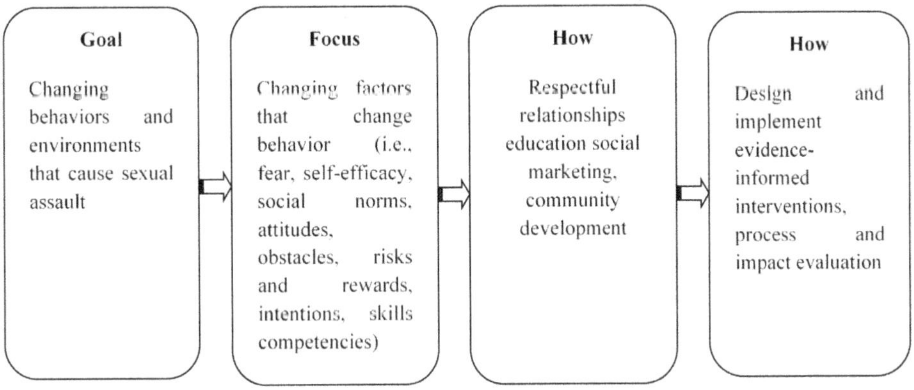

- Verbalize your resistance loudly,
- Exhibit confidence in potentially threatening situations,
- Never assume sexual assault can't happen to you,
- Travel in groups.

Learning how to control alleged 'innate' violent tendencies by men has been of great attention and more prominence in public policy circles in recent years. Programs are held in the U.K., Australia, North America and New Zealand, aimed at re-educating violent offenders.

To change the general attitude of blaming the victim and to provide more knowledge to the community, the strategies of public education have been applied. Many of these have been supported by government and are seen as major initiatives in preventing sexual violence. Public education is a part of prevention strategies used by many sexual assault services in Australia and overseas. An examination of some service-based programs suggests such programs aim at raising awareness about the facts of rape or the preventive measures women or children can do to protect themselves or to change attitudes and knowledge.

Another key strategy for reducing violence in society is education programs in schools. Changing attitudes has been the main focus of most of the programs, but some have also concerned changing behavior.

GROUNDED THEORY

Qualitative methodologies have a long history in sociology. However, during the 1960s, the quantitative research methodology was displaced with other methodologies (Charmaz, 2003). Having roots in positivism, quantitative methods assume a unitary scientific method of observation, experimentation, logic, and evidence (Charmaz, 2003). GT doubted this assumption and asked researchers to enter into the work without a preconceived hypothesis, allowing them to move back and forth between the collection of data and the analysis of the data.

Feminist studies have used GT since the mid-1990s. Researchers from a variety of disciplines incorporate feminist principles into their GT studies, with the claim of methodological compatibility. Contemporary forms of GT have shifted from its original positivist and post-positivist roots just as feminist perspectives have developed over time. This shift in GT is toward a more interpretive and constructivist GT position that is assumed to fit with feminist inquiry (Plummer and Young, 2010).

The main focus in constructivist GT and classic GT is reality. Constructivist GT is similar to the pragmatist tradition in perceiving reality as fluid and uncertain. While, the objectivist position of classic GT fits within a more positivist or objectivist position. Based on this position, it is possible to observe and describe reality from an un-biased viewpoint (Charmaz, 2009; Charmaz, 2006). According to objectivist GT researchers, like Glaser and Strauss, there is an external reality that can be incompletely discovered and described.

Objectivist grounded theorists concentrate on the role of data discovery. In contrast, constructivist grounded theorists hold that interaction creates data (Charmaz, 2009). Objectivist grounded theorists view themselves as neutral observers who witness the emergence of data. Constructivist grounded theorists assume an inseparable relationship between knowledge and social constructions. A constructivist grounded theorist, on the other hand, believes that the creation and dissemination of knowledge is not neutral but rather is created under the influence of pre-existing structural conditions, and surfaces in emergent situations (Charmaz, 2009). The perspectives, privileges, positions, interactions, and geographic locations of the researcher determine the creation of knowledge (Charmaz, 2009). Embracing the inherent messiness in the research process is characterized as the ideal constructivist grounded theory (Charmaz, 2009). According to a constructivist grounded theorist, a neutral position cannot be the creator of knowledge. In addition, they encourage an explicit discussion about the researcher's position, as well as an open and continuous effort to maintain reflexivity during the entire research process (Charmaz, 2009). As Charmaz stated, it is required to consider the research process and diverse perspectives of the participants and our own perspectives in order to provide a deeper, more complex, and reflexive analysis (Charmaz, 2009).

Both the stated and unstated meanings and actions of the participants are entered, understood and described by the constructivist grounded theorists. In this sense, researchers must decode the assumptions of the participants and themselves and examine them (Charmaz, 2009). In addition, a constructivist grounded theorist also considers the larger social structures or ideologies within which the participants' meaning and actions are uncovered and described. The personal thoughts and actions and the micro and macro levels of society are considered by the researchers in an attempt to interpret the connections between them (Charmaz 2009). The classic GT viewpoint, in contrary to the constructivist view, describes only the observable words and actions of the participants (Charmaz, 2009). Constructivist grounded theorists' focus is different from that of objectivist grounded theorists. The focus of objectivist grounded theorists is on creating context-free generalizations that can generate theory and maintain a micro focus. In other words, they focus on the observed world of the participants (Charmaz, 2009). While, constructivist grounded theorists emphasize on both the micro and macro (cultural scene) influences on participants.

Creating context-free abstract generalizations is the main objective of traditional grounded theorists. However, constructivist grounded theorists seek to create a theoretical explanation, within the historical and socio-political context, of a phenomenon that is credible and useful. Constructivist grounded theorists confirm the fact that their theories and explanations are partial and dependent on context (Charmaz, 2009). Traditional grounded theorists and constructivist grounded theorists have different views on the role of literature reviews and theoretical sensitivity. Traditional or objectivist grounded theorists are strictly adhered to the idea of theoretical sensitivity. Objectivist grounded theorists review the literatures strictly to support an emerging theory. In addition, they avoid any preconceived theories since they lead theoretical sensitivity to be lost. The stance of constructivist grounded theorists toward literature reviews and use of theoretical frameworks is a more nuanced one. Literature review is used as tool to enhance the constructivist grounded theorists' theoretical sensitivity and to support emerging theory (Charmaz, 2009).

Based on a constructivist epistemology, Charmaz created a different variant of GT, called constructivist GT. This epistemology differs from a positivist epistemology (Charmaz, 2006). In addition, the constructivist GT can be differentiated from classic GT based on three main features, as described by Glaser and Strauss (Charmaz, 2006). The three main areas include: foundational assumptions, theoretical sensitivity, focus and implications for data analysis.

GT AND SEXUAL VIOLENCE

The purpose of Lozano (2015) was to establish a theory to explain one part of a victim's life: the dynamics of the relationship of committed couple, specifically when the female partner was sexually victimized by someone other than her current partner. This study was conducted with the aim of gaining a better understanding of the effect of sexual assault on the couple relationship. A constructivist approach to GT was used in this study to allow the participants space to share their stories without agenda. First, an aspect of the GT approach, which distinguishes it, is the dynamic process in which, ideally, a substantive theory, based on the researcher's immersion in the data, is generated. According to constructivism, there are multiple realities that can be revealed through the interaction between the researcher and participants. Thus, although reality for couples where the female partner has been victimized is placed in the domains of social and cultural ideals, the constructivist paradigm allows the participants to maneuver on their lived experience. Second, since the GT method attempts to understand and potentially advocate for participants by examining how victims derive meaning from their experiences, it is well-tailored to a social justice perspective. Further, a constructivist approach will grant a space to the participants that they may not have had otherwise to share their experiences. Thus, the chosen research and methodology are consistent with Counseling Psychology's social justice aims. The GT approach is not only a methodological model of the scientist-practitioner due to embedding theory and practice, but it also enables Counseling Psychologists-as-advocates. Since GT allows for a greater understanding of lived experiences, such as the experience of being in a couple where one partner has a sexual assault history, researcher can disseminate this knowledge where it may facilitate change.

Developing a theory to explain the relationship dynamics of opposite-sex couples in which the female partner has been sexually victimized as an adult outside of the couple relationship, Lozano (2015) conducted a study. Four couples participated in the study and shared their experiences of disclosing the assault, communicating about the assault, physical intimacy, and impact of the assault to the relationship. Using a constructivist GT approach, the model emerged from the data. Overall, the women decided to talk about their experience because they felt secure in their current intimate relationship. Disclosing the experience happened for one of two reasons: (a) either to make sure that the relationship would last by testing the relationship and partner, or (b) because the women felt overwhelmed emotionally thinking about thc assault. The decision led to the response of both individuals in the relationship. General responses were positive for both parties, except the nuanced pieces that were relative to the sex of the person. After the disclosure, the relationship changed, but participants found it difficult to define it. The most noticeable change was in relation to physical intimacy and discussing the assault. When the female partner was triggered for various reasons, including during sex, discussing about the assault occurred. The previous literature in emotion-focused therapy, attachment theory, shame resilience work, and rape myth acceptance research supported the findings. Implications for counseling and future research directions are discussed.

Using GT methodology, Maktoubian and Khorasgani (2014) intended to explore sexual harassment in Isfahan and developed a paradigm modeling (Fig.2).

According to Tilley and Brackley (2005), intimate partner violence is a serious and pervasive problem in the U.S. society; 25% of women and 7.6% of men reported annually physical abuse by an intimate partner. To develop interventions to reduce partner violence, it is important to understand the risk factors for development of violence. Research with victims, rather than perpetrators, leads to a better understanding about the development of partner violence. The methodology used in the study was GT; it is a general methodology in which data is systematically gathered and analyzed. Studying issues such as the development of male violence in intimate partner relationships, which is categorized as issues with inappropriate or inadequate theories, GT is the most appropriate.

They studied men convicted of assault on an intimate female partner. The Violent Couples Model was developed by using the data. In this model, the primary elements included justifying and minimizing violence, childhood exposure to violence, ineffective anger management, childhood experience of

Figure 2. Paradigm modelling of sexual harassment in Isfahan (Maktoubian and Khorasgani, 2014)

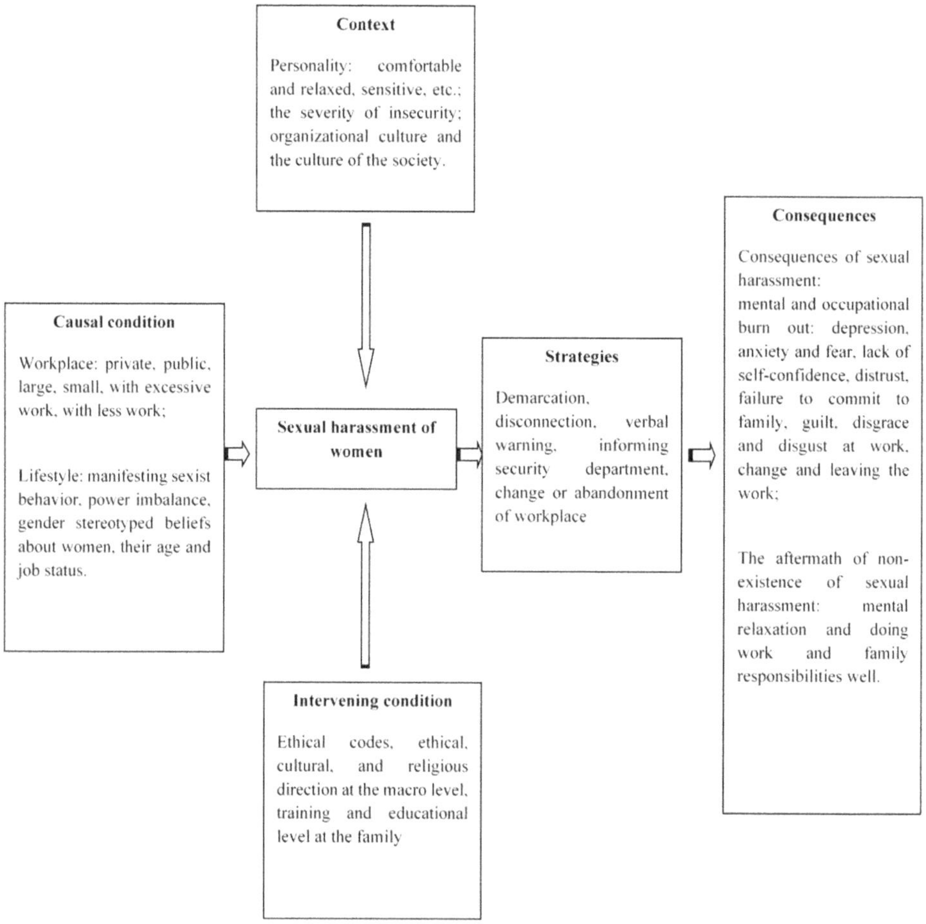

violence, and ineffective conflict resolution. The moderating elements in this model were social and familial factors. This model also included contextual elements including power and control, insecure maternal relationships, the view of violence as a private problem, ambivalent intimate relationships social isolation, jealousy, desensitization, objectification of women, immaturity, lack of awareness about what constitutes violence, mistrust, traditional views of the roles of women, and financial issues. The interventions used in the model were, in nature, primary, or preventive. The prevention efforts in this model focused on the family as a whole, rather than on batterers alone.

As Duma et al. (2007) declared, thousands of women and children in South Africa annually experience sexual assault trauma. The survivors of sexual assault, their families and the larger community of service providers are faced with the challenge of recovery from sexual assault. Yet, there is little research on recovery from sexual assault as a phenomenon. Aiming at discovering and developing the GT of recovery from sexual assault trauma within the first six months after the incident, Duma et al (2007) examined and analyzed the recovery undertaken by women who have been sexually assaulted. They sought to find answer to the question what the components of the recovery undertaken by women within the first six months following the incident of rape are. The principles of GT methodology were used in this longitudinal qualitative study.

Based on the ten women's descriptions of their journey of recovery from sexual assault, they discovered and constructed the substantive theory through the inductive and deductive analysis of data. This theory consisted of eight theoretical concepts or categories including 1) sexual assault trauma, 2) awakening, 3) pragmatic acceptance, 4) turning point, 5) reclaiming what was lost, 6) defining own landmarks of healing, 7) readiness for closure, and 8) returning to self. The GT contributes to the knowledge about the recovery by providing a process and language for understanding women's experiences within the larger social context of recovery. The findings suggested that women's journey of recovery is an individual experience; it is influenced by many and varied causal and intervening conditions such as personal biographies, relationships, supportive and non-supportive environments at individual, family, community and societal levels.

According to Carneiro et al. (2019), marital violence that is rooted in gender inequality has been experienced for many years and turned to a public health problem. They used a qualitative study through GT to understand marital violence in a municipality of the Brazilian Northeast. The study regarded the relevance of coping strategies based on institutional and social support in recognizing marital violence as a recurring problem in the life of women. It also showed that this problem has implications for women's health and that of their children. The findings of the study were consistent with the meaning of experiencing marital violence by women in criminal prosecution revealed by the phenomenon of experiencing marital violence as a progressive and recurrent process, with consequences for health and implications for social relations. Five components of the paradigmatic model contribute to understanding this meaning.

The data revealed a context of marital violence experienced in a recurrent way, in which women experience the phenomenon expressed in patrimonial, psychological, moral, sexual and physical forms. This experience takes place in a progressive process. First, it begins with more hidden expressions of violence, such as jealousy, control, humiliations and social isolation of women, and then gradually evolves into increasingly explicit expressions using physical force, such as hangings and battering. Following this apex event, the offender regrets and promises changes in behavior (Carneiro et al., 2019).

The consequences component, that is the impact of marital violence on women and children, indicates that experiencing marital violence in intimate relationships brings consequences to the lives and health of women and their children; For example, it can compromise children's school performance as children also tend to reproduce violent behavior as adults. From the category of unveiling the generation of violence, the situations in which the phenomenon was generated was revealed. It also showed how it affected the lives of couples, since both women and their aggressors witnessed and experienced violence in their families of origin, reproducing it in their relationships. Regarding the intervening condition that acts on the central phenomenon and increases its complexity, it was revealed that family support is absent during the experience of violence, weakening the woman's decision-making to break up the relationship. The strategies component of the paradigmatic model demonstrates that women seek to find institutional and social support, represented by family support and participation in support groups. It can contribute to coping with marital violence (Carneiro et al., 2019).

Using the constructivist GT, Wadsworth (2015) explored the perceptions of adult female sexual assault victims/survivors about their wellbeing. In this context, the study examined their definitions and descriptions of wellbeing, the impact of the assault on wellbeing; and barriers and facilitators to achieving wellbeing after the assault incident. The sensitizing concepts of this study were borrowed from feminist theory. The data were analyzed using first, second, and third level coding techniques, memo writing, and data displays. According to the participants, they were affected by negative effects of their overall wellbeing and the wellbeing domains of physical, mental, career/economic/financial, relational, and spiritual. The findings of this study indicated wellbeing as a core category that encompasses the five domains listed above. These domains were also described in the literature. Moreover, the dynamic, interactive, and overlapping nature of each of the domains of wellbeing as well as the participants' ability to enhance, maintain, or worsen health status and overall wellbeing were confirmed by the participants. In addition, a new construct, i.e. safety, emerged that cut across all domains. Furthermore, the distinguished significance of culture was recognized.

Sexual assault is prevalent in the United States and has many adverse health conditions. Though many of the harms experienced by victims/survivors of sexual assault have been uncovered in a variety of studies, most researchers have focused on only mental or physical health while neglecting the complex nature of wellbeing. In addition, there is little feedback on how sexual assault victims/survivors describe wellbeing and the improving or worsening factors. It is a need to regard what wellbeing means to the female victims of sexual assault in order to improve their wellbeing; how they describe it, what factors facilitate it, and what factors reduce it (Wadsworth, 2015).

CONCLUSION

Sexual violence and other forms of gender-based violence have been increasingly of great consideration as a significant public health issue since 2000. The global prevalence of sexual violence has been proved in various major reports and studies. Preventive strategies are increasingly attracted attention to prevent sexual violence since it is associated with individual empowerment, well-being, and societal prosperity.

Grounded theory (GT) methods have been recognized as standard social research methods. GT is used in qualitative research to provide explicit, sequential guidelines. It also offers specific strategies for handling the analytic phases of inquiry, and legitimizes qualitative research as scientific inquiry. Constructivist GT, on the other hand, seems more compatible with feminist inquiry.

An overview of the studies on sexual harassment and sexual violence was presented in this chapter. It focused on definitions, statistics, forms, consequences, and prevention strategies. Moreover, a comparison between GT and constructivist GT was developed. The impact of sexual violence on mental and physical health as well as social well-being was discussed; these impacts may be equally long-lasting. The preventive strategies suggested here included changing people's attitudes and behaviors by formulating and implementing appropriate policies and empowerment programs. In addition, in-depth discussions were presented on the application of GT in various studies such as understanding of the effect of sexual assault on the couple relationship, paradigm modeling of sexual harassment, understanding intimate partner violence, women's descriptions of their journey of recovery from sexual assault, understanding marital violence, adult female sexual assault victims/survivors' perception about their wellbeing.

REFERENCES

Acierno, R., Resnick, H., Kilpatrick, D. G., Saunders, B., & Best, C. L. (1999). Risk factors for rape, physical assault, and posttraumatic stress disorder in women: Examination of differential multivariate relationships. *Journal of Anxiety Disorders, 13*(6), 541–563. doi:10.1016/S0887-6185(99)00030-4 PMID:10688523

Bachar, K., & Koss, M. P. (2001). From prevalence to prevention: Closing the gap between what we know about rape and what we do. In C. M. Renzetti, J. L. Edleson, & R. Bergen (Eds.), *Sourcebook on violence against women* (pp. 117–142). Thousand Oaks, CA: Sage Publications, Inc.

Barker, K. (2017). *Sexual harassment experience, psychological climate, and sex effect on perception of safety* (PhD dissertation). College of Social and Behavioral Sciences, Walden University.

Brome, M., Saul, J., Lang, K., Lee-Pethel, R., Rainford, N., & Wheaton, J. (2004). *Sexual violence prevention: beginning the dialogue*. Atlanta, GA: Centers for Disease Control and Prevention.

Bularzik, M. (1978). *Sexual harassment at the workplace*. New England Free Press.

Carmody, M., & Carrington, K. (2000). Preventing sexual violence? *Australian and New Zealand Journal of Criminology, 33*(3), 341–361. doi:10.1177/000486580003300306

Carneiro, J. B., Gomes, N. P., Campos, L. M., Silva, A. F., Cunha, K. S., & Costa, D. M. S. C. (2019). Understanding marital violence: A study in grounded theory. *Revista Latino-Americana de Enfermagem, 27*, e3185. doi:10.1590/1518-8345.3116.3185 PMID:31596418

Center for Victim Advocacy and Violence Prevention. (2010). *Sexual harassment*. Retrieved September 02, 2019, https://www.usf.edu/student-affairs/victim-advocacy/types-of-crimes/sexualharassment.pdf

Charmaz, K. (2003). Grounded theory. In A. E. Bryman & T. F. Lia (Eds.), *The sage encyclopedia of social science research methods* (pp. 440–444). Thousand Oaks, CA: Sage.

Charmaz, K. (2006). *Constructing grounded theory: A practical guide through qualitative analysis*. London, UK: Sage.

Charmaz, K. (2009). Shifting the grounds: Constructivist grounded theory. In J. Morse (Ed.), *Developing grounded theory: The second generation* (pp. 127–154). Walnut Creek, CA: Left Coast Press.

Creamer, M., Burgess, P., & McFarlane, A. C. (2001). Post-traumatic stress disorder: Findings from the Australian National Survey of Mental Health and Well-being. *Psychological Medicine*, *31*(7), 1237–1247. doi:10.1017/S0033291701004287 PMID:11681550

Darves-Bornoz, J. M. (1997). Rape-related psychotraumatic syndromes. *European Journal of Obstetrics, Gynecology, and Reproductive Biology*, *71*(1), 59–65. doi:10.1016/S0301-2115(96)02605-X PMID:9031961

Duma, S. E., Mekwa, J. N., & Denny, L. D. (2007). Women's journey of recovery from sexual assault trauma: A grounded theory-part 1. *Curationis*, *30*(4), 4–11. PMID:18402415

Elliott, D. M., Mok, D. S., & Briere, J. (2004). Adult sexual assault: Prevalence, symptomatology, and sex differences in the general population. *Journal of Traumatic Stress*, *17*(3), 203–211. doi:10.1023/B:JOTS.0000029263.11104.23 PMID:15253092

HRPA. (2019). Doing our duty preventing sexual harassment in the workplace. *Human Resource Professionals Association.* Retrieved September 02, 2019, https://www.hrpa.ca/Documents/Public/Thought-Leadership/Doing-Our-Duty.PDF

Jewkes, R., Vundule, C., Maforah, F., & Jordaan, E. (2001). Relationship dynamics and teenage pregnancy in South Africa. *Social Science & Medicine*, *52*(5), 733–744. doi:10.1016/S0277-9536(00)00177-5 PMID:11218177

Kilpatrick, D. G., Saunders, B. E., Veronen, L. J., Best, C. L., & Von, J. M. (1987). Criminal victimization: Lifetime prevalence, reporting to police, and psychological impact. *Crime and Delinquency*, *33*(4), 479–489. doi:10.1177/0011128787033004005

Kilpatrick, D. G., & Seymour, A. (1992). Rape in America: A report to the Nation. Technical report, National Victims Center, Arlington, VA, and Crime Victims Research and Treatment Center, Charleston, SC.

Koss, M. P., & Dinero, T. E. (1989). Discriminant analysis of risk factors for sexual victimization among a national sample of college women. *Journal of Consulting and Clinical Psychology*, *57*(2), 242–250. doi:10.1037/0022-006X.57.2.242 PMID:2708612

Leserman, J., Li, Z. Z., Drossman, D. A., & Hu, Y. B. (1998). Selected symptoms associated with sexual and physical abuse history among female patients with gastrointestinal disorders: The impact on subsequent health care visits. *Psychological Medicine*, *28*(2), 417–425. doi:10.1017/S0033291797006508 PMID:9572098

Levitan, R. D., Parikh, S. V., Lesage, A. D., Hegadoren, K. M., Adams, M., Kennedy, S. H., & Goering, P. N. (1998). Major depression in individuals with a history of childhood physical or sexual abuse: Relationship to neurovegetative features, mania, and gender. *The American Journal of Psychiatry*, *155*(12), 1746–1752. doi:10.1176/ajp.155.12.1746 PMID:9842786

Lozano, N. M. (2015). The impact of sexual violence on intimate relationship dynamics: A grounded theory study (PhD dissertation). The Graduate College at the University of Nebraska, Lincoln, NE.

Maktoubian, M., & Khorasgani, A. R. (2014). How women are sexually abused in the workplace: Applying the qualitative methodology of the grounded theory to examine women's insecurity in the workplace. *Strategic Research in Security and Social Order*, *3*(7), 61–78.

Mollica, R. F., & Son, L. (1989). Cultural dimensions in the evaluation and treatment of sexual trauma: An overview. *The Psychiatric Clinics of North America*, *12*(2), 363–379. doi:10.1016/S0193-953X(18)30437-4 PMID:2748443

Plummer, M., & Young, L. E. (2010). Grounded theory and feminist inquiry: Revitalizing links to the past. *Western Journal of Nursing Research*, *32*(3), 305–321. doi:10.1177/0193945909351298 PMID:20040733

Quadara, A., & Wall, L. (2012). What is effective primary prevention in sexual assault? Translating the evidence for action. *Australian Centre for the Study of Sexual Assault*. Retrieved September 02, 2019, https://aifs.gov.au/sites/default/files/publication-documents/w11.pdf

Sorenson, S. B., Stein, J. A., Siegel, J. M., Golding, J. M., & Burnam, M. A. (1987). The prevalence of adult sexual assault: The Los Angeles Epidemiological Catchment Area Project. *American Journal of Epidemiology*, *126*(6), 1154–1165. doi:10.1093/oxfordjournals.aje.a114753 PMID:3500639

Stanley, L., & Wise, S. (1990). Method, methodology and epistimology in feminist research processes. In L. Stanley (Ed.), *Feminist praxis: research, theory and epistemology in feminist sociology* (pp. 20–60). London: Routledge.

The US Equal Employment Opportunity Commission (EEOC). (2011a). *Harassment*. Washington, DC: Equal Employment Opportunity Commission. Retrieved September 13, 2019, from https://www.ccoc.gov/laws/types/harassment.cfm

The US Equal Employment Opportunity Commission (EEOC). (2011b). *Sexual Harassment*. Washington, DC: Equal Employment Opportunity Commission. Retrieved September 13, 2019, from https://www.eeoc.gov/laws/types/sexual_harassment.cfm

The World Bank. (2018). Women, business and the law. *International Bank for Reconstruction and Development*. Retrieved September 01, 2019 from, http://pubdocs.worldbank.org/en/102741522965756861/WBL-Key-Findings-Web-FINAL.pdf

Tilley, D. S., & Brackley, M. (2005). Men who batter intimate partners: A grounded theory study of the development of male violence in intimate partner relationship. *Issues in Mental Health Nursing*, *26*(3), 281–297. doi:10.1080/01612840590915676 PMID:16020047

Tjaden, P., & Thoennes, N. (2000). *Full report of the prevalence, incidence, and consequences of violence against women: Findings from the National Violence Against Women Survey*. U.S. Department of Justice Office of Justice Programs National Institute of Justice. doi:10.1037/e514172006-001

Wadsworth, P. (2015). A Constructivist grounded theory exploration of wellbeing in female adult sexual assault victims/survivors (PhD dissertation). Arizona State University.

WHO. (2019). *Sexual violence*. World Report on Violence and Health. Retrieved September 02, 2019, Retrieved September 01, 2019 from https://www.who.int/violence_injury_prevention/violence/global_campaign/en/chap6.pdf

Chapter 10
Analysis of Corporate Social Responsibility With Grounded Theory Approach:
Focusing on CSR and Sustainable Behavior

ABSTRACT

This chapter is going to review and analyze the literature of the applications of grounded theory (GT) in corporate social responsibility (CSR). It is organized in three sections: definitions of CSR, the position of qualitative research methods and GT in the practices of CSR, and applications of GT in CSR. It particularly focuses on two paradigm models of CSR behavior and a paradigm model of sustainable behavior of farmers. Interviews, observations, and written materials such as CSR reports are the tools used to collect data in GT. Individuals, groups, or institutions can include the participants of studies in this regard and are selected regarding their relationship with the CSR-related phenomenon. The memos written by the CSR researchers are about the conceptual and theoretical ideas formed in the process of analysis. The phases of GT in CSR studies, including open coding, axial coding, and selective coding, are explained in this chapter.

DOI: 10.4018/978-1-7998-4252-1.ch010

INTRODUCTION

The concept of social responsibility is rapidly developed and should be considered as one of the most important indicators in countries; it is intertwined with policy making, sociology, business, management and accounting of companies. On the other hand, corporate social responsibility (CSR) is a key factor in an organization. The practices of an organization affect customers, suppliers of raw materials, government, and society.

It should be borne in mind that the responsibility of organizations towards society and the public lies beyond the provision of goods and services. Organizations reflect the concerns of the society and hence, they must feel responsible to resolve them by devoting parts of their financial and human resources to this matter. Numerous studies have indicated that the probable harms done to society by the organization may be the result of giving up on goals by the organizations. In this case, people's welfare will be lost for the benefit of the organization. Managers need to be competent in the perceptual, human and technical skills, and nowadays, must regard social issues.

CSR should not be considered as a luxury in the engaged business, which might or might not be afforded. CSR and sustainable development must be operated in respectful ways to the general population and their surrounding environment. Paying special attention to product quality and the impact of activities on the society can guarantee successful achievement for the businesses. It, at first glance, might be considered a simple operational cost. However, all costs are not equal and some corporations have learned that acting responsibly can bring them some advantages such as more innovation, increased revenue through higher quality products, and reduced costs by making smarter business decisions.

The emergence of CSR, which dates back to 1950s, in the debates of the sustainability, is considered as an important concept (Jansen, 2016). According to the latest analyses by Secchi (2007) and Lee (2008), great changes have been made in the meaning and practice of CSR developed in the definition of this term. What was on the main focus of the classical view of CSR was philanthropy and now, it emphasizes more on business-society relations and the contribution that a corporation or firm provided for solving social problems in particular. Social performance and market performance were, in the early twentieth century, closely associated.

Today, CSR not only contributes to resolving the economic and financial challenges, but also the problems in social, human, and environmental interactions. In this context, what can guarantee sustainable development of performance in a company is a social approach (Dakhili and Ansi, 2012).

CSR in business, which is considered to be voluntary in nature, refers to the activities beyond as abiding by law. The expectations in society have been changed and corporate social and environmental responsibility may reflect these changes (Babalola, 2012). Many involved people see CSR as a matter of legitimacy and acceptance, and few see it as a task that needs to be performed by applying higher standards of conduct by businesses, businessmen, craftsmen, and citizens (Wallace, 2003).

CSR – which is considered to be one of the most important challenges of the 21st century – may encompass many different things and has a variety of explanations in various sources, leading to a confusion. One source of such confusion is the existence of different connected or synonymous terms that overlap with it, such as corporate citizenship, sustainable business, environmental responsibility, the triple bottom line; social and environmental accountability; business ethics and corporate accountability (Gorski et al., 2017).

Reviewing literature on this issue, this chapter is organized in 3 following sections: the different definitions suggested for CSR, the position of qualitative research methods and grounded theory (GT) in the studies of CSR, and applications of GT in CSR. In particular, it also focuses on two paradigm models of CSR behavior, and one paradigm model of sustainable behavior of farmers.

CSR

The definition suggested by Freeman (1984) for CSR caused a broader understanding of this term; he asserted that the demand of society and stakeholders should be of greater consideration in business practices of companies. CSR plays an intermediating role between responsibility of organization towards society and the demands of society. According to Bonini et al. (2006), a social contract between business and the society can contribute to identifying these demands. At the same time, companies have different responses to the societal demands. Therefore, the answers to the following questions can provide solutions: how are the demand of society identified by companies, and how do companies choose to engage in these CSR practices.

The CSR is expected to do more than a simple good act. Differentiating CSR and philanthropy, Smith (2008) believes that the responsibility of the organizations towards society is broader than participating in some good actions. In addition, the results of a review study on CSR showed that the expectation and acceptance toward CSR practices have been recently changing (Lee 2008), indicating dynamic nature of CSR. Despite of advancements in the definition of CSR, new and developing definitions are still suggested in studies.

Furthermore, since CSR is a subjective concept, various definitions are provided for it (Yang and Rivers, 2009). Votaw (1972) asserts that the people's understanding of the definition of CSR is different from one to one. However, the variation in understanding CSR is not only in the domain of definition, but also in the way of CSR implementation, including a variety of practices, different perspectives, expectations and interpretation accordingly.

Companies manifest their CSR in their communities and abroad in many different ways. Most are based on discretionary or philanthropic activities, but some border is imposed to the stakeholders with whom they come into contact on improving ethical situation. Corporate contributions (or philanthropy), employee volunteerism, community relations, becoming an outstanding employer for specific employee groups (e.g. women, older workers, or minorities), making environmental improvements that exceed what is required by law can be mentioned, among others, as some common types on CSR. In practice, companies sometimes label CSR initiatives as good corporate citizenship, strong ethical practices, or sustainable business practices (Carroll, 2018).

The relevant studies usually use the terms "social responsibility" and "corporate social responsibility" interchangeably. Regarding the fact that the term CSR was emerged by large corporate businesses since the focus of this study was on small businesses, the term "social responsibility" was selected. Considering the matter of classification, the previous studies have focused almost exclusively on large corporations and the small businesses have not received as much attention (Masarira, 2014).

QUALITATITVE RESEARCH

The qualitative approach of analysis was selected for the present study since it, as compared to the quantitative approach, is the best to obtain knowledge from social scientific studies. The qualitative methodology requires the researcher considers this fact that the knowledge must not be treated as a mirror of reality rather different perspectives can have access to it while developing theory. The researcher plays an important role in producing (e.g. interviews, observations, text, pictures) and interpreting the data (Yerznkyan and Henriksson, 2010).

Researchers use this methodology to study human behavior and functioning. The significance of a situation can be best interpreted through the qualitative approach. The qualitative data focuses on ordinary events occurring in natural settings and provides a good understanding of real life situations. The arguments on the qualitative data indicated that it is rich and holistic and reveals well the complexity and meanings (Carter and Fortune, 2003).

The dominant approach in studying CSR is the positivistic stance in it and the qualitative methodology has been rarely used. Though the qualitative methodology is potentially best suited to study CSR, researchers have used it rarely in this regard. In particular, not enough attention has been paid to a contextualized study closely related to the event. The aim of qualitative research, according to Patten (2002), is providing a better understanding of the phenomenon under investigation; while, the quantitative methodology focuses on a tiny aspect. The reality is revealed within a contextualized framework by using the qualitative method and deep knowledge will be provided about the issue under investigation (Bazeley, 2007). Discourse analysis is used in the only research stream in the qualitative approach towards social and environmental disclosure and applied language was also studied in this approach (Coupland, 2006; Livesey, 2002). To provide a more understandable and wider picture of the phenomenon, different methods of study must be of great attention (Aguinis and Glavas, 2012).

GROUNDED THEORY

Grounded theory that is defined as a systematic inductive and comparative methodology is used to conduct inquiry aiming at developing theory. Based on three main reasons, it has been proved that GT is popular in management research: (a) it contributes to providing a new theory or fresh perspectives on the old theory; (b) it generates theory of direct interest and relevance for practitioners, and (c) it can reveal micro-management processes in complex and unfolding situations. However, it is relatively losing its popularity as a research method within the management discipline, and is rarely used in the CSR field (Anagnostopoulos, 2013).

One of the good research topics is CSR despite of absent studies on the tourism industry in India. The study by Jansen (2016) provides information about the industry of tour operator in India as well as the operators' views and practices on CSR. Regarding the explorative nature of the research, open coding was the first step of data analysis, through which a list of codes was created. The second step, i.e. axial coding, coded the data again and determined the main categories and subcategories. The purpose of such determination was finding any relationship in categories. The process of selective coding was the last step. The core concepts and the relationships between them were determined in this step. However, it should be noted that the process of coding was not always linear and sometimes merged, as typical in qualitative research (Jansen, 2016).

The sources of collecting data in GT include interviews and observations including transcripts and field notes and written materials such as documents, CSR reports, books, newsletters, diaries, letters, and websites. The preliminary observations are the first step of starting a GT research. Selection of the research participants (individuals, groups, or institutions) based on their relationships with the phenomenon or the concept they represent lies in the second step. Regarding the theoretical sampling, coding, and constant comparison of the qualitative data, the research ideas are recognized; they are considered to be the core of GT methodology. A research question should contribute to identifying the phenomenon under investigation as well as relevant information about the subjects, participants, or 'actors', and their realities in the society (Strauss and Corbin 1998). Another task left to the CSR researcher is providing some important insights into the realities of cultural participants. In this sense, the researcher has to produce a detailed description of the cultural scene (Žydžiūnaitė and Tauginienė, 2018).

APPLICATIONS OF GT IN CSR

Tyagi (2019) aimed at knowing the managerial decision making process in CSR formulation and implementation to develop a substantive theory on managerial decision making process by the use of GT. According to the results, CSR is recognized as a field within management, and not a discipline. Its theory provides guidance on the managerial decision-making process in formulating and implementing CSR in areas such as identifying and selecting stakeholders and partners, planning employee voluntary activities, and managing relationships. Nwanji et al. (2019) developed a substantive theory of ethical corporate governance by the application of GT approach.

As Aguinis and Glavas (2012) asserted, companies all over the world have engaged in communicating CSR principles, initiatives and activities. The stakeholders can be informed of the firms' CSR initiatives through the Internet. According to Isenmann (2006) an important transition is taking place in the CSR communication: it is entering a new digital online stage. The evidence show that various stakeholders like employees, customers, suppliers, investors, ranking and rating institutions, governments and local authorities, as well as pressure groups and other non-governmental organizations (NGOs) can be engaged and involved in this process through a new quasi-public online effort that is replaced for the managerial closed shop procedures.

Different studies have investigated the online communication of CSR. A few researchers, in the process of analysis, use first exploring websites and then provide the categories of analysis in the approach of GT. However, another stream in the literature analyzing online CSR communication of business firms is employing a discourse analytic approach and applying methods related to critical discourse analysis, GT or linguistics. In some of these studies the legitimizing role of corporate websites is the main topic. For example, the study by Coupland (2005) concentrated on examining the language drawn to describe socially responsible activities. The web-based CSR communication of five banking groups was the subject of another study by Coupland (2006). She identified three aspects of CSR in her GT research: doing good (activities, targeting communities), being good (environmental activities), and funding good (main financial operations). The findings showed that CSR, for traditional banks, is about community and the environment, referring to two aspects of "doing good" and "being good", respectively. Thus, little or no information can be found in the majority of banks' web pages on the issue of lending that is one of the main banking activities with high influence on the whole economy.

There is a little literature on the relationship between CSR and the core business of companies. The question, in this regard, is what the role of corporate strategy in CSR practices. In this context, Sadeghi (2013) explored, in the context of the annual report, the CSR practices (disclosures) of companies and their relation to various aspects of corporate strategy. She evaluated CSR practices and business practices through a multi-disciplinary approach. An appropriate analytical tool was applied in the research and GT methodology was adopted in the domain of interpretive tradition to develop the research within a subjective methodological underpinning.

Using the GT, the researcher can explore and analyze the data in a deeper level, and can generate a new theory within the multi-discipline approach that contributes to understanding the aspects cannot be explained within a single discipline. Most importantly, the application of two perspectives can help recognizing overriding problems in CSR implementation by companies. The new way of using GT methodology to analyze the annual reports is important for two reasons: 1) understanding CSR disclosures within the business context of the annual report, 2) evaluating the association between CSR practices and business of companies.

The annual report that is a formal report written with the agreement of CEO and the board of directors is the official voice of the company as well and presents information of various aspects in one report and the same context. Other means of communication such as standalone CSR report, on the other hand, does not reflect the business perspective of the company. The annual report contains information on business practices over the past year, main business decisions, business orientation, and anticipation of the company for the future of business. The shareholders and investors are considered to be the main target audiences of the annual report.

The examination of the possibility of developing a new CSR auditing system based on the analysis of current CSR literature and interviews conducted with a number of interested and knowledgeable stakeholders was the subject of a study by Morimoto et al (2005). This work aimed at creating a framework for social responsibility auditing consistent with the existing environmental audit system that is considered commercially successful. Tackling the complex issue of CSR auditing with a scientific approach through using GT, this project appeared unusual. Based on the evidence discovered to date in the literature review and the interviews, many perceive CSR as the social strand of sustainable development. However, there are controversies on its measurement. According to both the literature review and the interview analysis, developing an applied CSR auditing procedure, due to the lack of formal study of this complex subject, will be a challenging task. In fact, there could be found no single and broadly accepted definition, despite the widespread debate it has engendered. A prospective of CSR audit protocol was developed by considering the concepts from the findings of this research, together with the key factors identified in the literature review of CSR.

To outline the practice of CSR in a context with strong Islamic beliefs, Koleva (2019) identified unique CSR dimensions and constructs presented through an empirical framework. The framework was beyond the mere platform of the sense of Islamic philanthropy and was based on stakeholders and their related concerns as practices by the interviewed respondents. The study examined the CSR philosophy and approach in the Middle Eastern region based on the data collected from representatives of 63 organizations from Saudi Arabia, the United Arab Emirates and Oman and by employing GT strategy. The results indicated that the Middle Eastern understanding was largely based on social and altruistic actions. Such focus can be associated to the dominant role of religion in the examined region and the results in forms of non-structured or semi-structured approach to CSR.

Considine (2009) examined the way GT can be used to find empirically answers to the following questions: how do employees of a range of businesses make sense of CSR, how do they identify the initiatives and what business case, if any, can be made for CSR. He considered exactly an insight developed by GT into what CSR means to staff throughout a range of businesses and organization types and the design of a framework for considering a range of activities that might be classified as socially responsible by rigorous application of this methodology.

Examining the role of CSR and its influence on branding in the energy sector was the subject of a study by Michele (2015). The setting of this study was Hydro Ottawa because it is a power distribution and a power generation company, with a mixed private and public business model operating in a monopolistic context, and hence, it is a well-rounded example that can be transferred to other organizations and other sectors. Using GT, this research followed a case study approach. The findings indicated that a CSR strategy based on a healthy organizational culture, stakeholder needs, and the triple bottom line (financial, social, and environmental) resulted in CSR becoming the brand. The brand can then be communicated inside-out (from the employees to the external stakeholders)/outside-in (from external stakeholders to inside the organization) approach. Based on a GT analysis, a step-by-step prescriptive model was created, which could be used to enhance corporate social responsibility into Hydro Ottawa's brand and offer a critical perspective of the findings.

Alwahaibi et al. (2019) studied the practice of CSR reporting (CSRR) in Saudi Arabia. They described CSR perception, CSR implementation and CSRR in details as well as an interpretation for reporting practice, aiming at providing a GT to offer a plausible explanation for what shapes this reporting. Besides, the drivers and desired outcomes of CSRR were examined and linked in the study. There is no study on the use of the GT methodology exactly as instructed in the CSR literature. CSR practices were described in the first part of the findings. It revealed that CSR is perceived as an important concept though there were uncertainties on what CSR means to Saudi companies and what it involves. It was also proved that there is a gap between the perception of CSR and the way of its implementation as well as a lack of a systematic CSR strategy and performance measurements. CSR was still recognized and implemented as an ‘external’ factor to business operations and absence of creativity was clearly observed. The gap between CSR implementation/ activities and CSRR was evidenced as well. The arbitrary and inconsistent nature, absence of a formal mechanism, many transparency issues, and gaining less attention than CSR activities can be mentioned as features of CSRR. It presented a GT induced to interpret the reporting practices of Saudi companies. A textual and diagrammatical model that maps the territory of Saudi CSRR was used to illustrate the generated theory. What forms and shapes the reporting practices and accountability (both tacit and/or explicit) as the core concept/engine of the CSRR mechanism were explained and identified by the map, based on the managerial perspectives. The reinforcement of conventional importance of the concept and extension of its scope were the results of accountability in this grounded theory. In this sense, accountability is both society-centered and organization-centered.

PARADIGM MODELING OF CSR

Nourozi et al. (2014) used GT as the strategy for the analysis of the desire to implement CSR. Researchers use GT designs that are systematic, qualitative procedures to generate a general explanation (based on the participants' views, called a GT) explaining a process, action, or interaction among people (Creswell, 2000). Face-to-face in-depth interviews with open questions were used to interview with thirty informed executives and policy makers in the field of CSR. The interviews were repeated to share preliminary findings, make supplements, correct and modify the data.

Sampling was directed towards the generation and development of conceptual theory as opposed to creating a descriptive account (Breckenridge and Jones, 2009). Sampling from events, not necessarily individuals, is the focus of theoretical sampling method. The theoretical sampling is achieved by collecting data from people and/or data sources that are considered as relevant to answer the research question and the research objectives. Analyzing the primary collected data, the next subjects or data sources can be listed in accordance with the specific need to deepen the knowledge or the gaps to be filled; in this context, the characteristics of subjects, situations or events can be changed. One of the strategies to obtain theoretical sampling is using groups with different participants, but with relevant experiences in relation to the research phenomenon (Santos et al., 2018). When no new properties, dimensions, or relationships emerge during analysis, it can be said that the research has reached the theoretical saturation (Strauss and Corbin, 1998).

The core process in classic GT methodology is coding. The conceptual abstraction of data and its reintegration as theory happens in coding. The two types of coding in a classic GT study are: substantive coding, including both open and selective coding procedures, and theoretical coding. Substantive coding engages the researcher directly in working with the data, fracturing and analyzing it. in this step, open coding contribute to the emergence of a core category and related concepts and then the theoretical sampling and selective coding of data are used to theoretically saturate the core and the related concepts. The incidents (indicators) in the data are constantly compared to achieve the theoretical saturation and hence, the properties and dimensions of each category (code) are obtained. In this context, the indicators can be interchanged, indicating that no new properties or dimensions are emerging from continued coding and comparison (Holton, 2007).

The data is first involved in open coding whose core elements are posing sensitizing questions and constantly comparing data and codes (Setiawan and Darmawan, 2011). The CSR researcher, in open coding, writes memos about the conceptual and theoretical ideas emerging during the course of analysis (Žydžiūnaitė and Tauginienė, 2018). Breaking up the data into smaller parts to be deeply analyzed takes place in this first step of open coding. Then, the similarities and differences of these smaller analytical parts are compared. The same code can be used for the similar parts. The relationships that emerge in this process between the developed concepts need to be integrated into a general framework with one core category. The relationships between concepts (codes) and categories (concepts of higher order) developed in the open coding process must be investigated in axial coding (Vollstedt and Rezat, 2019).

Axial coding concentrates on a category (the phenomenon) as associated with the following aspects. First, the phenomenon is specified by causal conditions with respect to incidents or occurrences that lead to appearance or development of a phenomenon. Second, the phenomenon is incorporated in the context that is defined as the specific set of characteristics. Simultaneously, special set of conditions are characterized in the context; action/interaction strategies take place in these conditions to overcome, handle or react to a certain phenomenon. Third, the broad and general conditions that influence action/interaction strategies are considered as the mediate strategies, including time, space, culture, socioeconomic status, technological status, career, history, and individual biography, among others. Fourth, the aim of these action or interaction strategies is the phenomenon. These are neither always predictable nor intended, and also the results and consequences are resulted from the default of an action/interaction. Consequences can be either real or hypothetical in the present or in the future (Strauss and Corbin, 1998).

Selective coding integrates the different categories developed, elaborated, and mutually related during axial coding into one cohesive theory. A core category is selected by the CSR researcher and then, all other categories should be linked to the core as well as to the other categories (Žydžiūnaitė and Tauginienė, 2018). While selective and axial coding are quite similar, the selective coding needs a more abstract level. Thus, the core category is selected in the process of selective coding and linked to the other categories from axial coding. In addition, the validation of such links is needed and some categories might have to be refined and further elaborated (Vollstedt and Rezat, 2019).

Based on coding paradigm and experts' viewpoints, economic profitability, legal requirements, political influence, and managerial personality were identified as causal conditions of corporate social responsibility behavior.

- **Economic Profitability:** The economic factor, according to the interviews, was one of the causal conditions in the process of executing CSR. Some companies carry out social responsibility to achieve economic profitability; for example, to increase sales and corporate income.
- **Legal Requirements:** It is another principle of CSR. Some of the companies involved in this research have acknowledged that the laws and regulations issued by the government on CSR have forced them to implement CSR. This logic in countries with a high social responsibility index is less likely to be found.
- **Political Influence:** Political Influence is defined, by participants and interviewees, as they can influence on public affairs and change their regional activities sometimes.
- **Managerial Personality**: Another factor that is accounted for CSR in the companies and has a much stronger frequency is the personality of the executive directors, which puts the burden of responsibility on them.

The main category (phenomenon) is the "desire to do corporate social responsibility". The purpose of this category is to show the willingness of companies to respect their social responsibility towards the society and people and to create an appropriate corporate image. The participants had different views in this regard, some of which were in line with the literature of the subject.

Strategies: Based on the research participants' viewpoints, religious affairs, cultural affairs, social affairs, and implementation of appropriate government policies are identified as CSR behavior strategies.

- **Performing Religious Affairs** is one of the strategies proposed as a strategy in promoting CSR among corporate executives.
- **Performing Cultural Affairs**: The next matter that most interviewees agreed on was the need to pay attention to cultural affairs. The extent of social responsibility is declining among the people, due to people's concern about materials and luxuries.
- **Performing Social Affairs**: Encouraging the employees to do social work can enhance the social responsibility.
- **Implementing Appropriate Government Policies**: Most of the interviewees in this study focused on the need to implement government incentive policies and emphasized that the government could encourage companies to pursue social responsibility by implementing policies such as tax breaks.

The context of social responsibility behavior was identified, based on the participants' views, as education, government regulation, and technological factors.

- **Education**: Education can be divided into public and private. Public education is the formulation of appropriate education policies and private education can be identified as corporate education. According to the interviewees, one of the factors that underpin CSR is the perspective of practitioners to establish a proper education system to support CSR, so that it can bolster the culture of corporate responsibility among current management and staff.
- **Government Regulations**: A review of the literature on CSR also suggests that government regulations on CSR should always strive to create and encourage companies to comply with CSR, and in fact, to

adopt a much more appropriate incentive strategy that is more effective than other strategies.

- **Technological Factors:** Technological factors refer to the use of technologies that make less pollution and fewer errors and are expected to support technologies that reduce environmental pollution.

Intervening conditions were identified, based on the research participants' viewpoints, as market factors, promotion by media, socio-political factors, socio-cultural factors, and international factors.

- **Market Factor:** It is one of the influential factors on CSR and refers to manufacturers and suppliers.
- **The Media Promotion:** One of the means to promote CSR is focusing on promotion by media.
- **Economic-political Factors:** It is another intervening factor that is very influential since it is no doubt that the better the economic conditions, the more interest rate in social responsibility.
- **Social-cultural Factors:** Various interviews with CSR practitioners in European countries highlighted an interesting point: the gaps in CSR were more social–cultural. That is why, in some countries, social responsibility is strictly institutionalized among the people, while in some other countries, it is not recognized yet as a fact but as a ritual, luxury and fantasy activity. Therefore, building culture and trying to institutionalize social responsibility among the people must be one of the main priorities in every community.
- **International Factors:** One of the factors involved in the process of theorizing CSR for all companies, and especially for larger companies, is the extent to which they are engaged in CSR activities; companies such as Microsoft or Google provide voluntary work or free training for individuals to carry out their CSR mission.

Consequences were identified as the consequences of social responsibility behavior in companies, based on the viewpoints of research participants. They include credit sustainability, corporate sustainability, environmental sustainability, and political influence sustainability.

- **Credit Sustainability:** CSR ensures the firm's reputation and credit.

- **Corporate Sustainability**: Corporate sustainability is also the result of CSR. And one of the consequences that most companies may aim to achieve is corporate sustainability.
- **Environmental Sustainability**: The purpose of environmental sustainability as a result of CSR is creating clean air and a healthy environment, one of the major dreams for the big modern and industrialized cities.

Figure 1. The relationships between categories in the causal model (Norouzi et al., 2014)

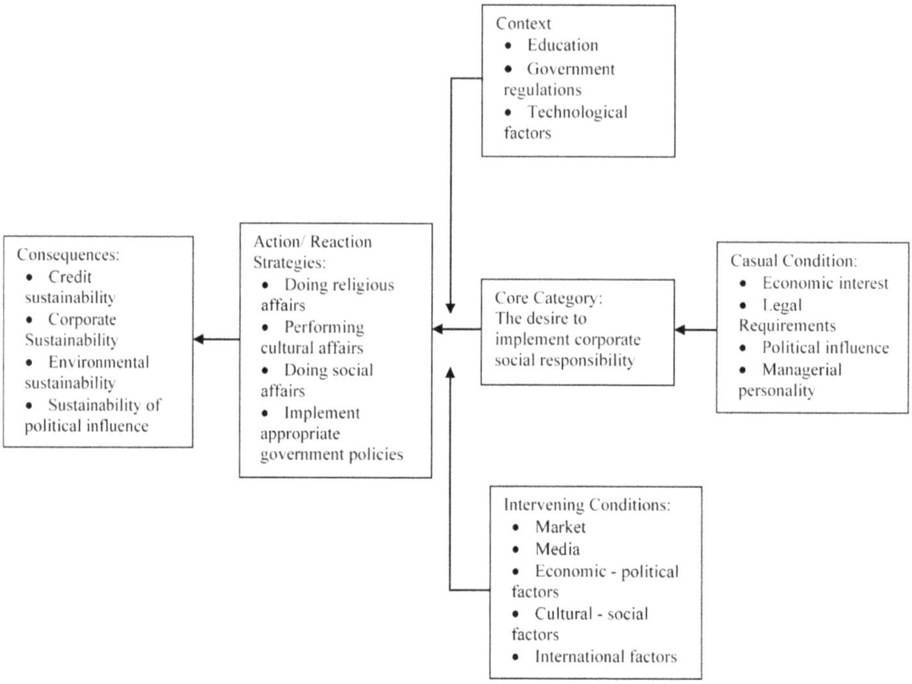

- **Political Influence**: CSR enhances corporate political power in the region. It is the great hope of larger corporations to influence in the region.

Todays, the companies all over the world are growing and, besides bringing very useful and productive results for their societies, they cause problems. In this context, the concept of CSR has been put forward with the aim of respecting and protecting the environment, helping to improve the quality and opportunities of life, empowering individuals and investing in societies so that the benefits of the organization can be met alongside the benefits of the society. The importance of this issue in societies is especially important because it has a long-term plan for business development. Alizadeh et al. (2014), through a qualitative approach, sought to provide a comprehensive model for the concept of CSR.

The open coding results of the contextual data indicated that totally 22 variables were identified around the concept of CSR: transparency and ethics in stakeholder engagement, balance between the interests of the organization and the society, sensitivity to social issues, efforts to reduce social problems, strategic vision, commitment and active role of the organization, religion, social responsibility as managerial responsibility, value nature of CSR, accredited reputation and credibility, impact of social responsibility on organizational commitment, task division with the government, social-economic context, profitability, the mental pattern of employees, education, acceptance of change, meritocracy, democracy, improving justice, the welfare of future generations, cultural context and corporate power over government.

These variables were grouped according to the paradigm model proposed by Bohem (2004) into four groups of related factors and one main category of CSR. Accordingly, the causal factors that make the existence of social responsibility essential include: the power of corporations over governments, strategic vision, sensitivity to social issues and efforts to reduce social problems. CSR is formed and activated by a set of factors that consist of the cultural context, the mental model of employees as proponents, the socio-economic context, and the value nature of CSR. Business strategies for accepting and conforming to social responsibility include: being based on meritocracy, being based on democracy, accepting change, education, tasks division with the government, accepting social responsibility as managerial responsibility, religion as criteria for decision making, commitment and active involvement of the organization, and transparency and ethics in relation to stakeholders. The consequences of this phenomenon include the well-being of future generations, improved equity in the distribution of income, profitability, the impact of social responsibility on the commitment of individuals within the organization, gaining a reputation for quality, and balancing the interests of the organization and society. Finally, according to the findings of the present study, the CSR was defined as follows:

"CSR is a set of activities derived from voluntary sensitivity and strategy-centered business to environmental events that are organized in the

Figure 2. Paradigm coding of corporate social responsibility (Alizadeh et al., 2014)

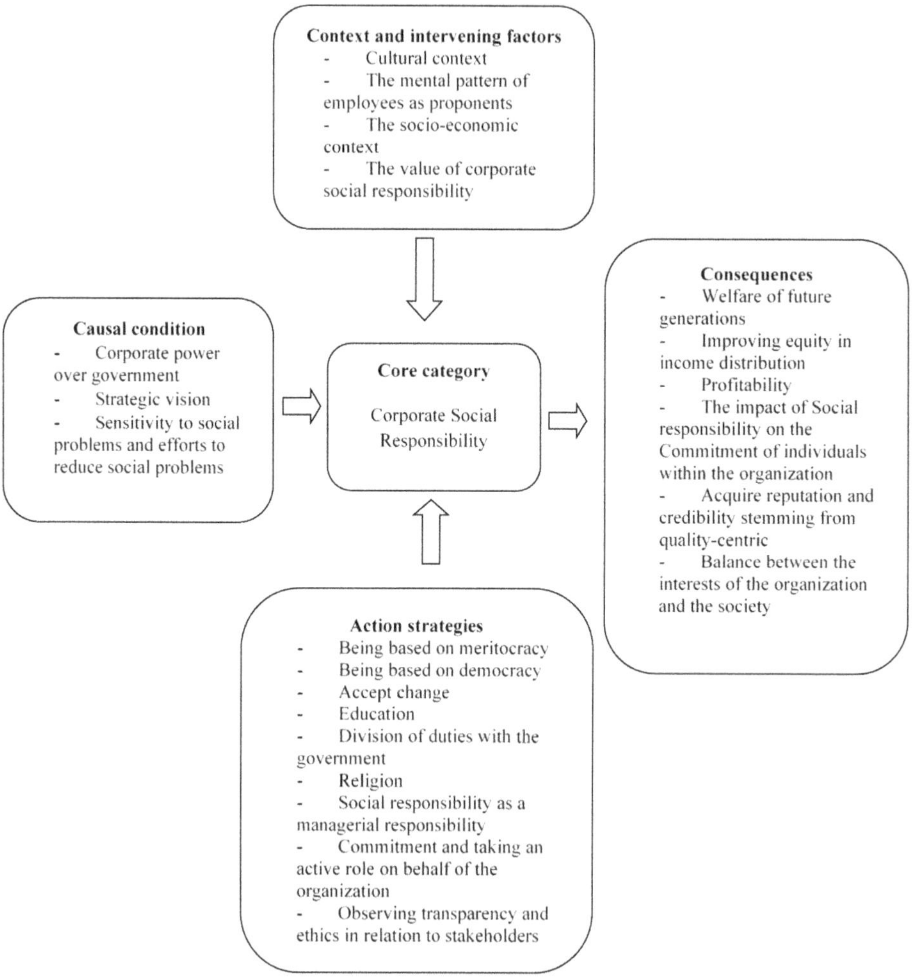

managerial, economic and social context of the organization in interaction with the environment. It emphasizes on meritocracy, democracy, change, human values, and balances the interests of the organization, society, people, and governments. ”

GT AND SUSTAINABILE BEHAVIOR

The purpose of research for sustainable development is to trigger or support sustainability-oriented change in the society, through which our knowledge and understanding will be improved to reconsider the way we meet our needs. This usually implies placing the scientific knowledge production in the same line with societal problem situations and hence, the disciplinary boundaries and the realm of science are not the case (Wuelser and Pohl, 2016).

According to the European Commission, CSR practices can play a key role in contributing to sustainable development as well as enhancing innovative potential and competitiveness in the European countries (Gorski et al., 2017). Corporations are expected to take action to improve the economy, society as a whole, and the environment. Innovation is the solution. New ways to make progress in the society can be uncovered by innovation and then, the private sector has a crucial role by engaging in CSR.

Besides the environmental factors, the concept of sustainability encompasses social and economic factors. The appropriate method to study sustainability and the meanings surrounding it is GT. The GT approach inductively contributes to a better understanding of the phenomenon of sustainability in the context of building projects (Carter and Fortune, 2003).

Namdar et al. (2017) identified the most important factors in the formation of environmental behavior. The farmers were selected by a qualitative approach based on the GT methodology. In the present study, 158 concepts were identified and classified, after 27 in-depth interviews with farmers in two villages of Sepidan County in Fars. Then, “environmental attitude”, “location” and “environmental policies” were identified as the main categories through axial coding and six categories including access to resources, contextual issues, education, technology, co-operation, partnership and the impact of peers, and domestic experience were determined. The native species and experiences were considered as sub-categories and finally, after selective coding, the paradigm model was presented by identifying the core category.

The analysis of the information gathered in this study and the resulting paradigmatic model showed that the environmental behavior of farmers was influenced by the causal conditions of “environmental attitudes”, “environmental policies and institutions” and “economic factors”. The attitude of farmers towards environmental issues influenced the environmental behavior of farmers. This category, which is one of the main topics identified in the research, includes concepts such as the viewpoints of peers, communication,

Figure 3. Paradigm model of environmental behavior of farmers (Namdar et al., 2017)

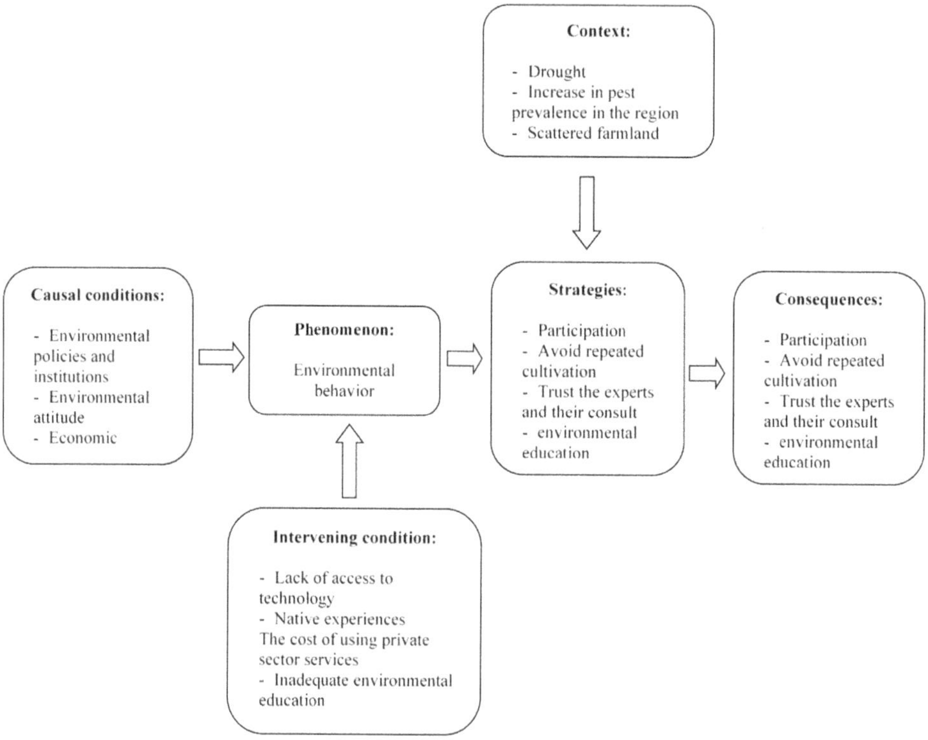

indigenous experiences, environmental responsibility, environmental education, which emerged in the sub-categories of research.

The economic and financial position of farmers plays an important role in making decisions about environmental measures. Low per capita agricultural land and, as a result, a strong dependence on income for measures such as burning straw land after harvesting for immediate action on next crop, lack of fallow land due to lack of land per capita is the decision of cultivation based on market position. Other causal factors affecting farmers' environmental behavior include agricultural management policies, including supportive institutions, environmental actions by experts, and existing laws that encourage or otherwise threaten environmental behavior of farmers. Also, in the midst of these conditions, the climate of the region, such as the current drought and the increasing prevalence of pests in the region and the small size and distribution of arable land, can be the contextual factors that affect the environmental behavior of farmers. That is, Farmers' decisions to use pressurized irrigation systems, which are some kinds of environmentally friendly behaviors and may be affected by the minor problem of land fragmentation and dispersal, and the farmers will inevitably use an alternate irrigation system.

Also, the weakness of government facilities and the high cost of environmentally friendly measures such as organic farming, lack of access to pressurized irrigation technology, lack of time, location or course content, appropriate education in the village, the costs of consulting in the private sector, etc., among others, are categories that appear to influence the environmental behavior and the adoption of farmers' behavioral strategies as intervening conditions.

In this model, active participation in environmental activities, attending in the relevant training programs, paying more attention and trusting the role of environmental experts and institutions, fallow lands and observing crop rotation, and the like, are some of the factors that can be considered as strategies. These strategies can ultimately cause decision making on the basis of sustainability rather than utility, attention and action to environmental friendly practices; in other words, a long-term view to the application of agricultural practices.

Léger and Pruneau (2011) provided a better understanding of skills needed to live sustainably as a family. Their instrumental single case study was qualitative in nature and started with a thematic analysis of interviews with family members to appreciate the experience of sustainable living as communicated by participants of the case family. According to the holistic examination of all findings demonstrated that competences such as collaboration, perseverance, self-efficacy, problem-solving, decision-making, self-regulation, and organizational skills play an important role during the involved processes in adopting new eco-sustainable actions, and are prevalent in families already living sustainably as well. Moreover, members of the single case family had perspective as consistent with the previous findings; they believed that the family values and harmonious family dynamics in maintaining a sustainable lifestyle are of great importance. Finally, a series of concluding hypotheses on a conceptual model of eco-sustainable change in the context of family were proposed through GT. The focus of these hypotheses was the interplay between three emergent constructs: collective competences, shared biospheric values, and collaborative family dynamics.

CONCLUSION

Corporate Social Responsibility (CSR) helps all companies which hold trust to do their business activities and hence, it is of great importance to them. All successful companies in the market use CSR as an inseparable part of their sustainability strategies to hold their business decisions and reputation. Grounded theory (GT) is a qualitative methodology, which borrows its name from the practice of generating theory from research grounded on data. The objective of this chapter was to examine the present studies on the applications of GT in CSR.

It focused on two paradigm modeling in the field of CSR. Casual conditions of CSR-orientation of corporations were found related to macro-environment and the organization itself; for example, its strategic vision. Context is typically relevant to culture. Intervening conditions were concerned with international and market factors. Strategies included policy making, performing cultural, social, and religious affairs, considering transparency and ethics in relation to stakeholders. The consequences were political influence, financial benefit, reputation, and having more justice and welfare in the society.

This chapter provided an explanation of the phases of GT in CSR research. The data analysis started with open coding, a list of codes was created in this step and the initial step of coding took place. In the second step, i.e. axial coding, the data was coded again and main categories and subcategories were determined. To find any association between the categories, they were analyzed. The process of selective coding was the last step through which the core concepts and the relationship between them were determined.

REFERENCES

Aguinis, H., & Glavas, A. (2012). What We Know and Don't Know About Corporate Social Responsibility: A Review and Research Agenda. *Journal of Management*, *38*(4), 932–968. doi:10.1177/0149206311436079

Alizadeh, M., Soheili, S., & Bamshad, V. (2014). Meta-synthesis position of corporate social responsibility in contemporary organizational research literature in Iran. *Entrepreneurship Development*, *8*(2), 353–369.

Alwahaibi, M., El-Tawy, N., & Theodosopoulos, G. (2019). A Grounded Theory to Map the Territory of Saudi Corporate Social Responsibility Reporting. Brunel Business School, Brunel University London.

Anagnostopoulos, C. (2013). examining corporate social responsibility in football: the application of grounded theory methodology. Handbook of research on sport and business, 418-431.

Babalola, Y, (2012). The Impact of Corporate Social Responsibility on Firms' Profitability in Nigeria. *European Journal of Economics, Finance and Administrative Sciences,* (45), 1450-2275.

Bazeley, P. (2007). *Qualitative data analysis with Nvivo.* Sage Publications.

Bohm, A. (2004). Theoretical coding: text analysis in grounded theory. In U. Flick, E. Kardorff, & I. Steinke (Eds.), *A comparison to Qualitative Research* (pp. 270–275). London: SAGE Publications.

Bonini, S. M., Mendonca, L. T., & Oppenheim, J. M. (2006). When social issues become strategic. *The McKinsey Quarterly, 2,* 20. http://passthrough.fw-notify.net/download/410337/http://www.yooyahcloud.com/MOSSCOMMUNICATIONS/qWE1bb/social_issues_that_become_strategic_report.pdf

Breckenridge, J. (2009). Demystifying theoretical sampling in grounded theory research. *The Grounded Theory Review, 8*(2), 1–14.

Carroll, A. B. (2018). Corporate social responsibility (CSR) and corporate social performance (CSP). In R. W. Kolb (Ed.), *The SAGE Encyclopedia of Business Ethics and Society.* Thousand Oaks: SAGE Publications, Inc.

Carter, K., & Fortune, C. (2003) Procuring sustainable projects: a grounded approach. In: D J Greenwood (Ed.), *19th Annual ARCOM Conference.* Association of Researchers in Construction Management.

Considine, P. (2009). The use of grounded theory to construct meaning in corporate social responsibility. *Proceedings of the European Conference on Research Methods for B,* 108.

Coupland, C. (2006). Corporate social and environmental responsibility in web-based reports: Currency in the banking sector? *Critical Perspectives on Accounting, 17*(7), 865–881. doi:10.1016/j.cpa.2005.01.001

Creswell, J. W. (2000). *Educational research planning, conducting and evaluating qualitative and quantities research.* Pearson.

Dakhili, H., & Ansi, H. (2012). The link between corporate social responsibility and financial performance: The case of the Tunisian companies. *Journal of Organizational Knowledge Management, 2012*(640106), 1–11.

Freeman, R. E. (1984). *Strategic Management: A stakeholder approach.* Boston: Pitman.

Gorski, H., Fuciu, M., & Dumitrescu, L. (2017). *Sustainability and corporate social responsibility (CSR): Essential topics for business education.* 8th Balkan Region Conference on Engineering and Business Education and 10th International Conference on Engineering and Business Education.

Holton, J. A. (2007). The coding process and its challenges. In A. Bryant & K. Charmaz (Eds.), *The Sage handbook of grounded theory* (pp. 265–289). Thousand Oaks, CA: Sage. doi:10.4135/9781848607941.n13

Jansen, P. A. M. (2016). *Corporate social responsibility: an exploratory research into views and practices of tour operators in India* (MSc Thesis). Leisure, Tourism and Environment, Wageningen University.

Koleva, P. (2019). An empirical model for Islamic corporate social responsibility grounded in theory and practice. Academy of Management Proceedings, 2019(1). doi:10.5465/AMBPP.2019.13934abstract

Lee, M. P. (2008). Review of the theories of corporate social responsibility: Its evolutionary path and the road ahead. *International Journal of Management Reviews, 10*(1), 53–73. doi:10.1111/j.1468-2370.2007.00226.x

Léger, M. T., & Pruneau, D. (2011). A grounded theory perspective on eco-sustainable change in Families. *Ecopsychology, 3*(4), 237–247. doi:10.1089/eco.2011.0042

Livesey, S. (2002). The discourse of the middle ground. *Management Communication Quarterly, 15*(3), 313–349. doi:10.1177/0893318902153001

Masarira, S. K. (2014). An analysis of small business social responsibility practices in South Africa (PhD thesis). Raduate School of Business Leadership, University of South Africa.

Michele, P. (2015). *Exploring the Role of Corporate Social Responsibility and its Influence on Branding: A Grounded Theory Case Study of Hydro Ottawa* (Thesis). University of Ottawa.

Morimoto, R., Ash, J., & Hope, C. (2005). Corporate social responsibility audit: From theory to practice. *Journal of Business Ethics*, *62*(4), 315–325. doi:10.100710551-005-0274-5

Norouzi, M. R., Danayifard, H., Fani, A. A., & Hassanzadeh, A. (2014). Theoretical processing of social responsibility based on grounded theory. *Journal of Management Improvement*, *4*(26), 5–34.

Nwanji, T. I., Howell, K., Faye, S., Agba, D. Z., Adewara, S. O., Lawal, A. I., ... Eluyela, D. F. (2019). Assessment of the effectiveness of ethical corporate governance in corporate decision-making: A grounded theory approach. *Achieves of Business Research*, *7*(1), 147–168.

Pataki, G., Szanto, R., & Matolay, R. (2015). CSR online and in real terms: a critical analysis of controversial sectors in Hungary. Corporate Social Responsibility in the Digital Age Developments in Corporate Governance and Responsibility, 7, 241-264.s doi:10.1108/S2043-052320150000007019

Patten, D. M. (2002). The relation between environmental performance and environmental disclosure: A research note. *Accounting, Organizations and Society*, *27*(8), 763–773. doi:10.1016/S0361-3682(02)00028-4

Sadeghi, M. (2013) *An exploratory analysis of corporate social responsibility and corporate strategy disclosure in annual reports: The grounded theory approach* (MPhil thesis). University of Sheffield.

Santos, J. L. G. D., Cunha, K. S. D., Adamy, E. K., Backes, M. T. S., Leite, J. L., & Sousa, F. G. M. D. (2018). Data analysis: Comparison between the different methodological perspectives of the grounded theory. *Revista da Escola de Enfermagem da U S P.*, *52*, 1–9. PMID:29668789

Secchi, D. (2007). Utilitarian, managerial and relational theories of corporate social responsibility. *International Journal of Management Reviews*, *9*(4), 347–373. doi:10.1111/j.1468-2370.2007.00215.x

Setiawan, M., and Darmawan. (2011). The relationship between corporate social responsibility and a firm financial performance: Evidence from the firms listed in LQ45 of the Indonesian stock exchange market. *European Journal of Soil Science*, *23*(2), 288–293.

Smith, A. D. (2008). Corporate social responsibility practices in the pharmaceutical industry. *Business Strategy Series*, *9*(6), 306–315. doi:10.1108/17515630810923612

Strauss, A., & Corbin, J. (1998). Basics of qualitative research: Grounded theory procedures and techniques (2nd ed.). Newbury Park: Sage.

Tyagi, K. (2019). Managerial decision making process in corporate social responsibility (CSR) (Doctor of Philosophy). College of Commerce and Economics, Goa University, India.

Votaw, D. (1972). Genius becomes rare: A comment on the doctrine of social responsibility Pt. I. *California Management Review*, *15*(2), 25–31. doi:10.2307/41164415

Wallace, A. (2000). Two models of corporate social responsibility to communities. *Mountain Plains Journal of Business and Technology*, *1*(1), 138–149.

Wuelser, G., & Pohl, C. (2016). How researchers frame scientific contributions to sustainable development: A typology based on grounded theory. *Sustainability Science*, *11*(5), 789–800. doi:10.100711625-016-0363-7 PMID:30174743

Yang, X., & Rivers, C. (2009). Antecedents of CSR practices in MNCs' subsidiaries: A stakeholder and institutional perspective. *Journal of Business Ethics*, *86*(2), 155–169. doi:10.100710551-009-0191-0

Yerznkyan, T., & Henriksson, A. (2010). *CSR policies from a communication perspective* (Master Thesis). University of Lund.

Žydžiūnaitė, V., & Tauginienė, L. (2018). Grounded theory in corporate social responsibility research. In D. Crowther & L. Lauesen (Eds.), Handbook of research methods in corporate social responsibility. Elgar.

About the Author

Maryam Ebrahimi currently is an independent researcher in Germany. Her post-doctoral research was in the area of Information Systems Management funded by the Alexander von Humboldt Foundation, Germany. She has oriented her studies towards the application of modeling and simulation methodologies especially system dynamics and agent-based modeling for the purpose of policymaking. A few of her publications are 'hybrid simulation approach for technological innovation policymaking in developing countries' and 'modeling and simulation techniques for improved business processes'.

Index

M

O

P

Q

R

S

T

www.ingramcontent.com/pod-product-compliance
Lightning Source LLC
LaVergne TN
LVHW081325300926
849161LV00008B/1876
* 9 7 8 1 7 9 9 8 4 2 5 2 1 *